Tony. A

Formidable, Compelling & Overwhelming Evidence

Johnny Chesney

PublishAmerica
Baltimore

First printing

ISBN: 1-4137-2410-8
PUBLISHED BY PUBLISHAMERICA, LLLP
www.publishamerica.com
Baltimore

Printed in the United States of America

Dedication

I'm sure a dedication to my former solicitor, Gordon Spofforth, may seem more than a little strange. However, without his assessment of me as being a complete and utter gob-shite moron, neither he nor his associates at Warrington Crown Court would never have dared to perpetrate their nefarious deed.

There wouldn't be a need for me to have written this book,
if there hadn't been a cover up!

There wouldn't be a need for a cover up,
if somebody didn't have something to hide!

There wouldn't be something to hide,
if my trial had been legal
and false evidence wasn't used against me!

There wouldn't be a need for an illegal trial,
using false evidence, if there had been any real evidence!

There wasn't any real evidence,
because Johnny wasn't guilty!

Dead simple! Init!

Acknowledgments

Tracey Rooney - You were and remain a better friend to Frances, than any of her sisters.

Chris Lloyd - Ditto Tracey

Mary Fitzpatrick - Frances couldn't have asked for a better mother, nor the children a better grandmother.

Michael Fitzpatrick - Frances couldn't have asked for a better father, nor the children a better grandfather.

Mr. Hawkins - Taffy, retired, thanks for getting me started on the appeal.

Mrs. Frances Chesney! For Everything!

CONTENTS

Introduction

This book is based entirely upon actual and **factual** event; the author has religiously adhered to keeping the retelling of his story as factual as possible, especially as to the events leading up to the trial, the trial itself, the appeal efforts and the consequent cover up by the courts.

At first glance it may appear a little odd that the author should choose to write his true life, come true crime story with an apparent fictional component (albeit minimum) within it. Initially, I did set out to present nothing but true, pure, hard facts. However, hard facts don't make very good reading and then there's the added bonus of filling in memory gaps as well as also helping to add a little colour to the story. In addition, at the early stages of writing I soon realised that there was too much me, me, me; I did this and I did that, this happened to me and that happened to me. Altogether a much too self-centred approach. So in order to attempt to deviate from such self-centeredness I made myself the third party and tried my best to change the theme of the book, from what had happened to me and instead tried as much as possible to concentrate on the effects of my imprisonment, on my family; who were after all the real victims of the entire affair.

But, what's probably a lot more important is that, despite the fact that **all claims made in the book can be verified and backed up 100%, with genuine documentation and real physical proof**, what you are reading may still (probably) be presented to a mainstream publisher and through the grapevine I've gleaned that *legal technicalities* may well force me to publish it as a fictionalised version of actual events, if it's ever to reach a wider audience. Meaning that the story will probably need to have the names changed in order to protect the guilty. All of the above have influenced the way in which I've chosen to write the story, which still remains at least 99% true. Which is a hell of a lot more than can be said about the *evidence* that was presented as fact to the jury during my trial!

The author does not purport this book as being a literary masterpiece, although before any attempts were made to publish the book, he passed it around various friends and family, asking for a critique on his work. Stipulating that they would need to be as harsh as possible in their criticisms, in order that he could iron out any problems with the manuscript before he sent it off to publishers etc. Alas! Either none of them wanted to upset Johnny or it may just have been an exceptionally well written story, because he only managed to get good reviews back. So the entire book remains largely unedited from it's original first manuscript. The one main point that did come out from these appraisals was that *it was supposed to be a true crime book and Johnny did not make enough mention of the crimes.*

So here's my chance to put the record straight and outline the whole point of the book. Although without the theft of the wagons there wouldn't be any reason for writing the book. The book is NOT primarily about the theft of the wagons: *the real crime was perpetrated by Gordon Spofforth et al.* When you put your entire life in the hands of a solicitor. You expect him to tell you the truth and not to get himself embroiled in stitching you (his client) up! If Gordon Spofforth had carried out his duties towards his client in accordance with all (or indeed any) of the rules and regulations set down by the British government; neither Adrian Westerman, or much more importantly Geoffrey Robert Travis would ever have been presented to the jury as honest witnesses with credible evidence and; therefore, Johnny would never have been convicted. Which in turn means that there would never have been a miscarriage of justice and there wouldn't be any need for the consequent cover up. And if there was no stitch up or cover up, then there certainly would be no basis for the book.

I feel that I have to emphatically stress the point that I'm not quite so stupid that I don't realise that unless any **claims that I make in the book can be verified and backed up 100%, with genuine documentation and real physical proof,** then I could indeed be digging myself into an even bigger and deeper hole, than the one that I'm already in. I'M NOT THAT STUPID! I've taken a great deal of care to ensure a wide distribution of multiple copies of both said documentation and the real physical proof! Read the book and it'll become very clear that I, more than your average Joe Bloggs have plenty of reason to justify my apparent paranoia! I DID NOT CHOOSE OR SET OUT TO BE THIS UNIQUE INDIVIDUAL I'VE BECOME! I've only become unique thanks to the efforts of Gordon Spofforth *et al.*

The only reason that I can consider myself to be unique is because during the entire total of nine months that I spent in prison, I spoke to several dozen other prisoners, who like myself had quite obviously been through unsuccessful trials; from them I gleaned that I am indeed the one and only person that anyone has ever heard of that **DID NOT get disclosure on a witness**.

Most of us for the most of the time are masters of our own destiny and *only reap what we sow*. Which sounds fine, in theory at least. However, in the real world circumstances and events can often overtake us, leaving us at the mercy of fate or in the hands of the Gods and therefore outside the bounds of our own control. Or worse, at the mercy of our fellow man, or much worse still, at the mercy of particular members of our fellow man that we've been foolhardy enough to put our trust in. The author of this book found out the hard way that leaving his own destiny at the mercy of fate would have been by far the best choice of the above.

Once upon a time the author of this book was a wagon driver who had two separate loads stolen within the space of six months. So, the police naturally looked at him as being the main suspect and decided to charge him. Consequently he went to trial at Warrington Crown Court between the 1st and 12th of July 2002, for three counts of theft; the third charge being made up of stealing a consignment of 41 bicycles, that would have been impossible for him to have stolen; as he was later able to prove, they had never been in his possession.

Prior to the trial Johnny's barrister warned him that the prosecution case would be based primarily upon there being just too much coincidence, for one lorry driver having so many problems with missing loads or part loads, in such a short space of time. He also warned Johnny that Warrington Crown Court had an 85% success rate for gaining convictions; which was apparently the highest rate in the entire country. Unfortunately for Johnny, he was about to learn exactly how this exceptionally high success rate was achieved.

At the beginning of the trial Johnny was led to believe that he'd been given access to ALL of the disclosed material and that he was aware of every witness that was to give evidence against him. However, during the course of the trial it transpired that vital **FALSE** information had been deliberately withheld, as to the identity of an **undisclosed witness** and the apocryphal evidence he was to give at the trial. Consequently the case for the defence suffered to the extent that he was found guilty on counts one and three, but not guilty for stealing the 41 bicycles that he'd never had in his possession. Some eight weeks later on the 6th of September 2002, he received two years imprisonment, for each count to run concurrently.

Prior to sentencing Johnny informed his solicitor and barrister that he intended to appeal against both convictions. However, the solicitor and barrister were surprisingly absolutely vehemently opposed to having any involvement in an appeal, despite the fact that Johnny was more than willing to put a very substantial amount money into their pockets and pay for said appeal by himself; as he'd been informed that legal aid would not fund an appeal.

Having plenty of time at his disposal whilst in prison, he decided to have a go at a DIY appeal. This decision was partly based on the experiences with his former legal advisors; in the belief that he couldn't possibly do a worse job than them and the much more obvious reason being lack of cash, which in turn **partly** contributed to his appeal failing. The author willingly supplied the single Judge Court of Appeal with a multitude of separate points as to why he did not receive a fair trial, all of which could be proved without any kind of doubt. However, the British appeal system has a well developed method of **'selecting'** which points it chooses to reply to and which to 'misinterpret' and which points it chooses to completely ignore, including anything that it feels even the slightest bit uncomfortable with. By far the most important of these uncomfortable points has been and always will be the issue of the **non-disclosure** of a witness called **Geoffrey Robert Travis**, who gave completely false evidence at the trial.

Despite the fact that in every single piece of correspondence connected to the appeal he repeatedly elaborated his complaints in great detail, especially the issue of the **non-disclosure**. It was then and still remains the one single point that has never on any occasion been tackled by either the former solicitor or barrister, the single Judge, the Honourable Mr. Justice Langley, the appeal court's outside lawyer, any of the three appeal court Judges, or the Criminal Cases Review Commission. This ignoring tactic by the appeal courts was entirely consistent throughout his appeal efforts since day one! He came to the conclusion that they all must obviously think that just by ignoring the issue it will somehow just go away.

After almost three months of persistently chasing up the appeal whilst in prison, a date was eventually set for his case to be heard. The single Judge, the Honourable Mr. Justice Langley, supposedly considered his grounds for appeal and refused the application for leave to appeal, stating:

"The reality was that you were convicted on compelling if not overwhelming evidence after a full and fair summing up because the jury were sure of your guilt and that you were not telling the truth. Your solicitor's counsel have dealt clearly and convincingly with what you say. I see nothing at all unsafe in the jury's verdicts".

The evidence could indeed be deemed to be both compelling and overwhelming, to those who chose to view it as such, but only in the same sense as Tony Blair's compelling evidence of Saddam Hussein's huge stockpiles of weapons of mass destruction, and every bit as overwhelming as the evidence that Saddam was about to launch a nuclear attack on Britain within the next forty five minutes. The parallels between the two statements and the calibre of the evidence that both Tony Blair and Mr. Justice Langley based their statements upon were then and still are, exactly the same. The compelling and overwhelming evidence had in fact been confusing and false evidence; given by the **secret, undisclosed witness** who had biased the jury with what the jury must have presumed to have been verified and accurate evidence. Mr. Justice Langley inadvertently added himself to an ever growing list of court officials who consistently refused to acknowledge the issue of the **non-disclosure**.

In Britain there is **no automatic right to an appeal**, you might think that such a right exists, but take Johnny's word[1] for it, no such right exists in Britain. In order to get anywhere even remotely close to an appeal, you first have to be granted **leave to appeal.** If you don't have untold bucket loads of money to throw about, then you have got absolutely no fucking danger of getting past this first crucial stage. This doesn't just apply to Johnny; it applies to every single poor person in the whole of Britain.

The British appeal court's most favoured tactic for denying anyone wrongly convicted any chance of an appeal is simply to prevent them from getting past the first stage in the *alleged* process. Thereby effectively denying them a *proper appeal*.

Furthermore, anyone foolhardy enough to persist and attempt to further an appeal without first being granted leave to appeal, runs the very real risk of having their sentence increased, should the appeal court decide that the initial appeal was frivolous and groundless. This tactic usually succeeds in deterring the overwhelming majority of people from trying to take their appeal any further, regardless of how justifiable their case for appealing was in the first place.

Sure of both his innocence and the fact that he'd been wrongly, if not illegally convicted, Johnny took the plunge and continued on regardless, despite the fact that the appeal court refused him leave to appeal a second time.

---

[1] Unfortunately, Johnny had to find out the hard way!

Johnny's sentence was not increased; for the most obvious of reasons being that, his case for appeal was well and truly justified. The refusal to grant Johnny leave to appeal simply served to silence him from being able to bring the *activities* of Warrington Crown Court in to the public domain.

Undaunted by the failures, he continued on unaided to a third appeal. When that failed he went onto his current fourth appeal.

Some may decide to allow themselves to believe that Johnny was guilty anyway, and that in the absence of any real proof he deserved to be framed, and assent to such practices, thereby giving their approval to those at Warrington Crown Court, who decided to break the British governments own rules as to the supposed rights of defendants at trial. In which case where does that lead to? If it becomes all right to frame a poor penniless gob-shite lorry driver, like Johnny; then it must follow that it is also acceptable to frame the next guy and the next after that. When that becomes acceptable, where will that lead to? Where will it end? Who's next?

Tony Blair, a former solicitor himself, would be among the first to publicly denounce such practices as deliberately withholding evidence, especially false evidence as being much more in keeping with the former regimes in countries such as Iraq or Afghanistan and most certainly not something that should be either expected or tolerated in Great Britain. So perhaps you should carefully consider just what happened to Johnny Chesney, because unless a hold is put upon these practices; they'll become accepted as the norm.

Definition of disclosure

Johnny's own understanding of and the general consensus of the definition of the rules governing disclosure of evidence in Britain are that: everybody that is due to stand trial in a court of law in Britain is *supposed* to have full access to all of the evidence that is to be used against them at the trial. If new evidence arises at any point, which is intended to be added to the prosecution case; then that too must be disclosed BEFORE it is given as evidence at the trial. This means that the defence team is supposed to ask for sufficient time to examine the new evidence and it is well within their right to call a halt to the trial if any new evidence arises during the course of the trial. AT ALL TIMES THE DEFENDANT IS *SUPPOSED* TO BE MADE AWARE OF **ALL** THE EVIDENCE AGAINST HIM!

Chapter I
Why Be a Wagon Driver?

It was mid-June and slap bang in the middle an unusually glorious warm and sunny English summer. The window of the army 'four tonner' was fully wound down, in order to allow some ventilation within the wagon's cab, as Johnny drove along with his right arm hanging out of the window. He could feel the extremely hot summer sun burning into his typically Celtic, light coloured skin and noticed a deep red colour, beginning to appear, especially on the lower part of the arm. He drove through the disused airfield, that for now at least, was being used as a safe training area for novice wagon drivers, his mind began to wander to thoughts of home, #19 Avis Walk, Field Lane, Fazakerley in Liverpool; thinking to himself that by the time he got back home in just a little under two weeks time; both arms will be the same colour.

The left arm was already tanned, as Johnny and Frances had been on holiday on the Greek Island of Crete, for two weeks with their small *angelic* son Jack, immediately prior to the commencement of his annual camp with the Territorial Army (TA). Whilst in Crete they had hired a car and had driven all round the island, with Johnny's left arm hanging out of the opened window of left-hand drive car; thus he had returned back home to Liverpool with a 'lop-sided tan' on his arms.

It was the summer of 1992 and Johnny had been in the TA for over two and half years when 151 Queens Own Highlanders regiment's C company's Colour Sergeant had asked him if he would like to do a *four tonner* course whilst at annual camp. Johnny had almost bitten his hand off at the chance. After all, a class III HGV licence would have cost over £600 at the time in civvy street and not only was he going to get it for nothing, but also get paid for doing the driving course into the bargain. Besides he was pretty sure that it would be quite interesting and something that he'd enjoy and he didn't the fact that the driving course was going to be a hell of a lot easier than yomping around the Norfolk countryside digging trenches, getting soaked wet through, doing mock battles and getting at the very best two hours sleep a night whilst on exercise. No way José; this year Johnny boy was going to have himself a nice easy camp.

The annual camp had indeed turned out to be even easier than Johnny had hoped for. Other than going for the three mile battle fitness test (BFT) run before breakfast on alternate mornings; although possibly as many as 90% of the other guys in the company complained about having to run such a vast distance, before breakfast, this was not in the slightest bit difficult for him as he had been well used to running each Wednesday night with Neil, Billy and Murphy, the company's physical training instructor (PTI). The small group ran from the TA unit in Score Lane to Sefton Park, then ran around it once and returned via Rose Lane, which was chosen as being the route with the steepest possible hills; i.e. '*uphill both ways*', or as near as damn it.

Most if indeed not all of this group also complimented this weekly effort with their own individual training regimes. In Johnny's case it was a five mile run along the Leeds-Liverpool canal, a stretch of which was located close by his Fazakerley home, at least twice a week in addition to regular training of twice a week at the local Ju-Jitsu club.

As he'd already been told to expect, the first week of the driving course consisted mainly of classroom work with the highway code. Johnny was quite taken aback as to just how much of the highway code he'd managed to forget since passing his car test some eleven years earlier. He also had to learn plenty of new stuff, such as axle weights and additional rules and regulations governing the army's vehicles whilst driving in convoys and night driving, etc. At the end of this week the group of trainees had to sit a theory test, which each individual needed to pass, before being allowed to go on to the second week and from there ultimately finish off with the practical driving test. This was the first major hurdle to overcome which, although Johnny had managed it easily enough, had quickly despatched several, if not all of the less capable trainees.

The second week was a much more hands on driving affair; which pleased him greatly. The little boy inside him was just dying to burst out of him and he eagerly looked forward to having a go at driving a *big lorry*.

Luckily enough there was only a relatively small number of trainees on the course, so the guys who had been fortunate enough to have been selected for the course had ample opportunity to get plenty of real driving practice done. There were no real hic-cups other than when Johnny 'lost' a mirror against a high hedge; this was later to become his most common accidental damage when driving lorries.

On the second and final Friday morning came the actual driving test which Johnny passed, but he was left with the uneasy feeling that he had only done so by the *skin of his teeth*. The TA paid for the cost of applying for the new licence along with all the other relevant fees and a few weeks later his new driving licence arrived in the post. So Johnny began looking around for wagon driving jobs.

His initial worries as to not being able to use the HGV licence, due to lack of experience, now proved to be completely and utterly unfounded as he had neglected to consider just how poorly paid these jobs were and the fact that they were quite so *ten a penny*. Therefore Johnny soon found that he could easily come and go as he pleased with these jobs, especially on the agency, which he soon found out formed at least 80% of available wagon driving jobs. This of course fitted in very nicely with his house-husband duties and as he was about to start a course at Liverpool University in September that year; he envisaged that he could still carry on a bit of lorry driving on the odd days here and there. So despite the meagre earnings; both Mr. And Mrs. Chesney were more than happy with the situation, as it was.

The following weeks and months saw the Chesney family's income rise, once Johnny had rooted out the really bad paying agencies (the vast majority) and only accepted jobs from the very few and far between agencies that were likely to pay that little bit more money for his or indeed any other wagon driver's services.

September was upon them in what seemed like a flash, Johnny started his course at the university and the wagon driving took a back seat, with Johnny only doing the odd days here and there, whenever possible, i.e. at the weekends when he was not away with the TA or during the month long inter-semester breaks.

Over a year had passed since the annual camp in Thetford. The British army has a policy that all *four tonner* drivers with the class III licence should also have an HGV class I licence after they've held the class III license for a minimum period of one year. This is for a very practical reason which is because, if one *four tonner* breaks down then it has to be towed by another *four tonner* by means of a straight bar, effectively making it into an articulated lorry, hence the need for the class I license. So now that a year had elapsed; Johnny applied for the class I course. After all, it cost just over a grand at the time in civvy street, and as with the previous course, he was getting paid for doing the course and it wouldn't cost him a single penny. Within three months, he'd been on the course, passed it and had the new license delivered in the post.

Soon after Johnny was well pleased to be earning that little bit extra with his newly acquired licence and everything seemed to be going fine with the family's finances looking even healthier. Until one bitterly cold October night during his second year at university, when out of the blue Johnny received a phone call from the Liverpool Royal Hospital telling him that his wife Frances, who had been on a night out with her friends in town, had been involved in a traffic accident. The nurse on the phone assured Johnny that Frances wasn't too seriously hurt and Johnny was extremely relieved when he was able to speak to her on the phone. However, she needed to stay in the hospital overnight and because he had to remain at home in order to baby-sit Jack, it wasn't until the following morning that he was to learn the full details of the accident.

Frances and her friends had been retuning from their night out in a taxi, when it had stopped at the traffic lights, on the corner of Victoria Street and Stanley Street. The taxi was suddenly struck from behind by a drunk driver, apparently at great speed. The force of the impact had thrown Frances violently from the back seat, face on into the driver partition, with her knees taking almost the entire force of the impact on the floor of the passenger compartment. As a result of the crash, Frances' injuries were so severe, with her knees and lower back being by far the worst affected, that she remained on sick leave for six months. Eventually leading to the loss of her job as a care assistant, at Boaler Street old peoples home, which she loved so much and had enjoyed doing for the past thirteen years.

Frances had always been an extremely active person throughout her life; in addition, she had always been an extremely attractive woman with a full womanly, voluptuous figure, which was complimented with captivating beautiful bright blue eyes and absolutely naturally straight and perfectly white teeth which produced an overpoweringly beautiful smile. Johnny had always acknowledged the fact that he'd been much more than just extremely lucky to have such a gorgeous, babilicious, foxy chick for his wife. Not only that but, on the whole she also had a loving, caring and intelligent personality (providing of course, that she remained unriled and wasn't due to start her period). However, the crash had resulted in a great deal of loss of the mobility in her legs, so all the other problems created by her injuries were exacerbated with the loss of her beautiful, trim, healthy figure, which in turn was exacerbated even further by what was to eventually become a huge increase in her weight, which had utterly destroyed her beautiful voluptuous figure but fortunately had left her endearing personality and wonderful sense of humour completely unscathed.

All of this left Johnny, much more than Frances herself, with a strong aversion towards those who either drink and drive or drive recklessly for whatever reason. His feelings on the matter were that these people should make some attempt at considering the consequences for those who are likely to become the unfortunate and unwilling victims of their wholly inconsiderate and reckless actions. Whilst still being able to acknowledge that the vast majority of such people did not initially set out to deliberately destroy other peoples lives. In Johnny's opinion and in an ideal world, drink drivers and the like should receive a taste of their own medicine which in turn, would definitely result in a much reduced number of driving accidents overall.

During the ensuing months Johnny's household duties increased to the extent that his studies suffered quite drastically as a result, which contributed to him leaving university with a mere third class degree. Needless to say Johnny was absolutely devastated by this result and consequently ended up back on the agency driving lorries, instead of getting the high-flying well paid job both he and Frances had aspired to for the past four years.

Chapter II
Scary Monster

Johnny and Frances had barely just stepped through the door, after having collected the kids from school, when the phone began to ring.

"I'll get it darling, you make us a cup of coffee, love", said Johnny.

"Hello"?

"Hello, can I speak to Johnny"?

"Yes, speaking".

"Johnny, this is Lesley from Best Connexion agency. According to our records, you've done a couple of jobs for us in the past. Are you free for work tomorrow morning"?

"Yeah, sure", he quite happily answered, knowing that Best Connexion paid just that little bit better than most of the other agencies.

"OK fine, have you got a pen and paper ready"?

"Yeah, sure, go ahead".

"It's a class I job, tomorrow morning at 07.30, at Heinz's in Wigan. Do you need the address"?

"No, I've been there before".

"OK fine, you'll need to be there at 07.30. Remember to take your driving licence and wear working boots and a high-viz jacket. There'll be some of our time sheets already there in the office. So no need to worry about that and report to the duty manager, Liam Gallagher. Do you have any questions; for me"?

"No, no I'm fine with that, don't worry yourself; I'll be there at 07.30".

Johnny put the phone down and turned to Frances as she passed him his coffee. Despite the fact that she'd never been any further than the kitchen he had to go through the entire conversation again as she was quite severely deaf, as a result of a childhood illness and as usual wasn't wearing her hearing aid.

After a light dinner Johnny went out to the Ju-Jitsu club for the evening.

When he returned around 21.00 his wife scowled, asking him if he had enjoyed himself, with a great deal more than just a subtle hint of sarcasm detectable in her voice. "Cos 'YOUR SON'S' been fucking acting up again"!

Immediately sensing that all was not well in the wifey wifey department, Johnny's seven years previous experience of her mood swings prevented him from making the reckless mistake of daring to venture asking as to exactly what the nature of 'YOUR SON'S' misbehaviour had been and offered to have a 'word' with 'OUR SON' when he returned from work the following evening. Besides, all three sons were now in bed and he knew that if they weren't already asleep, they'd certainly be pretending to be had Johnny entered their bedroom now that 'BIG DADDY' was back. Besides Johnny had no intention of getting 'HIS SON' out of bed.

"I'll speak to him tomorrow night, after work".

In a vain, almost desperate, attempt to try to lift her spirits, Johnny told her that he had a really good work out at the club and had got *well battered* on the mat. He tried to further involve her into a conservation about his evening at the Ju-Jitsu club, in order to take her mind off whatever was worrying her. When it became obvious that she wasn't in the slightest bit interested in his evening, he thought that maybe cooking will shift her mind off whatever it is that's bothering her and said, "I'm starving darling".

"There's plenty left over from dinner, in the fridge; you know how to work the microwave", she snarled.

Oh Jesus Christ, wrong approach there Johnny boy; she's determined to remain in this mood, wallowing in her own depressive state. *Low profile time, Johnny,* he thought to himself. Without making the lethal mistake of prolonging the conversation any further; he made a hasty retreat to the relative 'safety' of the kitchen, with an obsequious "yes my love, would you like a cup of cocoa"?

"No! (without the thanks) I've just had one", she said as she continued her almost vacant malicious glare towards the direction of the television.

Prudently Johnny remained out of sight of the enraged creature from the black lagoon whom he feared may well have murderous intentions towards him. He prepared his meal in terrified silence, taking at least twice as long as was actually necessary, in the vain hope that Mrs. C's mood might have lifted just enough for him to be able to venture back into the living room without the fear of the dreaded tongue. He made sure to wash up himself, so as not to evoke further fury from the *furious fraulein* whose festering anger just might erupt into another of her almighty temper tantrums at even the slightest provocation. Alas, by the time he cautiously crept back into the room, her mood had deteriorated even further as she refused to acknowledge her husband, still scowling towards the television.

Despite the fact that she was watching some moronic drivel, Johnny had the good sense not to dare asking if he could change the channel. Instead he just said that he was "off to bed, as I'm up early in the morning" where he hoped that he would be just that little bit safer.

His goodnight kiss on his wife's cheek, which was the best he could think of to try to obsequiously appease her, was greeted with a malicious askance and smouldering silence.

The well intentioned early to bed paid no dividends for poor old Johnny, as Patrick, the baby, seemed determined to deprive him of as much sleep as possible. Patrick had Johnny up at least four times through the night, while Frances slept just like the proverbial baby. Patrick was the baby of the family, he was their third and final child, who had just turned two years old. He had his mother's beautiful eyes, but had also inherited his daddy's dogged determination and tonight he was determined that he was not going to sleep alone; oh no he was getting into the comfort and security of his parents bed, no matter what; and that was that! Eventually a completely exhausted Daddy had to accede to Patrick's demands and lift him into the bed, where he slept soundly for what precious little was left of the night.

The next thing Johnny heard was some unmemorable boy band blaring out some trite bland drivel about the girl of their dreams, from the radio alarm. *Oh Christ, here we go again, another day, another half a dollar to be earned*, he sleepily thought to himself as he dragged himself from the warmth of the extremely comfortable and still inviting bed. Only the memory of Frances' foul mood from the previous evening, dissuaded him from jumping back into the bed and leaving some other *lucky fellow* the honour and privilege of driving one of Hienz's wagons half way round the country.

By 06.50 Johnny was sleepily doing his best to finish off his breakfast cereal, when the fearsome creature from the previous evening appeared in the doorway of the kitchen, asking, "what time do you need to be in work for"?

"Half seven", he replied.

"Well hold on; make yourself another coffee, while I make you up some butties".

Johnny never gave this change of mood a second thought, as she had now returned to her usual considerate self; last night's *face* had been quite out of the ordinary 'YOUR SON' was of course 'OUR SON'. He had obviously been particularly naughty; if not extremely bad the previous evening; hence the *face* that Johnny had to endure on returning from the Ju-Jitsu club. As previously stated they had in fact three sons, of which

Jack was the eldest at nine years of age. It was invariably to Jack that she alluded, when she used the term 'YOUR SON'. You've heard of *Jack the Lad,* haven't you? Well this was *Jack the Twat.* Although he was by no means out of control, he was however the *handful* of the three sons and both parents were concerned that the other two might go through the same phase when they got to about Jack's current age. *Jack* was a *kid and a half.* Johnny knew that he could write a trilogy on *Jack the Twat's* escapades so far and he was only nine years old at this moment in time. Out of the three sons Jack might have looked the least like his father; but by Christ, he acted the most like him. The same fiery Celtic temperament, stubbornness, determination and he also had a few of Daddy's other attributes that we shall not go into.

Before Johnny had the chance to ask what *Jack the Twat* had been up to the previous night, he was informed that at about 18.30 Frances had answered a loud knock at the door, to two very irate parents of a child that *Jack the Twat* had bitten during a fight. As Jack was still out and was either playing or perhaps munching his way to victory in another life or death battle, at that point whilst Johnny had been out gallivanting as she chose to describe it; she'd been left to defend herself against these abusive parents alone, hence the *face.*

"All right! Like I've already said, I'll see him as soon as I get in from work tonight", replied Johnny.

"What's the point? By tonight the fucking horrible little bastard will have added something else to his list", She added, woefully.

"Well keep him fucking in then". Johnny snapped back gladly as he *escaped* to work.

"I can't stand the little shit in the house".

"Well I can't do anything until tonight". He angrily retorted as he fled to the tranquillity and safety of the garage.

Chapter III
Bradford

In order to avoid another bout with the newly riled *Dragon,* Johnny drove off as soon as he was in his rusty twelve year old Ford Escort banger. Before he had even driven out of his own street, the seven o'clock news came on the radio and he realised that he would need to get a shift on if he was to get to Wigan even remotely close to the appointed time. Luckily enough the traffic was nice and quiet on that particular morning; so quiet that there was no need for the kind of reckless speeding usually associated with someone as desperate as he was to get to work. Knowing that while at work, he'd be a safe distance away from Frances for at least the rest of the day, *Thank You sweet Jesus for making me a lorry driver and keeping me out of harm's (Frances') way*, he thought to himself.

Somehow he managed to get to the Heinz yard at Kitt Green in Wigan a little after 07.40. Another ten minutes later and he was presenting himself to the traffic manager, who was completely unconcerned and made no mention about Johnny being twenty minutes late, for which he was more that a little relived. Thus avoiding either the need to make up excuses, or worse still being sent away and having to return home to the *Furious Fire Breathing Dragon.*

After hanging around in the office for a few minutes he was told that his load wasn't ready yet and to go wait outside with the other drivers who were loitering around in an impromptu smoking area awaiting loads and/or paperwork. Whilst talking to these other waiting drivers the conversation, as always, degenerated into a whinging match over the pay and conditions that they each had to endure. Including the fact that all of them were on the agency, as there was no such thing in existence as real, well paid, full time jobs.

Johnny could never understand why so many people in the job complained about it so much. He didn't agree that it was as terrible as they all made it out to be and just as he was about to wander off on his own in order to escape from the pointless bitching, he was saved by someone from the office calling him back in to tell him that his load was now ready. He was promptly given a big brown envelope containing the paperwork and a set of keys.

As always, despite knowing that Johnny would need to break the law in order to do so, the traffic clerk tried to encourage him to get to the delivery address as soon as possible which, as always, Johnny agreed to comply with, and as always he had no real intention of doing any such thing. In the past he'd seen far too many gob-shite drivers getting fined, points on their licence, banned, sometimes jailed, and on rare occasions even killed by complying with such *requests* and when the police became involved, the employers invariably denied all knowledge, leaving the gob-shite driver to take the rap alone.

The clerk had told him that the trailer was still on bay number 15 and it would therefore be easy for him to locate it amongst the myriad of trailers scattered throughout the extremely large depot. Once he was fully hitched up and his paperwork had been checked for the delivery address, etc., Johnny set off from Kitt Green at about 08.50. Realising that he had no chance whatsoever of reaching Bradford before the 10.30 delivery slot, he deliberately ambled his way along the busy M60. Besides, he had no real choice other than to go slowly anyway due to the usual heavy morning traffic. However, once clear of the Rochdale area, the traffic eased enough for him to get up to a reasonable speed. It was now 10.30, which was his delivery slot time and he still had at least another 25 miles to go before reaching Bradford.

Johnny arrived in Bradford at about 11.15 and underwent the usual routine of going round in circles and getting lost but finally managed to find the delivery address of Family Hampers in Holme Lane. As he approached the entrance to the yard he could see another wagon facing out of the yard, which given his view from the cab of his wagon, travelling at speed, appeared to be leaving the yard. So Johnny pulled his vehicle past the entrance round a sharp bend and parked up at a safe point on the road outside.

No sooner had Johnny parked the vehicle and began to prepare to walk the short distance back to the yard with his paperwork for the delivery, when he was approached by two young Asian men, both in their early twenties. Johnny only took any real notice of the more talkative one who was a bit heavier and darker skinned than the other. He appeared to be a quite cheerful, likable guy, unlike his friend who was just a bit too reticent for Johnny's liking. At the time it struck Johnny that the talkative one looked ever so very slightly like a darker version of George Michael, especially because he had the same type of designer stubble type beard. He approached Johnny and asked him.

"Which one are you delivering to mate"?

"Family Hampers", replied Johnny.

"Can I have a look at your paperwork"?

"Yeah sure", replied Johnny, as they were so close to the Family Hampers yard he had tacitly taken it for granted that the young Asian man was an employee of that particular firm.

Looking at his watch and the delivery time written in big bold capital letters on the outside of the big brown folder, the young man added, "You've missed your delivery slot mate, we've been waiting for this load all morning. It was supposed to arrive yesterday, just hang on and I'll phone my boss to see what he says. He'll probably still want you to make the delivery anyway".

The young man dialled a number on his mobile phone and spoke to someone on the other end of the line. At the end of his telephone conversation he turned to Johnny and said, "Sorry mate we can't fit you in at this warehouse today, but since we've been waiting on this load, my boss has said I can unload you at our other building, it's only a few minutes down the road. Is that ok with you"?

"Yeah...Well...Eh, well I suppose so", replied Johnny.

"Well here I'll write down the address for you. Do you know where it is"?

"Well I've got an *A to Z* in the cab..."

"...Tell you what mate, you're going to have turn around at the bottom of the road. By the time you've done that I'll go get my van...it's a white Mercedes sprinter fridge van...I'll wait for you out on the main road; when I see you come out of the side street I'll drive off and you can follow me. How does that suit you"?

"Yeah ok, thanks mate", replied Johnny who quickly jumped into his cab, eager to catch up with the young man so as to avoid getting lost in Bradford for a second time that morning.

As he drove down the road, he noticed several other delivery vehicles parked in a large lay-by type area of the small industrial estate. *I hope that's not the place where I'm supposed to turn*, he thought to himself as he continued to look for somewhere big enough for his large vehicle to turn. Undaunted by his inability to find the elusive turning place, he continued down Holme Lane, perhaps for about another quarter of a mile. Eventually, the road began to narrow as he passed an as yet unfinished new housing development, until the road became so narrow that he decided to stop. *Oh Christ! I reckon I must have missed the turning point*, he thought to himself. Just as he pondered his dilemma, someone from the building site came over to him. He was probably only about thirty-five, but had the appearance of a much older man, mainly due to his shabby clothes and the fact that he walked with a shuffle. He had a perceptibly stooped posture and looked as if he hadn't seen soap and water or a razor for quite some considerable time, neither had his greying hair had seen a comb recently, never mind shampoo or a pair of scissors. Overall this character could easily have played the part of Scrooge or Fagan in a Christmas pantomime play.

"Hello mate, where are you looking for"? Enquired the dishevelled pedestrian who had a look of obvious concern on his face.

"I know where I'm going". Johnny quickly replied, trying to avoid entering into too much conversation, with 'Scrooge'. "It's Family Hampers…It's back up at the top end of the road, but I missed the entrance and someone from the yard told me that I could turn around if I came down Holme Lane a bit".

"Well I used to be a lorry driver and I can assure you, you'll never get turned down here", replied the man and he offered to assist in stopping traffic as Johnny reversed in order to turn.

In spite of the stranger's appearance and added to the fact that most people that try to give you assistance whilst reversing a lorry end up creating more problems than they solve, Johnny had no real option other than to gratefully receive *Scrooge's* offer, as a queue of waiting cars was by now beginning to developed both in front and behind of his wagon.

The man momentarily disappeared out of his sight in the mirrors, behind the back end of the trailer. When he returned into his view he began beckoning Johnny to reverse, by waving his arms around, in various directions, presumably with the intention of directing him. Although Johnny found it extremely difficult to decipher exactly in which direction Scrooge expected him to turn, at least Johnny was able to derive some amusement from this poor man's well intentioned efforts, as his tattered appearance made him look like a scarecrow in a storm. Tears of laughter began to well up in Johnny's eyes and he had the greatest difficulty in trying to control the vehicle and his laughter at the same time.

The first thought that came into Johnny's mind was his recollection that one of the first things they drummed into him on both of the TA driving courses was: always guide a moving vehicle from in front of the driver, with the driver looking forward and not into the mirrors, so as to avoid the banks man getting run over. *You couldn't have been much of a lorry driver mate, you'll end up being a squashed ex-lorry driver*, he thought to himself as he struggled to keep his *assistant* in view as he kept switching from side to side in his inadequate but well intentioned attempts to guide the reversing wagon. From pure chance alone, Johnny managed to catch a glimpse of *Scrooge* as he shot off to one side in order to open gates leading to the building site, before returning and continuing to guide the wagon into the building site.

Eventually Johnny managed to reverse into the site without causing either death or serious injury to his new found *friend.* Grateful for the help this hapless man had afforded him, Johnny gave him a toot on the horn and the thumbs up as he began his journey back up the road, in the direction from which he came.

The security guard on the gate of the Family Hampers yard, a man in his early fifties and a little overweight, gave Johnny a discernable nod as he drove past, which Johnny interpreted as his having been a little concerned as to the length of time it had taken him to get turned around. Johnny returned the nod as he drove past without bothering to stop as he feared the young Asian man would have given up on him by now and gone onto the second yard without him. As Johnny turned back onto the busy main road he was relieved to see the white fridge van waiting, just past the traffic lights. The driver waved him to follow and drove off at a speed that Johnny found extremely difficult to keep up with, so difficult that he soon lost sight of the speeding van by the time it took to get through just two sets of traffic lights.

He hoped in vain that perhaps the van driver would be waiting a short distance along the road. However, once he realised that he must have completely exhausted the van driver's patience, Johnny stopped the vehicle and reverted back to using the *A to Z* and the address that the dark George Michael look alike had given him previously. Soon he found himself driving into an even smaller, tighter, industrial estate than the one he had just come from in Holme Lane. As he drove in he could see the two men already waiting there for him, with a red fork lift truck. The taller one beckoned him to park alongside one of the buildings. Johnny could see from the pot holes created from years of dropping trailer legs in the tarmac, exactly where he was expected to park up. He'd only just got out of the cab when the shorter, darker one approached him and offered to help unclip the trailer's curtains. He then added that they could unload the wagon completely by themselves and suggested that perhaps Johnny could go and get himself a bite to eat while they unloaded.

After the sleepless night before, food was the last on his mind. Anticipating that they would take about half an hour to unload, he took this golden opportunity to jump back into the cab, whip his boots off and leap onto the bed. Almost immediately he could hear and feel the movement of the unloading going on inside the trailer behind him, but before he had even the slightest chance to begin to doze off, the shorter man was knocking on the cab door.

"That's us done now mate, have you got the paperwork"?

Jesus Christ man! Are you two on a mission or what? He thought to himself as he clambered out of the bed and handed the paperwork to the

George Michael look-alike, who signed the proof of delivery documents and began re-clipping the curtains. By the time Johnny had managed to get his boots back on and got himself out the cab, the resealing of the curtains was all but finished and within a few minutes, he was reversing the wagon so as to enable him to leave the small industrial estate and start on his return journey. He was soon leaving Bradford and back on the motorway, but almost immediately, he felt himself beginning to doze off, so pulled into Hearts Head Moor which was the nearest available services. Parked up, boots off, and back onto the bed. This time he fell asleep, almost immediately and woke up about forty-five minutes later. Refreshed from this revitalising nap, he set off for Wigan again.

When a company books a driver from an agency for a day's work it is usually for a minimum of eight hours. Looking at the clock located within the tachograph head he saw that it was now almost two o'clock, and he was already approaching Warrington. He knew that if he returned too early, he would very likely get sent back out on another job. In which case it could be well after eight, nine or perhaps even as late as ten o'clock before he could hope to make it home that evening. Despite the fact that he was painfully aware that the family could well do with the extra cash, he was determined not to be quite so late tonight, because he was going to have to sort *Jack the Twat* out and didn't want any more pressure on his disabled wife. He knew several good spots in Warrington where he could park up and get a bit more sleep. However, as he drove into the town he remembered that he needed to get a spare key cut for his own car, for his wife, so decided to go on that particular errand in order to kill some time and get up to the eight hour limit. Besides, a bit of skiving never killed anyone did it? Johnny parked up as close to the town centre as he possibly could, and by the time he had the spare key cut and had returned to the wagon, it was almost half past two and he reckoned that his eight hours would expire at about half past three. Estimating by his own calculations that if he set off now and travelled directly to Heinz's depot, by the time he refuelled the wagon, did his paperwork, etc. then he would be bang on for getting away at about four o'clock, which had the added bonus of just missing the rush hour traffic, albeit by the skin of his teeth. The plan appeared to be going ever so well as he approached the Wigan turn off at junction 26 on the M6 northbound, when suddenly the cab phone began to ring. Johnny answered using the hands free facility, to someone who introduced himself as Ian Lythgoe, a traffic clerk at the Hienz's Wigan depot. He was enquiring as to when Johnny expected to make the Bradford delivery, as the customer had been on the phone with the same enquiry. Johnny's answer was that he had already made the delivery earlier that day and that he would shortly be returning to Heinz's depot. Ian Lythgoe asked him to make a point of coming to see him before he left the yard for home, to which Johnny replied, "Yeah sure".

On arrival at the yard he parked and dropped the empty trailer, refuelled the tractor unit and then went straight into the transport office, specifically asking for Ian Lythgoe, who seemed at a first glance quite anxious to meet him. He immediately asked Johnny about the delivery that morning, as Johnny began reciting the morning's events, he sensed that this traffic clerk was becoming increasingly concerned as to the load's whereabouts. He told Johnny that he felt something was really wrong and whilst in Johnny's presence he phoned Family Hampers and recited Johnny's story. They in turn told him that they had no second yard at the address Johnny had described, and from what Johnny could make out were demanding that the goods be delivered as soon as possible. As Johnny knew the address where he had been to only that morning and was confident that he could find it again, he felt sure that the *mistake* would sort itself out in due course. After going into the day's events in further detail with Ian, Johnny asked him if there was anything else he could do to assist, to which the reply was no.

"Well if that's all mate I'm off, can you sign me a timesheet please"?

The timesheet was duly signed by Ian Lythgoe, and Johnny left the yard still entirely confident that the *mistake* would sort itself out in due course and that he had nothing more to worry about.

No sooner had he left the yard when his own mobile phone began ringing, it was Ian Lythgoe stating that both he and his superiors in the company had discussed the matter. Since Johnny had left the depot, and they had come to the conclusion that the load had been *misappropriated*, they asked Johnny to go to the Wigan police station and report that the load had been stolen. Ian stressed that it needed to be Johnny himself that made the report to the police, as the load had been in his possession at the time it had apparently been *misappropriated.* At this point Johnny was still only a little worried and agreed to go and make a statement. When he arrived at the police station and told the policeman on the desk the reason why he was there, the policeman stated that it was a Bradford matter, nothing whatsoever to do with the Wigan police and that he didn't want to take a statement from him.

Johnny left, jumped back into his car and phoned Ian Lythgoe using his own mobile phone in order to relay the message back to him. He ended the conversation and continued on his homeward journey; which took him via the M58 motorway. He had travelled less than three miles and hadn't even got quite as far as the Skemersdale exit when the phone started ringing again; this time it was Lesley Brough from the agency, asking *20 questions* about the delivery he had made that morning. As Johnny was still driving he told her to phone him back on his house phone in about half an hour or so. As he walked up the garden path Johnny could hear the phone ringing and as soon as he stepped through the front door his wife handed him the phone saying "...here he is now". Johnny had correctly guessed that it was Lesley Brough. With a continuation of the *20 questions*, this time with the added request to return to Wigan and from there go back to Bradford with Ian Lythgoe, in order to show him the exact spot where Johnny had made the delivery, she even offered to pay him for the extra hours involved.

Johnny realised that a refusal to comply with this request might well be construed as him having been involved, if indeed the load had been *misappropriated.* Besides the load had after all been his responsibility and he accepted that he was indeed under a duty of care to take all reasonable steps to ensure it's security. So he told her that he'd return to Wigan as soon as he had eaten and put the phone down. However, the *Jack problem* still had to be sorted out, and as usual Jack was nowhere to be seen. So Johnny went over the day's events with his Frances, while he waited to see if and when *Jack the Twat* might decide to bless the family with his presence and return home. Under normal circumstances Jack's belly would have told him when it was time to come home; at least it usually did when he went missing. Besides, Johnny had no intention of getting stuck in the rush hour traffic. Almost a whole hour had elapsed, still with no sign of *Jack the Twat*, so Frances told Johnny to go back to Wigan regardless and leave the *Jack problem* until the following morning. Johnny reluctantly set off for Wigan, fearing that if he didn't have words with Jack tonight there could well be a repeat of the previous evening's incident which would in turn bring even more pressure to bear onto poor beleaguered Frances, who had quite enough on her plate already.

Johnny arrived back at Hienz's yard at about 18.30, where Ian Lythgoe seemed more than a little anxious to be getting a move on and Johnny could see that he was very relieved to see him. Despite his having to wait around for Johnny for some time, Ian Lythgoe remained perfectly amicable with him. They set off for Bradford in Ian's car less than ten minutes later. On arrival in Bradford, Johnny took him on a *guided tour* of the places that he had been to that morning, in the correct chronological order that he had visited each location. However, as it was now night time all of the warehouses were by now closed, including Family Hampers and the units in the small industrial estate where he had delivered at the *second over-spill site.*

Ian took lots of photographs of both sites, then told Johnny that he required him to accompany him to the local Bradford police station, in order to make a statement there. After an hour or so in the police station, he had given the policeman a quite comprehensive statement. At the end of which, Johnny asked the policeman to make a special note of the man who had helped him to reverse, for the simplest of all reasons. Johnny was now painfully aware that he hadn't actually entered the Family Hampers building and so it may have become difficult for him to prove that he had been anywhere near the Family Hampers yard, let alone Bradford. He hoped that surely the man that had been kind enough to help him reverse would remember such an unusual event as having to help a big wagon turn around. Once finished, they were both relieved to be done and dusted and back on the return journey to Wigan. On arriving back at the Heinz depot, Ian thanked him for his willingness to co-operate and duly signed a new time-sheet, even insisting on adding on a couple of extra hours to help Johnny with the additional costs involved for his repeated journey.

By the time Johnny got back home to Fazakerley in Liverpool it was well past midnight and the house was in complete darkness. When he crept into the house he found the kids fast asleep in bed. Frances was also fast asleep on the couch in the living room but woke up as he entered the room and got up and offered to make them both a nice cup of cocoa, after which they both went to bed. Thankfully *Jack the Twat* had managed to get through that evening without any more bloodthirsty incidents.

The following morning Johnny insisted on having the long awaited *chat* with *Jack* before taking the two eldest boys to school. Later on in the morning, Johnny received a phone call from Lesley Brough, specifically thanking him for "helping to save the Heinz contract for the agency" and told him to phone her anytime if he wanted any more work, from the agency.

At the end of the week Johnny sent in his time sheet that Ian Lythgoe had signed. The Friday that Johnny was due to be paid on came and went, without any sign of a payslip from the agency. So he went to the cash machine at the bank in order to obtain a mini-statement, which showed no record of a payment having been made. So he patiently waited until the following Friday, checked his bank mini-statement, but still no payment from the Best Connexion agency. Naturally he phoned the agency, specifically asking to speak to Lesley Brough on the matter of the overdue wages. She informed him that due to the unusual circumstance of that day, the agency would require him to send them his tachograph chart for the day in question. The same afternoon he posted the tachograph chart by first class post and awaited payment. The following Friday arrived and still no wages. Johnny was straight back on the phone to Ms. Brough. This time she claimed that they had examined the chart and found discrepancies with the recordings on said chart. Both of them knew that this was pure bullshit, if Johnny had anything to hide on said chart, he could simply have not bothered to send it to Ms. Brough.

FORMIDABLE, COMPELLING AND OVERWHELMING EVIDENCE

After listening to another half dozen or so bullshit excuses from Ms. Brough, Johnny put the receiver down and resigned himself to never being paid by the agency. If he'd taken the non payment to court it would have cost him several times the amount of any wages he was due anyway. He knew it, the agency knew it and the small claims courts knew it. This is exactly what all agencies that have no intention of paying former employees rely on, thereby assisting them to make many millions of pounds every year at the expense of the British working class.

This was the last that Johnny was to hear about the Bradford incident for over a year to come.

Chapter IV
United Carriers

The long school summer holidays came and went, without too many serious incidents involving Jack (now referred to as *Jack the Nice Little Boy!*). The Chesney family could not afford to go on holiday during the peak season, but at least they had managed to get away the first week in September to Majorca on a cheapo, from which the entire family returned refreshed and relaxed. Even Frances' condition seemed to improve, a little. The following months passed and Christmas rapidly approached. December was always the busiest month of the year on the agency for wagon drivers and by mid-December Johnny was literally run off his feet with offers of work coming at him from all directions, from agencies galore.

He had been at one particular company (United Carriers) for almost an entire fortnight, which he now considered to be a long time at one company; on the agency. He was actually reasonably happy to be there, despite the fact that the firm was quite literally run by monkeys. Although the job involved multi-drops and the company had a nasty habit of always giving you far too many drops to do; that even Superman could never achieve in a million years, never mind be able to do in a single day. However, he was quite content to be going there as it meant he could avoid having to chop and change by going to new companies almost every day and he had every intention of making the job last until Christmas was out of the way.

Due to the quite often overpowering workload, with just too many parcels being heaped onto each driver, invariably at the end of each shift, Johnny would need to return various parcels back to the depot as he never had anywhere even remotely near the time needed to get them all delivered in a single day.

Another recurring problem that he often encountered when attempting to deliver United Carrier's parcels was that he would have delivery notes for parcels that were not to be found on the wagon. On other occasions he would have parcels in the back of the wagon without the corresponding paperwork with which he could make the delivery. He had long since come to the conclusion that United Carriers was truly a complete and utter shambles of a firm. Which didn't really get him too bothered, as he knew that after the Christmas rush it would be very unlikely that he would be retained by the company. So he was able to take all the 'fuck ups' that he was expected to tolerate with a pinch of salt.

One morning Johnny arrived for work at the pre-arranged time and when he asked for his paperwork for the day's work ahead, the traffic clerk had made a point of asking him about one delivery in particular that hadn't been made on the previous day. It was for a consignment of forty-one bicycles, due for delivery in Holywell in North Wales. As they hadn't been on the wagon, which was as previously stated, after a very regular occurrence for items to be missing from the load. Johnny had thought nothing of it on the previous day and merely marked the delivery notes with "not on load". The traffic clerk however insisted that they had been on the wagon when Johnny had left the yard the previous morning. When Johnny in turn insisted that he would have noticed if forty-one bikes had been on the lorry or not the previous day. The traffic clerk completely lost touch with any semblance of professionalism and said that he was going to get the person who had been responsible for loading the bikes onto the truck to confront Johnny. To which Johnny replied, "Yeah well go ahead then, bring him here"!

The night shift loader duly arrived in the office and a ridiculous three way pantomime-like argument developed, with "oh yes, they were on the wagon"—"oh no, they weren't"—"oh yes, they were", etc. Johnny soon tired of this ridiculous farce, said that he wasn't prepared to suffer any more of this abuse and announced that he was returning home.

At about lunch time on that same day another traffic manager who gave Johnny the impression that he was somewhat considerably higher up the food chain in United Carriers than the traffic clerk who had instigated the morning's palaver, phoned Johnny at home, with more questions as to the mysterious disappearing bikes; to which Johnny reiterated that he did indeed have paperwork for a delivery in Holywell on that day but didn't have any packages inside the vehicle with which he could make the delivery. Again, he reminded this more senior traffic manager that in his extremely badly managed firm, this was an everyday occurrence. Later the same day, a policewoman phoned Johnny at home, asking more or less the same questions over again, to which Johnny gave exactly the same answers. She finished the conversation with stating that she "wasn't even sure that a criminal offence had taken place" and that indeed a mix up may well have occurred.

Johnny never returned to that particular firm, nor did any more work for that particular agency and as far as he was concerned, that was the end of the matter.

Chapter V
Nottingham

Unperturbed by the recent incident at United Carriers, Johnny continued to work as a lorry driver throughout December and up until Christmas. Knowing that come January when the Christmas rush would be over, the work would go really slack, so he might as well *make hay while the sun shone* and earn as much cash as possible before the forthcoming drought in January.

On the evening of Thursday, the 21st of December 2000 at around eight o'clock Johnny received a phone call from Jenny Callaghan of Hexagon employment agency, asking him if he would be available to go to work on the following morning. As he'd always been on good terms with both Jenny and the agency, from whom he'd never had any kind of the usual trouble normally associated with agencies, he was happy to be getting another day's pay before the Christmas break. She went on to tell him that it was for TNT logistics and informed him that they did the transport for a chain of off licences, in Looters Lane in Warrington. She continued by asking Johnny not to let her down and be at the yard at seven o'clock sharp, the following morning. After assuring her that he would definitely be there on time, he looked forward to relaxing for the rest of the evening and thought to himself, *Thank Christ, after tomorrow, that'll be me finished until after Christmas.*

By the time the following morning arrived his enthusiasm for the day ahead had diminished, and he reluctantly dragged himself out of bed, crawled downstairs and while still quite literally half asleep, sat nodding off into his cup of coffee. Sensing that the clock was ticking away, he tried to down his bowl of cereal as quickly as possible and swallowed down yet another cup of coffee, in a desperate attempt to try and wake himself up. Wishing that he'd never agreed to do the job in the first place, he got the car out of the garage and reluctantly set off to Warrington as quickly as he could manage, still trying to keep awake and beat the worst of the rush hour traffic.

By the time he'd arrived at the TNT yard he was late, as usual, but at least had managed to wake up properly and immediately went straight to the transport office where he was subjected to a much more than usual amount of paperwork, including the signing of declarations relating to drivers' hours, and unusually they took the extra precaution of taking a Polaroid photograph of him, which he was assured was 'bog standard' procedure for that company, as the transport company carried high value goods, i.e. alcohol and cigarettes.

After a few of the usual delays, he was given what seemed to him like a *ton* of paperwork and a set of keys for a rickety old seventeen and a half tonne rigid, ERF wagon and told that he was going to Nottingham on his own. At this point, something piqued him because the "on your own" seemed to have been particularly stressed by the traffic manager, who had handed him the keys and paperwork. Johnny was left with the uneasy feeling that something just wasn't quite right. However, he was eager to have the last day's work before the Christmas break over and done with, so he carried on, disregarding that annoying irritation at the back of his mind.

Something else struck him at the same time; Johnny had previously been to a similar company in Huyton in Liverpool, which also supplied deliveries to off licences. That firm would never have entertained the idea of sending out new or agency drivers on their own, especially not *one day wonders* like himself. TNT would in all probability never see him again after that day's work. In the case of the Huyton firm, a van boy or second man always went with a driver, whether he be a new driver or otherwise. Security of the load (from the driver) was not the only reason for the additional expense of an extra man in the cab. In addition, as was the case on this particular day, Johnny was given between ten and fourteen pallets of ale, all of which would need to be handballed into two separate shops. Were these people really expecting him to do this all by himself?

Realistically, to undertake such a task on his own would have taken several hours at each shop. Another cause of annoyance to Johnny at the time was that he knew that TNT must have had several van boys in their employ and he'd never previously heard of any occasion when a *one day wonder* was sent on his own. So why didn't they send out a van boy with him, leaving one of their own more trusted drivers who would have known the location of the shops to go out on his own, as part of the van boy's job is also to guide new drivers to the shops. Regardless Johnny set off for Nottingham, contenting himself with the thought that this would be his last day driving lorries this year before the long Christmas break that he was already beginning to yearn for.

There were some maps among the reams of paperwork he had been given, but as always, he decided to go via his own route. The problem with these type of company maps were that they were almost invariably computer generated printouts, which invariably did not take into account traffic conditions, road works, and one way systems. Weight and height restrictions were non existent to these computers; the maps were more often than not out of date anyway and had specific timings which were always without fail completely unrealistic to be able to comply with.

As previously stated the wagon was a battered old ERF, fitted with a semi automatic Eaton twin splitter gearbox, which even when the wagon had been brand new, it would have been extremely difficult to operate. Now in the year 2000 it was extremely old and obsolete. The Eaton gearbox was the predominant influence in his decision on which route should be taken to Nottingham. Wanting to keep the gear changes to an absolute minimum he decided to travel to Nottingham via the M62 eastbound and from there go south on the M1; ignoring the computer generated directions, which suggested the best route to Nottingham was via the M6 southbound, then east on the A500 to Stoke, then bypassing Derby via a newly constructed stretch of the A50 and onto Nottingham.

Johnny's journey was as always slow due to the grid-locked motorways that these days, we accept as being the norm. Plus he had also skived en route, having a sleep on the services, which allowed him to miss the tail end of the rush hour traffic.

At perhaps around 11.00 he eventually reached the outskirts of Nottingham. He tried and failed at all the usual methods of finding his way, by stopping and asking directions. However, as with all major English cities he found it difficult to find anyone from Nottingham itself, let alone anyone that could actually speak any English and now found himself in a city that he was completely unfamiliar with and consequently found himself lost. He almost got to the point of feeling dizzy with the excessive amount of going round in circles. *I'm never going to find this place, it's time I bought an 'A to Z', I suppose it might come in handy at some point in the future*, he thought to himself. He knew he was close to the city centre and looked around for a newsagents or similar shop to by an *A to Z*. This however led to him getting his knickers in an even worse twist, as the wagon was too big to find an easy parking place without the real danger of Johnny himself getting a parking ticket, which he knew only too well he would be left to pay on behalf of the wagon's owners. He became increasingly exasperated, as he found himself going round in a different set of circles looking for a shop, until the point where he decided to simply park the wagon at the nearest available parking spot, get out the vehicle and search for the up to now elusive newsagents.

The place which he had chosen to park the vehicle, he assumed was very close to the railway station, as he had seen the British Rail sign on several occasions whilst circling around lost in the vicinity, although he couldn't actually see any railway tracks and assumed that they were probably underground. He parked the wagon in what appeared to an unused loading bay which was part of a big warehouse, opposite to a large block of high-rise flats and then set off walking in the direction where he thought he had already seen a group of shops earlier. He'd been unable to park there before due to the lack of available parking places for such a large vehicle. However, the group of shops tuned out to be nothing more than a printers, building merchants and just about anything other than a newsagent, so he continued on in the direction of the train station, knowing that he was sure to find a W. H. Smiths or similar type of shop there. He was later to recall that he had zigzagged through a couple of streets and crossed over a canal to get to the train station, once there he soon found a newsagent, bought the *A to Z* and began his return journey back towards the wagon.

By now the reader should have at the very least a reasonable idea of what follows next. He retraced his steps with ease; however, finding the wagon proved a little more difficult. Although he couldn't be absolutely one hundred percent certain about exactly where he'd parked the wagon as he had neglected to take note of the street name, he was nevertheless pretty good at getting his bearings. Moreover, the now empty space on the unused loading bay and nearby high-rise flats bore more than a passing resemblance to the place where he thought the wagon ought to be. The eternal optimist inside him told him to scout around the vicinity, as he may indeed just have lost his bearings. He began by methodically working his way around the immediate area as best he could, in an ever increasing spiral, for perhaps twenty minutes or so, until he found himself back in the immediate vicinity of the train station. With a remote glimmer of hope still in his heart, he then set off back in the direction of where he believed the wagon ought to be, praying to God that this time he would manage to find it. He was fast becoming much more familiar with the area and with an increased pace, quickly found himself back at the now familiar empty loading bay adjacent to the block of high-rises. The sight of which made his heart sink.

Now despondently conceding to himself that in all probability some dirty fucker had stolen the wagon, he began making his way back towards the train station. Knowing that with it being so close to the city centre, finding a policeman on the street should surely be a relatively easy task. On returning to the train station his enquiries led him to a British Transport police station, located within the confines of the train station building itself. Although finding an actual policeman proved to be a more difficult task. The small entrance to the police station was locked and he had to ring a bell and wait for someone to come to the door. When he eventually managed to get an answer and relate what had happened to a policeman, the result was complete disinterest, with him being told that it was not a British Transport police matter and he was given directions to what was described to Johnny as being a proper police station, only a few minutes walk away.

Realising that time may very well be of the essence, as by now perhaps as much as an entire hour had elapsed since he had last seen the wagon, he made his way there as quickly as possible. On reaching that particular destination, he was curtly informed by a security guard/policeman seated in the reception area of this building that it was not in fact a police station, but was actually a magistrates court building. Once more he was completely taken aback by the court policeman's disinterest and lack of initiative on the matter. This second policeman's opinion was that the British Transport policeman had merely fobbed him off and that in actual fact the nearest real main, police station was located right at the other side of the city centre. As Johnny still had the *A to Z* that he had purchased earlier, in his possession, the second policeman circled the exact location of the main station and advised him that the quickest way to get there was to proceed there on foot. So for the second time Johnny set off as quickly as he could, in search of some semblance of even a slightly more interested reception.

En route to the next location, he encountered a policeman and woman who had a scruffy young man in handcuffs who was obviously under arrest and was ranting and raving. Johnny made the mistake of approaching this group to ask either policeperson if he was still going in the right direction to the main police station. When he bought the *A to Z* he had also bought a bottle of water, and when Johnny asked his question to the two police personnel, the loony under arrest began screaming abuse at Johnny, including asking him if he'd "paid for that water"? The incident provided Johnny with a moment of levity, but no help in getting to his next location as the policeman just answered Johnny's request for directions with "can't you see we're a bit bust at the moment mate"? leaving Johnny to continue towards the main police station with only his newly acquired map for assistance.

His route took him directly through the city centre shopping area, past a bright golden carousel, that seemed to be part of the Christmas festivities. There was still no sign of any patrolling police, right up to the point when he had finally found the main police station.

Once inside, he proceeded to a high counter, where he informed a policewoman on the reception desk as to the relevant parts of the days events. She at least appeared a to be bit more interested and told him to wait while she passed on the relevant details to someone who would deal with his predicament. Johnny then asked if he could use the phone, in order to inform the of what had happened. His request was granted and he phoned Jenny at the agency, as he had no idea what TNT's phone number was and knowing that she would know who should be informed inside the TNT company. Her first question for Johnny was had he left the keys in the wagon? To which he replied, "Of course not! I've still got them on me". Jenny related her relief to Johnny's answer to her question.

Johnny waited patiently in the police station's reception area for about half an hour to forty minutes, until being called back to the desk and directed to an internal phone which upon picking up, the receiver was immediately answered by a male police officer who took a short statement from Johnny about the theft of the wagon, via the internal phone. In addition to being more than a little surprised at the manner in which what he considered to be a fairly serious matter was being dealt with, his other most pressing concern at this moment in time was how he was he supposed to get back home to Liverpool. The policeman on the phone was unable to offer any assistance on that matter, telling Johnny that surely it would either be his employer's or Johnny's own responsibility to arrange his return transport. When he related this same concern to the girl on the reception desk she gave him more or less the same answer as the policeman on the internal phone. She did however offer him the use of the telephone again, in order for him to arrange some kind of transport for himself. Again he phoned Jenny at Hexagon, telling her that as he still had his own bank card on him, he would withdraw some more money from a cash machine and pay for his own ticket home, then return the keys to TNT on the following morning when he went back to pick up his car from the TNT staff car park.

As he had just come from the train station, he knew it would be easy enough to retrace his steps and catch a train to Liverpool. On setting off towards the train station he easily found a cash dispenser in the city centre. Having absolutely no idea how much a ticket home would cost, he drew £100 out and continued on towards the train station. On arrival there the ticket clerk informed him that a train directly to Liverpool would be leaving in forty minutes and cost £28, which he found to be a great relief, having always thought that rail travel was much more expensive than it had now proved to be. He was pleasantly surprised to find the train arrived forty minutes later and departed bang on time. It was also modern, clean inside and wasn't in any way overcrowded; in fact it bore no resemblance whatsoever to the service on dilapidated antiquated scrap that was constantly being screened on the television news.

During the journey home he began pondering the day's events, in particular the emphasis that the traffic manager had placed on the words "you'll be going to Nottingham on your own" and the most unusual, if not completely unheard of instance, of not having a van boy with him that day. The fact that no matter what the circumstances, the agency gob-shite always gets the blame for absolutely anything that goes wrong, played on his mind a great deal throughout almost the entire journey back towards Liverpool.

Johnny had never been a rail traveller, save on the odd occasion, and so had no idea of the route that the train was to take nor that it would stop in Warrington on its way to Liverpool. However, about an hour and ten minutes into the journey, the train pulled into and stopped at a Warrington train station. Hoping that surely he couldn't be too far way from the TNT yard, Johnny decided to alight there and then. He intended to call into TNT that evening and return their keys, thereby avoiding the need to return the following morning in order to retrieve his car.

He walked for approximately two and a half miles to the TNT yard which took him about thirty minutes. Upon arriving at the TNT yard, he had to introduce himself to the security guard and explain why he was there, as there was no shift change at that time in the evening, before being permitted entry into the depot. He walked around the main building, in a clockwise direction before eventually reaching the traffic office, located at the rear of the building.

Once inside the traffic office, from where his shift had started earlier that day, he introduced himself again, this time to a man who appeared to be in his late twenties and had all the appearances of being the manager. Johnny explained why he was there and returned the wagon's keys to him.

"I'm going to have to ask you to fill in some forms before I can sign your time sheet and let you go".

"Yeah sure".

The forms appeared to be some type of insurance document, in which Johnny wrote a short script on where he had parked the wagon, etc.

Before he had a chance to complete this task, an older man, perhaps in his late fifties, quite literally thrust a mobile phone into Johnny's face, saying, "Here, there's somebody wants to speak to you".

Feeling a little disconcerted by this man's behaviour and attitude, Johnny paused momentarily before speaking.

"Hello"?

"Who's this"?

"My name is Johnny Chesney".

"Are you that fucking driver that went to Nottingham"?

"Yeah, that's right, I'm that fucking driver that went to Nottingham".

Looking on the bright side of things, at least from this moment onwards, the relationship between these two men couldn't possibly have deteriorated any further.

"So tell me this cocker! You went to Nottingham on your own and somebody stole your wagon, is that right? That is what you're telling me. Right! Cocker"!

"Yeah, that's right".

"And tell me cocker! How many of the two deliveries did you make"?

"Well none, and just who the fuck are you"?

"I am Mr. Richard Johnston, HEAD OF SECURITY at TNT in Warrington, cocker".

"Well Mr. Head of Security, strange as it may seem to someone quite so high and mighty as yourself, I am not prepared to tolerate being spoken to in such an abusive, condescending manner", Johnny replied and thrust the mobile back towards *Mr. Thrust the Mobile in Your Face* in exactly the same manner in which he had received the mobile. "Here"! Johnny snarled.

By now a small group, of what were presumably other TNT employees had gathered on the driver's side of the office area, all of whom appeared to be gleefully enjoying the evening's entertainment. This little charade being played out before them must have added a little excitement for them and provided them with a little levity, during what would presumably otherwise have been a pretty mundane night.

Turning to the quieter, younger man who was certainly a great deal much more socially competent than either of the two people that he had just spoken to, he asked, "Have you done my time sheet yet"? in an extremely impolite and forceful manner.

"Yes there you go; listen mate, we really do need you to come back here in the morning", he replied in a deliberately extremely demure tone, not wishing to cause any further hostility than had already been created by both *Mr. Thrust the Mobile in Your Face* and TNT's head of security.

"Well it's good to see that at least one of you lot have a sense of humour. You know you've got absolutely no fucking danger of me coming back here in the morning".

"Well if you don't come back under your own steam, we'll see to it that you'll be coming back with the police", chirped in *Mr. Thrust the Mobile in Your Face*.

"That's fine by me arsehole; you go ahead and do your very worst".

With this Johnny spun on his heels, left the office, crossed the yard to the staff car park, got into Effie, his faithful old heap, and left the TNT yard for what he knew would surely be for the last time.

Driving home his mind returned to the niggling question that had been bothering him all day. Why had that bastard firm sent him—*a one day wonder*—out on his own, without a van boy, in the same way that every other similar company would have insisted on doing when carrying such a high value load? *Too late now to go worrying about that, what in the name of Jesus Christ am I going to say to Frances? As if she doesn't have enough on her plate already! Why the fuck did this have to happen to me right on top of Christmas? I can only blame myself for being such a dickhead and for being prepared to put myself at such an incredible risk for such a fucking pittance,* he thought to himself, feeling more and more miserable, downhearted and full of self pity by the minute.

On arriving home he had to undergo the unenviable task of retelling the day's events to his poor beleaguered wife. This was going to be far more difficult than any possible police interrogation, that he knew he would almost certainly have to go through at some point in the near future.

Frances, as you would quite naturally expect was completely overwrought with her concerns over her husband's latest dilemma; she bombarded him with a multitude of all the predictable questions and comments, none of which were to be of any help whatsoever. Why didn't you park it up somewhere safer? Why didn't you tell the TNT manager in the morning that you needed a van boy with you? Why didn't they just give you a van boy in the first place? Why this? Why that? Why the other? Etc.,etc.,etc. You know you're going to be the gob-shite that's going to take the rap for this, don't you! Thank Christ you still had the keys on you!—Neither of them realised just how important the fact that Johnny had retained the keys was later going to be. At this exact moment in time they were both assuming that retention of the keys may well be Johnny's redeemer in this case. However, as you will later learn, this was most definitely Johnny's biggest drawback.

Every bit as dumbfounded as Frances, Johnny had no reply to offer to any of her questions nor could he offer any real comfort to his tearful spouse. Devoid of any solutions, both he and Frances opened a bottle of red wine that was supposed to be for Christmas dinner in a few days time and both got absolutely plastered. What else were they supposed to do at a time like this?

Chapter VI
The Police

Around nine o'clock one evening during January of 2001, about three weeks after the Nottingham incident involving the TNT delivery, Frances answered the phone, to a withheld number. She knew it was a withheld because the Chesney's phone was fitted with a caller display panel that showed the number of any call, whether incoming or outgoing. The person making the call introduced himself to her as Detective Constable Jimmy Johnston, and informed her that he was a policeman from Nottingham. He continued by saying that he wished to speak to a Mr. Johnny Chesney. This was the inevitable moment that she had been dreading for the past three weeks. At least this wasn't quite as bad as she had previously imagined, that the police would actually come marching up to the front door in front of the entire street.

"Here, it's for you", said Frances, holding out the phone, with an outstretched arm and a look of almost sheer horror on her suddenly ashen face.

Although those were her only words to Johnny, he could immediately sense the dread within her; the expression on her face told him something was very wrong.

"Hello".

"Hello, am I speaking to a Mr. Johnny Chesney, a former employee of TNT logistics in Looters Lane, Warrington, Cheshire"?

"Well kind of yeah, I only worked there for one day and that was it".

"Allow me to introduce myself, I am D.C. Jimmy Johnston of Nottinghamshire police in Nottingham, I must apologise for interrupting your evening, mate; however, I'd like for you to help me with a few questions that I'd like answered, if it's not too much trouble, for you, mate".

The political correctness of this policeman, his attempts at being friendly and much worse still, the word "mate" sent alarm bells ringing in Johnny's head. In all Johnny's previous experiences with the police, the word "mate" and civility didn't go hand in hand with policemen. *Be careful what you say to this fucker*, Johnny thought to himself before answering.

"Yeah sure thing, go ahead, anything I can do to help".

"I have a report in front of me, concerning a vehicle that was stolen in the central Nottingham area, whilst said vehicle was in your possession. Do you remember anything about that"?

The alarm bells were now ringing out at full blast. *This twat is pussyfooting about just a little too much for my liking...he's fucking up to something*, Johnny thought, almost out loud.

"Yeah well of course I'm going to remember having a wagon stolen from me, especially when it was only three weeks ago. How can I help you"?

"Can you just remind me of how you got back from Nottingham to Warrington"?

"On the train"

"What train was that then"?

The one that goes from Nottingham to Liverpool, you stupid fucking twat, he thought to himself before allowing himself to continue, out loud. "If my memory serves me right then, it left Nottingham at twenty minutes before five, bang on time, I might add. I had originally intended going straight home to Liverpool and then returning the keys for the wagon to TNT the following morning and had no idea that it would stop in Warrington, but when it did I decided to save myself a journey and go hand them in, there and then".

"Yes ok, then can you tell me about how you left the wagon when you parked it"?

"Well I've got to assume that I left it locked, haven't I? I mean it's got to be extremely unlikely that I didn't, if you know what I mean"?

"Well the thing is *mate* we've got a bit of a problem with the wagon. You see, when it was recovered and examined it, the contents as you'd quite naturally assume, were missing. However, the locks on the vehicle had no damage done to them whatsoever, but the vehicle had been moved from where you said you had parked it. Since then I've been reliably informed that stolen vehicles usually have had some kind of damage done to the locks when they're recovered. Can you give me any help on that Johnny"?

"Well I'm afraid that all I can tell you is that I believe the wagon was left locked and secure, in the location that I described to the policeman that I gave the original statement to in Nottingham, on the day of the theft. I'm sure you'll agree that's about as much as I can possibly do under the circumstances".

"Yes, ok Johnny, we'll leave it there for the moment and we'll have to see where we go from here. Again I must apologise for having troubled you so late at night, goodnight".

After the phone call, Johnny had to undergo a proper gruelling interrogation, this time by Frances. Although he did his very best to placate her, telling that the policeman seemed to be quite a nice chap, that he didn't appear to be too biased against him and may even be on his side, she remained totally unconvinced that all would turn out well for them. They both tried their best to allay any fears concerning the phone call, but it was still always niggling away at the back of both of their minds over the next week or so.

One night Frances answered another late night call from the same policeman, again asking for Johnny and again went over more or less the same questions. During this phone conversation, D.C. Johnston stated in an extremely unconvincing manner that he would be *passing through* Liverpool within the next few days and politely asked if Johnny would mind coming to a local police station within the Liverpool area so as they could have a *chat*, as there were some things that he needed to *go over* with Johnny in person. Johnny knew only too well that to refuse this request would only increase D.C. Johnston's suspicions that he may have had some involvement in the theft of the wagon and it's contents; so he had no real choice but to agree to the interview. D.C. Johnston finished the conversation by telling Johnny that he would arrange an interview room at either Huyton or Aintree police station and phone him back within the next day or two, in order to give him the details of the time and date. He finished the conversation by saying that it would be a very informal 'chat' and that he estimated it would take up thirty minutes of his time, at the very most. Again he apologised for having disturbed his evening and ended the conversation.

Totally unconvinced and extremely sceptical about D.C. Jimmy Johnston's motives himself, Johnny had to endure another bout of trying his best to allay Frances' fears; this bout however was only to last a mere twenty minutes, when Johnny received yet another phone call from D.C. Johnston stating that he had arranged to come to Liverpool in order to have our *chat* at 10.30 on Wednesday 26/1/01. After asking Johnny if that day suited him alright and receiving an affirmative reply, he again apologised for having called at such a late hour and ended this conversation with "I'll look forward to seeing you on the twenty-sixth of January, in a few days then".

Johnny could easily discern that something had quite obviously biased D.C. Johnston into believing that poor old Johnny didn't have a single functioning brain cell in his head. *This wanker must undoubtedly thinks that he can smell a rat. Well if that's the case, then I can smell a ten ton mutant fucker*, Johnny thought to himself. So the next morning Johnny took the seemingly sensible precaution of phoning a solicitor and made arrangements for him to be present with him on the twenty-sixth of that month. At the time this seemed like the most sensible thing to do under the circumstances.

Ten days or so later, at the appointed date and time, Johnny duly arrived at Copy Lane Police Station in Aintree, Liverpool, where he was met by John Hinchcliffe, a solicitor, from the firm of Maxwell, Entwistle and Byrne. He was an extremely well dressed man in his late forties who gave Johnny the impression that he was the type of person that was only too glad to be taking the money for it, but haughtily felt that this type of work was beneath him. They had both arrived about ten minutes early, giving Johnny ample time to give the solicitor a quick run through of the reasons for his being there. However, the policeman from Nottingham was not anywhere near as punctual and they both had to wait for another thirty minutes for D.C. Johnston and his companion to arrive in the reception area of Copy Lane. Johnny estimated that D.C. Johnston was possibly in his early thirties, about 5 foot 10 inches tall, with collar length hair that was in a tidy 1970's type hairstyle. In Johnny's opinion, he just looked too normal to be a policeman. He was accompanied by another policeman from Nottingham who was much older and had only a smattering of hair on the top of his head. On arrival, both these policemen cordially introduced themselves to Johnny, leaving the solicitor to have to introduce himself. D.C. Johnston immediately realised that his *extremely cunning ploy* had been rumbled and the Mr. Nicey approach, that he had previously employed during the telephone conversations with Johnny, quickly disappeared and he began behaving in a manner much more in keeping with that normally associated with the police.

Fifteen minutes later, Johnny was charged with the theft of the wagon that had been stolen from him in Nottingham. He was assured this was merely a procedure that anyone being interviewed under caution had to undergo. A few minutes later, all four men were sitting in an interrogation room and a taped interrogation duly began.

The interrogation focussed on several main points; the first of which being as to why hadn't he taken the computer generated printout's suggested route to Nottingham, which in turn tied in nicely with his next question, concerning the time that it had taken for Johnny to travel from Warrington to Nottingham, which in turn also tied into why had it taken Johnny almost a whole hour to report that the vehicle had been stolen.

Johnny repeatedly went through each stage of all the same details several times over and over again during the interrogation and added that, with respect to the time he estimated that he had arrived in Nottingham, he had called into the services, probably Trowel Services, immediately before leaving the motorway for the Nottingham exit. He explained that whilst there, he had made a transaction using his bank card in the services shop and therefore that if they assumed that he'd left the services shortly after the time of said transaction; then it should give them a reasonable estimate as to time he must have arrived in Nottingham. He went on to further explain that the time of said transaction should be noted on his bank's computers. Johnny was extremely surprised to see the instantaneous effect that his mention of banks and computers was to have on both policemen's faces, as he quite literally watched both faces light up like the Blackpool illuminations, right in front of his very eyes. D.C. Johnston's next question was would Johnny agree to sign a document, allowing them access to examine his bank accounts? To which Johnny answered, "Yeah alright, sure, providing you promise to put something in there, while you're at it". Neither of the two policemen chose to share in Johnny's spontaneous moment of humour and passed him the relevant forms for signing. The policemen had obviously come well prepared in advance.

Another major focus of their questioning was on their assertion that there was no apparent damage to the locks in the vehicle when it had been recovered. Johnny's answer to this was (as it has persistently remained since and from which he has never since deviated) that if he was not present at the time when the wagon was stolen, then it would be utterly impossible for him to make any kind of conjecture as to how it was stolen, or by whom. This was to be a line of questioning that all of those involved in trying to have him found guilty would repeatedly try to draw him into.

Another point that they banged on about relentlessly was about a video tape they claimed to have, which apparently showed the stolen wagon as it was in the process of being abandoned. They went on to claim that the driver of the wagon could be seen. However, due to *technical difficulties* with the video machine at Copy Lane and the format of the video tape, they were unable to show him the video tape at that point. *What a load of bollocks!* thought Johnny. Even D.C. Johnston could see that his format story was received with silent, astonished disbelief and decided that trying to trick Johnny into an admission with such tales was a complete and utter waste of time, for him at least, especially as he knew that Johnny must have been on his guard.

The task of tricking Johnny would need to be left to someone that Johnny was much more likely to trust!

The interrogation came to an abrupt end, with D.C. Johnston informing Johnny that he was being released on police bail pending further enquiries and that he would be required to attend another interview which was to be held at the main police station in Nottingham, where he'd given the original statement over the internal phone. The date was arranged for the fourteenth of February, Saint Valentine's Day.

Johnny stated that he was very much looking forward to seeing him in Nottingham, as that being in the locality of the actual events, would give him the opportunity to give D.C. Johnston a *walk through talk through* of the exact spot where he had parked the wagon when he'd set off looking for a place to buy the *A to Z*. He added that they could both look for closed circuit television camera (CCTV) on buildings in the area, which would ultimately give a great deal more credence to Johnny's version of events for that particular day. Thus ended the 30 minute *chat*, some four hours later than D.C. Johnston had apparently originally anticipated.

Almost three weeks went by, until the day before Johnny was due to travel to Nottingham, when he received a phone call from the solicitor telling him that the appointment for the following day had been cancelled and that the police would contact Johnny through the solicitor, in order to arrange a new date and time. A few days later the solicitor called again with the new appointment. As the time for the next appointment approached, Johnny received yet another call from the solicitor, with news of another cancellation. This time he had the date for the next appointment ready prepared, which was not to be held in Nottingham, but back in Copy Lane in Aintree, again. Johnny was relieved that at least he wouldn't need to travel all the way to Nottingham for the next interrogation. By now several weeks had elapsed since first meeting with D.C. Johnston and his buddy. Yet again the date for the next appointment approached, and yet again another phone call from the solicitor with yet another cancellation. On this occasion however there was no new date as yet and he was assured by the solicitor that he would inform Johnny of said date as soon as he became aware of the new date.

More than a month elapsed since the last cancellation and still no news as to when or where the new date was to be arranged. The Chesney family wished to book a cheap late holiday. So Johnny very reluctantly took the initiative, feeling that perhaps he should let sleeping dogs lie and that no news was good news, and phoned the solicitor with an intense aura of trepidation, that Frances was later to say she could feel in the air exuding from him, to ask if he had heard anything from Nottingham. The reply that came back quite literally had Johnny and Frances dancing in the street. Apparently only thirty minutes earlier the solicitor had opened a letter from the Nottingham police, stating that the conditions under which Johnny had been on police bail had now expired and for the foreseeable future, no further action was to be taken against Johnny. The quick getaway cheapo was booked in a micro-second and two days later the elated Mr. and Mrs. Chesney were lying down, under a canopy, on a beach in Santa Elulia in Ibiza, whilst the children splashed about in the sea. The biggest worry that Johnny and Frances now had to contend with was which one of them was having the Bud and who was having the Smirnoff Ice. It turned out to be the most relaxing holiday they'd ever had, now that this enormous weight had been lifted off both of their shoulders, from here on in they could take anything in their stride after what they'd had to endure since before Christmas. Neither of them had a care in the world.

When they returned home from their well earned break, both were 'chilled to death' and Johnny returned to work as a lorry driver. However, Johnny had decided that there was to be no more driving around with high value loads that just might go astray, no more irritating agency jobs, instead he got himself a full time job driving waste tippers. It was extremely dirty and smelly. Each night when he arrived home from work, he had to remove his clothing in the back garden regardless of the weather conditions, put them into a bin bag and deposit them in the garden shed until the following morning. None of this bothered either Mr. or Mrs. Chesney in the slightest because at least they could sleep soundly at night; sheer heaven!

The summer came and went without any more incidents. Johnny had definitely picked the right job this time, after all who was going to steal a smelly wagon full of other peoples rubbish? Johnny's thirty-ninth birthday, on the sixteenth of October, approached, the last one before the 'oh no! the big four 0'. Johnny and Frances made plans to visit friends that had moved to a small town outside Sarragossa, in Aragon, Spain for his birthday, as they had never been away without the children and Frances' parents had volunteered to look after the children and make sure they got safely to and from school each day for the midweek five day period they intended being away for. It was going to be yet another cheap getaway, as all they'd need would be two £79 plane tickets and a little spending money.

On the evening of the second or third of October Johnny received a completely unexpected phone call from the solicitor.

"I've got a bit of bad news for Johnny I'm afraid"

"Well go ahead, lets hear it then". In less than one single milli-second from uttering these words it suddenly dawned on him what the solicitor was referring to. It seemed like an eternity before the solicitor spoke again.

"We've contacted the police…It's pertaining to the Nottingham incident, I'm afraid Johnny. The Nottingham police have passed it on to the Cheshire constabulary and they have decided to take it further, a lot further in fact. They want you to appear at Northwich Police Station on the seventeenth of this month. As far as I can make out, they want to ask you questions on the load you lost in Bradford, as well as something about some cycles in Holywell. They seem to be trying to connect these with the Nottingham wagon, which they also want to question you about".

"But I can't recall ever being in Northwich; what the fuck has Northwich got to do with anything"?

"It's the branch for the National Crime Squad in Cheshire, besides other than that it's just a police station that's got an available interview room, that's all"

"I thought all of this was over and done with"?

"It doesn't seem like it, does it"?

"It doesn't look like I've got much say in the matter then, does it"?

"No look, just come up here to their office on the morning of the seventeenth, before ten o'clock. That'll give us plenty of time to go over what they are likely to ask you at the interview, which isn't until half past eleven".

"Yeah, right, I suppose so". Johnny put the phone back on the receiver.

Johnny's immediate worry was the effect that this was going to have on Frances; she hadn't been keeping particularly well lately and was excitedly looking forward to going to see Rita and Frank in a couple of weeks time. "What in the name of fuck am I supposed to tell her? Why can't these fucking wankers just leave me and my family alone"? he muttered out loud to himself. Something niggled him at the back of his mind, something he just couldn't put his finger on! It grigged him for an entire hour, he didn't know what was bothering him so much, but just could not get rid of a niggling doubt at the back of his mind. Suddenly the front door swung open, Frances entered, in a much more cheerful mood than was usual for her.

"All right darling"? she chirped as she kissed his cheek. "The baby's asleep in the car. Go get him, will you? But don't put the car away, yet".

Johnny went out through the front door, as he did so he almost fell over Frank, their middle son, as he sleepily ambled through the doorway in the opposite direction. Jack was doodling about in the garden. "Don't play outside in the dark Jack, go on inside". Picking the sleeping baby up from the back seat of the car, he was left in no doubt that his family was growing up around him and that he wasn't getting any younger. The strain he could feel on his back, due to the ever increasing weight of Patrick reminded him of that.

Once back inside the house, Johnny took Patrick straight upstairs before he had the slightest chance to wake up, and put him straight into bed. As he descended the stairs, the older two sons crossed him on their way up. "Goodnight boys", he said as he kissed each of them on the head when they passed each other. On reentering the living room Frances passed Johnny a freshly made cup of tea and announced that she was going to sneak back out and get them both a kebab, now that we've got rid of them three for the night!

There's a coward and a hero lurking inside each and every one of us. Tonight the coward inside Johnny was the predominating factor which refused to allow him to break the news to his wife and spoil her otherwise happy evening. He was never to find out just exactly why she had come in in such a particularly good mood. Regardless he could find no reason to spoil her night. *Leave it until tomorrow, by then I just might have built up the courage to tell her, besides if I tell her now I'll be lucky to get a jam butty out of her, never mind a kebab*, he thought to himself in absolute silence.

Frances left the house and duly reappeared twenty minutes later, with the munchies from the chippy. Later as they were preparing to retire to bed, Johnny ascended the stairs and Frances began groping his buttocks. "Hi baby, tonight's your lucky night", she said in a big gruff voice, her own imitation of a cross between Barry White and the giant from the *Jack and the Beanstalk.* Johnny was first into bed and eagerly awaited her arrival, upon which she began fondling his genitals. *There ain't no way she's getting told tonight*, he reminded himself as he enthusiastically pounced on top of her.

The following morning as Johnny scrunched up the wrapping paper left over from the previous evening's chippy meal, he apprehensively began to mentally prepare himself for the unenviable task ahead. That although he dreaded the thought of doing so, he knew he must perform this awful task, and the sooner the better.

After making her a cup of tea, he tentatively sat down next to her and announced, "Darling, listen, I've got something to tell you…"

"Well get on with it then".

"…it's about that wagon that I had stolen from me in Nottingham…I've got to go to Northwich police station on the 17th of this month".

"Oh wait a minute; you've got to be joking".

"Please believe me Frances, I really do wish to fucking Christ that I was only joking. I got a phone call from Gordon Spofforth, just right after you left to go to your Mary's last night".

"Johnny please, for fuck's sake, just tell me you're just kidding! You've got to tell me you're kidding"!

"No can do babe".

"Right, I'm going to phone him myself, you are absolutely dead fucking meat if I find out you're winding me up"! She growled with an ever increasing temper and volume in her voice, as she stormed towards the phone.

Johnny could see her visibly tremble as she fumbled through the phone book, unable to locate the number she was almost frantically searching for. Exasperated, she tossed the phone book onto the phone table. Finally she managed to find the solicitor's phone number using the last incoming calls menu on the phone's memory.

As she pressed the fast dial facility, she tried her best to gather her thoughts and control her anger, in order to prepare herself in anticipation for the forthcoming ordeal that she would much rather not have had to endure. When she managed to get through, Gordon Spofforth wasn't even in the office and another solicitor confirmed what Johnny had previously said. She informed the solicitor that they had already arranged a trip to Spain for that week.

His response was, "If you start to mess them (the police) about then I'm sure they can make your life very difficult for you".

Frances correctly interpreted this as meaning—you'd better go or else! And resignedly put the phone back on the receiver.

"What am I supposed to tell my parents, never mind Frank and Rita? We both need this fucking break".

"Well phone them; tell them what's happened, I'm sure they'll all understand. Surely to Christ we must be able to sort something out between us. Maybe we can go a week early, or maybe even a week late".

"Oh shut up", she scowled, venting her anger and frustration out on her husband.

Later that day she somehow managed to bring herself to make the two phone calls, one local number and one international number, and all their plans were put on hold.

The sixteenth of October arrived and the Chesney family did their best to celebrate Dad's birthday. Next day was the dreaded seventeenth, Johnny went to Huyton at the appointed time, met with the solicitor, then travelled with him to Northwich. On arrival at the police station they had to wait in the reception area. Johnny was dressed in his usual casual attire, track suit bottoms, trainers and a tee-shirt. The solicitor, Gordon Spofforth was typically dressed for any solicitor, two piece suit, shirt, tie and dress shoes. They waited for about twenty minutes. A plain clothes policeman appeared from within an internal door; went straight over to Gordon Spofforth and asked the question, "Mr. Chesney"? As in Mr. Chesney, I presume. This blatantly deliberate mistake, that even a five-year-old child with average intelligence wouldn't have made, served to reinforce Johnny's initial feeling that this guy had seemed somehow very familiar from the very moment he had set eyes on him. His thoughts momentarily alternated between *What the fuck do you think you're playing at, twat*? and his concerns over his wife that he knew almost certainly, would at this very moment be fretting over him.

Johnny was the type of person that very rarely forgot a face; he had never been very good at remembering names and was worse still when it came to guessing peoples ages, but faces were definitely his strong point. Mr. Deliberate Mistake had a mild, but discernable Scouse accent, was probably in his late thirties with thinning ginger, as opposed to red, hair. Johnny also noticed several grey hairs among the ginger hair, especially around his temples. He was probably just over six foot tall, with legs that seemed just a bit too skinny, relative to the rest of his body. It was his demeanour and even more so, his mannerisms than his actual physical appearance that Johnny seemed to notice more than anything else, which made him seem so familiar, each and every time he looked at this man.

The apparent problem with the mistaken identity was quickly resolved and Johnny underwent the same procedure as in Copy Lane some ten months earlier, before they got down to the nitty gritty of the interrogation. During which Mr. Deliberate Mistake and his side kick bombarded Johnny with a multitude of questions. Each of them would take it in turn to keep the pressure up on him, thus allowing the other to rest, whilst denying their quarry any repose. Another of their tactics was to question him on the Bradford incident, then within a split second switch to Nottingham and within another split second, onto United Carriers and from there back to Bradford, in an instant yet again. They would pause deliberately every now and then, exchanging silent glances with each other, giving each other an occasional knowing nod, sometimes with a deliberately poorly concealed minuscule fraction of a smirk. On other occasions they would scribble little notes and exchange them with each other; the recipient of said note would in turn raise his eyebrows, just enough so as to be discernable, in full view of the interviewee.

Johnny of course realised that all of this was purely an act, aimed at trying to disconcert and confuse him. Far from achieving their goal, these techniques served purely to reaffirm his belief that if they really had any real evidence on him then there would be no need to act out the charade being played out in front of him, and rather than weakening his resolve their charade only served to bolster it. The mainstay of their suspicions rested on Johnny having been just that bit too unlucky to be believable. They maintained their techniques relentlessly for well over two hours solid, whilst their victim remained both steadfast and consistent with his answers throughout the entire ordeal.

The crux of their questioning on the Nottingham wagon focussed mainly on the length of time it had taken Johnny to get from Warrington to Nottingham and the apparent lack of damage to the locks on the vehicle when it was recovered. He answered the time issue by explaining the route he'd taken and his reasons for doing so. As for the locks, Johnny had previously stated that if he hadn't been there when the wagon was stolen then it would be impossible for him to say how it was stolen, and as he'd never seen the locks or indeed the vehicle after he parked to go and look for the *A to Z*, then he couldn't possibly comment on the condition of the locks either.

. As for United Carriers and the non existent bicycles, the police asserted that they had a video tape which showed that theses bikes were loaded onto Johnny's vehicle. Johnny's only reply to this was to challenge them to show him the video. They declined the invitation.

They appeared to be a lot more shaky and much less sure of themselves when it came to their questioning for the Bradford wagon. They were altogether a great deal more taciturn when questioning him over this incident, during which they merely skimmed over the readings on his tachograph chart for that day and mentioned that they had checked with the owners of the unit where he had been unloaded by the two young Asian men. Their enquiries revealed that the unit had been empty for some considerable time prior to the incident and it was in no way connected to the Family Hampers firm. They continued that the owners of the unit had given them access to it and there was no sign of any of Hienz's goods by the time they had got round to visiting the premises.

After a total of three and a half hours in the interrogation room, the interview finally ended, with Johnny being told that he was to be charged with three counts of theft; Bradford, United Carriers and Nottingham. He and both policeman then underwent the formalities of completing the entire charging procedure again, only this time it was very definitely for real.

Mr. Deliberate Mistake's parting words to Johnny were, "I'm going to pass on my report to the Crown Prosecution Service (CPS) and we'll have to see where we go from here, it's up to them now from here on".

The eternal optimist inside Johnny took some comfort from these words, as they encouraged him to hope that this policeman did not really believe that he had a very strong case against him and that the case may very well get abandoned and thrown out of court at some later stage. Failing that he always had the chance that a jury would find him not guilty anyway. Despite his limited experience with courts, he knew from the type of questions that they had been asking him earlier that the evidence they had against him at very best weak and unsubstantial. In addition, the fact that these two policeman had to rely on their underhand tactics and interrogation methods, seemed to give credence to his heartfelt belief rather than just hoping upon hope.

As Johnny left Northwich he remembered that same niggling feeling that he had seen Mr. Deliberate Mistake somewhere before their meeting today. It wasn't his face that Johnny remembered, but something in Mr. Deliberate Mistake's demeanour, his mien, his attitude, his posture, his what?—that disturbed Johnny. What the fuck was it?

During the return journey to Huyton, Johnny and the solicitor discussed the interrogation. Gordon Spofforth didn't tell him anything that he didn't already know. Which was that the police had singled him out as the main suspect. Primarily, if not entirely on the pretext that they found it difficult to believe that any lorry driver could be quite so unlucky in such a relatively short period of time. Therefore any case put before a jury would therefore need to be based upon purely circumstantial evidence, based upon there being just too many coincidences for one lorry driver to have been so unlucky in such a short space of time. However, Gordon Spofforth informed Johnny that under British law it was perfectly acceptable to be convicted on circumstantial evidence alone and that the Crown would therefore probably have to base their case against him on those grounds. Gordon Spofforth also informed Johnny that he was not aware of any other evidence against him and that if any new evidence were to come to light, then both the police and the Crown Prosecution Service were under an obligation to disclose any new information to the defence, who in turn were under the same obligation to forward any other new or additional information to Johnny himself.

Johnny then went home, telling Frances what he had been charged with and that he had been released on police bail, but had to appear at Warrington Magistrate's Court in three weeks time. Both had yet another sleepless night, but the following morning the world was still turning and life had to go on as usual regardless of what the future may have held for him. The three weeks passed and Johnny duly turned up at the magistrate's court at the appointed date and time, as always with his ever faithful wife at his side. It was only an extremely short hearing, in which Johnny pleaded not guilty to all the charges and another date and time was set for him to return to the magistrate's, while the CPS decided their next move.

Chapter VII
Mr. Spofforth and Mr. Watson

During the intervening period Johnny made what was to be the first of a great many visits to the solicitor's offices, during which both he and Gordon Spofforth repeatedly went over the sequence of events for each of the three counts. On one particular occasion Gordon Spofforth insisted on coming to Johnny's house for one of these meetings. This request seemed more than a little strange at the time to Johnny, but realising just how reliant he was on the solicitor, he was reluctant to cause any animosity between them by forcing an answer as to why the need for the *home visit*. Consequently Johnny never found out the answer to his vexing question, which still irritates him to the present day. Following several more court appearances, spread out over a period of a few months, a date was eventually set for his trial to begin at half past ten on the morning of Monday the first of July 2002.

Throughout the course of these regular visits to the solicitor's offices, Johnny asked for and received a regular supply of **pre-disclosed** deposition material, which he scrutinised in the most incredibly minute detail, as he had no intention of being tripped up by the crown's Barrister on any single point. He knew that he was innocent and was determined not to go to jail for these crimes which he did not commit. Eventually Johnny had a very substantial amount of this material which he was assured by Gordon Spofforth was the sum total of material that the Crown intended to use against Johnny at his forthcoming trial.

In relation to the Bradford charge, the main worries caused to Johnny in the pre-disclosed information included police witness statements by Ian Lythgoe. Although there was a definitely discernable negative change of tune in Ian Lythgoe's statements towards Johnny himself, from the time Johnny had last seen him, he said absolutely nothing that could possibly have caused him to be convicted.

The police witness statement made by Ms. Lesley Brough however, was filled with pure undiluted poison. In July 2000 she had been ever so chummy with Johnny, phoning him to thank him for his co-operation. It had after all, in her own words, been him that had helped "to save the

Heinz contract for the agency". Not even the ruckus over the non-payment of Johnny's wages could possibly have brought about the malice that she now bore him, especially considering that it was her agency that owed him money and not the other way around. According to her, in a completely uncorroborated statement, she was now claiming that during the phone call she made to Johnny's mobile phone when he was driving home on the M58 motorway, near Skemersdale, he had seemed strangely unconcerned about the apparent loss of the load, in addition to having supposedly said "companies like these lose millions every day". Johnny took careful note of this and the next he met with Gordon Spofforth, questioned him as to the legality of her statement. On a previous meeting with him and the barrister, Johnny had remembered seeing notes on Tom Watson's table, among which were the names of several witnesses. One stood out in particular at the time, as it was marked BROUGH - HEARSAY. All three men had been talking about something else at the time and Johnny had never got around to asking what HEARSAY meant. However, the word hearsay stuck in Johnny's mind because it was the name given to a manufactured pop group in the television series *Pop Stars* which Frances had been an avid fan of. Despite the fact that he had not been in the slightest bit interested in the show, he must have passively watched it on several occasions.

Before bothering Gordon Spofforth with what could well have been a trifling, insignificant question, Johnny took the time and trouble to look the word up in the dictionary; which gave the definition as:

hearsay *n.* information or evidence derived from others rather than based on direct experience.

Johnny assumed that the term must have had another definition in legal terms, so he asked the solicitor about it. The answer that he received was that in relation to Lesley Brough's statement, <u>it could only be used in a trial if was corroborated by another witness</u>! He added that as there were no corroborating witnesses to back up her statement, the solicitor assured Johnny that he need not worry about it as she could not possibly corroborate it and therefore it couldn't be used against him at a trial.

Other evidence which he received was a video tape from the CCTV in Family Hampers yard, which showed Johnny's wagon as it drove past on both occasions. Once, before his meeting with the two Asian men, and once as he drove past again, on his way to the 'second site'. Johnny was to make perhaps a lethal mistake of not paying too much attention to this video, because he had a much more intriguing witness to contend with from the Bradford incident.

It turned to be none other than *Scrooge* himself. When Johnny had given the statement to the police officer in Bradford, on the night of the offence, way back in July 2000, he had made the point of asking the policeman to take particular note of his meeting with a man from a building site, that had assisted him in reversing. He had made this specific request to the policeman because he had no way of knowing that the entrance to the Family Hampers yard had been so well covered by CCTV, nor that his wagon would have been seen on said video. Therefore at the time of giving the statement, he was unsure if he could prove that he had even been in Bradford that day, let alone anywhere near the Family Hampers yard. He therefore thought it extremely fortuitous that he had met someone (by pure chance alone) who could not in any way be connected to the Family Hampers company, but that could independently verify that he had been in the immediate vicinity of the Family Hampers yard that day. So Johnny insisted that the scruffy man from the building site being included in his statement.

To Johnny's complete and utter amazement, not to mention despair it appeared that both he and the police had accidentally stumbled across the biggest liar and romancer in Bradford if not the whole of Yorkshire. Astonishingly the police and the prosecution were now intending to use what Johnny had hoped would be his redeemer in the Bradford case, against him as a prosecution witness. Much worse was yet to come, Scrooge's real name turned out to be Adrian Westerman, but in police witness statement he added that he also had an alias of Andrew Westerman.

Practically everybody is well aware that lorry driving is an extremely poorly paid job. Under the driver's hours regulation as laid down by law in this country and indeed throughout the European Union, an HGV driver is not permitted to drive more than ninety hours in any fourteen day period. In plain English this means forty-five hours per week. In addition to this, lorry drivers can boost their legitimate income by adding another fifteen hours per week roping and sheeting, loading, unloading, etc. and by doing their administrative paperwork.

In July of 2000, at the time the Bradford incident occurred, wagon drivers were being paid £5.50 per hour. Security guards and/or utilities officers and the like were paid the standard minimum wage of £3.10 per hour. Professional, well educated personnel that had earned expert status in their field of work, on the other hand, earned much more than the combined earnings of both lorry drives and security guards.

In his police witness statements and later in a British court of law, Adrian Westerman stated that his occupation was as a utilities officer and described his duties as "having to take care of the day to day health and safety of the building site". Although he was never asked to elaborate as to the detail of what his duties actually entailed. In plain English, a utilities officer is an ever-so-nice, modern and politically correct title for a building site labourer, who also has the honour and privilege of cleaning out the shithouse. He continued that he had previously been employed as a lorry driver for eighteen years until the March of that year. He had however, found it difficult to find another job as a lorry driver so had sought out employment as a utilities officer.

The evidence to be used against Johnny was as follows: Mr. Westerman had a vast and comprehensive knowledge of the transport industry. In addition to this, he had qualifications galore, specifically pertaining to wagons and to almost every other aspect of the haulage industry. So many qualifications that Johnny knew exactly what they were and that if he really had them, he should have been a highly paid executive in a top class blue chip transport company, rather than him having to be reduced to cleaning out the shithouse for a living. In addition to all this he claimed that due to his wide experience, he could also estimate the apparent weight of a wagon just by examining the clearance between the arches of the mud flaps and the tyres below. He went on to claim that he clearly remembered that the wagon's wheels had a very high clearance. Thus indicating to him that the trailer was in fact empty. In Adrian Westerman's view this was reinforced because as Johnny had reversed, he noticed that both the trailer and tractor unit wheels were skidding on the road surface as the driver of the wagon attempted to reverse into the entrance of the building site. He continued suggesting that only a loaded trailer would have sufficient weight to prevent skidding when reversing. Johnny was utterly flabbergasted that evidence of such dubious quality could possibly be introduced as reliable, credible evidence in a court of law.

Johnny became increasingly annoyed at the solicitor's and barrister's insistence on the retention of the shield issue. They repeatedly insisted that it would be wrong to harass this witness, because the prosecution would portray him as "having no axe to grind" and that he was not connected to the complainants. It would therefore be difficult to find a motive for him to lie and they "preferred to question his accuracy, rather than his honesty".

Also as part of the pre-disclosed information, Johnny had supposedly received details of all the Crown's intended witnesses' previous convictions. Including those for Mr. Westerman, which in addition to several other convictions, included burglary, theft, obtaining property by deception and impersonating a police officer. Johnny's initial reaction to the suggestion that anyone with such a notorious character could actually be allowed to give evidence against him was one of sheer amazement.

Gordon Spofforth however, informed Johnny that although Mr. Westerman's previous history could be put to the jury; there was for Johnny at least one significant drawback, to carrying out his defence in this manner.

Johnny himself was no angel, in his misspent youth, he had been convicted for stealing cars on several occasions and therein lay the dilemma for poor old Johnny. If he was to insist on Mr. Westerman's previous criminal record being put before the jury, then his own "shield" would have been removed, meaning that the jury would also become aware of Johnny's own previous criminal record. Unperturbed by this, he still insisted that he had no real need of his shield anyway, as he himself had not been in trouble with the police since 1986. However, the barrister and solicitor still insisted that they knew best, and vehemently insisted that Johnny retain his shield.

There were of course some other witnesses from the Bradford case, but Johnny was to lose almost entirely all his focus on the other aspects of the evidence against him due to his preoccupation with Adrian Westerman's incredulous evidence. He lost his focus not only for the Bradford case, but with all three counts because astoundingly, the prosecution was actually intending to present *bona fide* evidence from this man.

***

Even with the most cursory glance, with respect to the charge for count two, the theft of forty one bicycles from United Carriers, Johnny could see that prosecution intended to use this charge as a pointless added extra which would be thrown in, in order to create a detrimental impression on the jury for the outset of the trial.

There was, at very best, extremely weak and altogether dubious evidence that the bikes had ever been on his wagon when he left the United Carriers yard on the day in question. When he examined the interrogation notes, he noticed something that he had previously forgotten, which was that in a seemingly desperate attempt to weaken Johnny's insistence that the bikes were never on his load on the day in question, the police had tried to trick him by saying that they had video tapes from the loading bay which clearly showed the bikes being loaded onto that particular wagon. Johnny knew this to be completely false and the police never produced any such video either as part of the disclosed material or later at the trial.

The pre-disclosed material for the United Carriers case included CCTV footage from within the United Carriers buildings which did not show any such thing as the bikes being loaded onto that particular wagon, never mind any other wagon.

***

With respect to the Nottingham charge, the major point that Johnny had to worry about that he had been given disclosure on was an astonishingly poor quality CCTV tape from a company called Thyssen, that did not even have any timers on it, outside whose premises the Nottingham wagon had been abandoned. This video tape supposedly showed the driver of the stolen vehicle in the process of abandoning it. However, Johnny was only given a complexed version of it (without the timers).

A complexed video tape is one where several cameras have all of their images stored onto one single tape and a sophisticated high-tech piece of equipment is needed to decipher and separate each image, so that they can be viewed separately. The tape Johnny was given to view also seemed to have the added problem of being in time lapse mode. Needless to say, the video machine in Johnny's living room was fine for recording and watching Clint Eastwood and *Fawlty Towers* and the like, but was totally useless with the complexed tape that he had in his possession.

He knew that the Thyssen video must surely have been specifically chosen by the Crown quite simply because it did not have any timers on it. One of the major concerns the barrister repeatedly reiterated to Johnny was that the Crown would strongly suggest the same as they would for the Bradford case, that the wagon was already empty when Johnny had arrived in Nottingham because he had already emptied it somewhere else and then he had dumped it in Nottingham himself. The barrister added that there was too little time between the time Johnny had told the police he had parked the vehicle and the time it had been abandoned. The crown reckoned that despite the absence of timers on the Thyssen video, they could prove their theory, because the Thyssen company had finished early that day as it was the last working day before the Christmas holiday and that cars could bee seen emptying out of the staff car park at approximately half past one that afternoon, which according to the police was shortly after Johnny had said he had parked the wagon. So the Crown could claim that there was not enough time to steal the wagon, take it somewhere to be unloaded and from there drive it to the Thyssen yard and dump it. Johnny however, insisted that any times he gave to the police during the interview were of course, as he had stated at the time, only approximate. The barrister also added that the crown would make great play of the fact that Johnny himself had stated that he had parked the wagon close to the train station, yet the abandoned wagon had been found so close to the very same train station.

FORMIDABLE, COMPELLING AND OVERWHELMING EVIDENCE

Johnny was now becoming increasingly concerned that a jury would believe the Crown and not him and was becoming increasingly painfully aware that he would have to show some very strong evidence to counter this. So without any encouragement and completely under his own steam, he arranged for the baby, Patrick, to be babysat by his grandmother and for the older two boys to be picked up from school. As soon as they dropped off the two older kids at school, both he and Frances got into the car and drove off, intending to visit Bradford and Nottingham armed with both a still and a video camera.

Bradford being the much closer of the two, was first on the list. They made video tapes of the Family Hampers site, paying particular heed to the sharp bend in Holme Lane that was so close to the Family Hampers gate where he had pulled past in order to park up safely. He also tried to show that a vehicle moving at speed past the yard would have a different view than that as seen by the yard's CCTV camera.

Next stop was the Square Street Industrial Estate, where the actual unloading had taken place. Johnny took video and still shots similar to those taken by Ian Lythgoe on the actual night of the incident. Including the exact spot where he had been unloaded and where the marks of a reversing wagon could be seen in the IL15 photograph, despite the police's insistence that no one that they had chosen to interview from the industrial estate had seen a wagon being unloaded there on that particular day.

One very important point stuck in Johnny's mind as he viewed the sites in Bradford that hadn't previously occurred to him on his previous visit with Ian Lythgoe, which was, that whoever had led him to this specific location must have had an extremely intricate and very detailed knowledge of the Bradford area, and in particular, of the small obscure industrial estates like the one in which they were now standing. For two very specific reasons, one being how could anyone not from that area possibly know the location of such a conveniently empty industrial unit where their activities would go unnoticed, and equally important was that as with most industrial estates these days, most are extremely well covered by CCTV cameras, with the exception of Holme Lane and Square Street.

The Bradford expedition took up an hour at most of their time and they were soon back on the motorway, heading towards Nottingham. On arrival there, the first stop was the Thyssen building. Whilst taking pictures of locations around the Thyssen camera that Johnny assumed the complexed video must have been filmed from, he immediately noticed several other CCTV cameras located within the immediate vicinity. Johnny took careful note of these and even made a sketch of a map, showing their exact locations, knowing that there had to be at least one of these cameras that would have provided a much clearer picture of the person who had abandoned the vehicle.

The next stop was the loading bay where he had parked the vehicle before going to look for the *A to Z*. On this occasion, he found the location easily enough and this time he made sure to make a note of the street name (Manvers Street). *En route* to this location, they had to pass directly through an industrial estate which was made up primarily of small industrial units and warehouses. This industrial estate was located immediately to the south of the main train station and was slap bang in between Manvers Street and the Thyssen building. So whoever stole the wagon would probably have needed to pass through that area in order to abandon the TNT vehicle. However, despite all this new information Johnny was still blissfully unaware of just how important this location of the Manvers Street site was.

From Manvers Street they both walked to the train station, then on to the Magistrates Court and from there on to the main police station, taking note of the time it took to get to each destination.

Following that, Johnny drove from the Thyssen yard to the train station and using the car's odometer measured the distance, which was 0.3km. From there he reset the odometer and measured the distance between the train station and Manvers Street, a distance of 1.4km. Thus he calculated that the wagon had probably moved no less than 1.7km. This calculation did not take into account any other detours that would have been necessary to go to a warehouse to unload.

On the return journey from Nottingham, Frances made a couple of videos of wagons on the motorway as they were travelling along. This was done with the intention of showing that self-levelling air suspension automatically readjusts itself and thereby maintains the clearance between the tyres and wheel arches of both the tractor unit and the trailer, whether or not a load is being carried by the trailer. By sheer good fortune one of these was a MAN diesel tractor unit of exactly the same age and model, and not that it would make the slightest bit of difference, but it was even the same colour as that driven by Johnny on the day of the Bradford incident. To add to their good fortune, not only was it a six wheeler, the same as the Bradford wagon, but the video also clearly showed that the trailer of said wagon had a load on board it, because it was a flat bed trailer which had the load sheeted on top of it. Although it was not possible to see through these sheets, the shape of the load beneath them could clearly be made out without any difficulty whatsoever.

His good fortune on finding this particular lorry continued, because as Johnny's car passed this wagon the air suspension which is fitted to all except the most antiquated (i.e. dating back to the 1970's) wagons and trailers, clearly and indisputably showed that said self-levelling air suspension had maintained the clearance between the tyres and wheel arches, despite the obvious load on board the trailer.

With his having a considerable amount of roping and sheeting experience himself, Johnny made an educated guess, but only a guess, that said trailer would most likely have been carrying a full load of two tonne steel coils. Despite this educated guess, he was later to be in complete agreement with the barrister, who said that because he could not see beneath the sheets he could not make a judgement as to what may have lay beneath them. Nor, that because it had self-levelling air suspension, could it in any way be possible to estimate the weight of the load on board the trailer. In fact Johnny himself agreed that to do so would be absolutely absurd. In which case how could Warrington Crown Court possibly be permitted to present such evidence as being credible to a jury?

In addition to the visits to the solicitor's offices, Johnny also had three meetings in total with the barrister at his chambers. On each occasion he was accompanied by Gordon Spofforth. Following the trip to Bradford and Nottingham, Johnny made his third and final visit to the barrister's chambers, armed with the newly made video tape and all of the other information that he had gathered during his big day out to Nottingham and Bradford. He informed the solicitor and barrister of the many small industrial units between the Manvers Street area and the Thyssen building which could easily have afforded adequate facilities to unload a seventeen and a half tonne wagon in a very short space of time. He also strongly emphasised that he wished the barrister to show the jury the distances that he had measured, which could easily have been verified, simply by calculating the distances on a map, such as an *A to Z*, in order to counter the crown's obvious point that Johnny had in his own words told the police that he had parked the wagon close to the main train station.

So at the conclusion of their final meeting the case against Johnny appeared to be crumbling, even before the start of the trial. The solicitor and the barrister were all of the opinion that he would be found not guilty of all three charges and each and every one of the three men were in complete agreement that the evidence against him was extremely weak and totally reliant on circumstantial evidence. However, Tom Watson, the barrister, did forewarn Johnny that the most likely cause of a guilty verdict against him would be due to the jury being unconvinced that he could be so unlucky, so as to lose either entire loads or parts of loads, on three separate occasions within six months. Gordon Spofforth said that in both his and the barrister's opinion, which was after all based on considerable experience, none of these charges against him could possibly stand up in court on their own and that the court would have to rely upon a jury that did not like the idea of too many coincidences.

So as the date for the trial loomed ever closer, Johnny remained relatively unconcerned, believing that even the most inexperienced or hopeless barrister should be able to tear apart any so called evidence such as Adrian Westerman's *fantasy world evidence* and Lesley Brough's hearsay evidence, which should not be allowed in court anyway. Additionally Johnny was assured that in the absence of any real hard evidence, the prosecution would have to rely upon a jury, biased against just too much coincidence, alone. The barrister added that as the police had never recovered any of the missing items, never mind in Johnny's possession, they would have to come up with something else if they were to make a viable case against him.

Chapter VIII
The Trial

Johnny, Frances, the solicitor and barrister were all in court nice and early so as to sort out any problems before the trial began. They apparently went over all of the main points yet again. Frances was extremely tense and Johnny tried his best to conceal his own anxieties from her and tried to put her at ease and assure her that this was going to be a doddle and that he would definitely walk free from court.

After a seemingly pointless, endless amount of legal gobbledegook, the trial eventually got underway during the afternoon session. Firstly Mr. Lewis-Jones for the prosecution gave his opening speeches and from almost within his first breath, he had informed the Warrington jury that they were dealing with someone from outside their own community and not only that, but the defendant was apparently a Scouser.

Ian Lythgoe was the first witness to take the stand. Johnny had obviously somehow neglected to read between the lines with the police witness statement by Ian Lythgoe. The man who had been so eager to add on a couple of extra hours when signing Johnny's time sheet almost two years earlier was now berating Johnny with the utmost bitterness and prejudice that would only be equalled by one other witness, the following day. He refused to acknowledge the co-operation that Johnny had given on the day in July 2000 and also refused to acknowledge that there had been any imprinted holes on the road surface where the trailer had been unloaded by the two young Asians.

In an astonishing denial of the bleeding obvious, in an even more blatant show of his bitterly prejudiced bias against Johnny, he refused outright to admit that tyre marks that could clearly be seen on his own photograph, labelled exhibit IL15, could have been made by a reversing wagon. He even denied that they showed the direction in which the vehicle had moved. Basically he swore blind that these tyre marks were from anything other than a reversing wagon. Unfortunately for Johnny, the barrister's failure to tackle this witness properly served as prelude to the standard of service he could expect from the barrister.

George Platts, the Family Hampers security guard was the final witness for that day. He turned out to be one of very few witnesses that was able to give completely dispassionate evidence. Without any encouragement he stated that wagon drivers who were unfamiliar with the Family Hampers site often missed the gate as it was on a bad bend and that they needed, as Johnny did on the day, to go further down Holme Lane in order to turn around so as to gain entry into the yard. From the questions he answered, he informed the jury that there was a Kays Catalogue warehouse next to Family Hampers, in addition to other firms that had their premises in Holme Lane. At this moment in time Johnny didn't fully realise the significance of this particular statement. So ended the first day of the trial; both Johnny and Frances were relieved that he had the chance to fight another day.

On the second day Johnny had his second chance to see Mr. Westerman again, each of the three counts had it's own specific raconteur, who stood out against all the other witnesses for each count. Adrian, alias Andrew, alias Mr. Wagon Expert that miraculously does not need weighing apparatus in order to determine the weight of a wagon, alias reformed petty criminal, alias Walter Mitty, alias Mr. Utilities Officer was very definitely count one's raconteur.

Johnny did not recognise the man who walked into the room and made his way to the stand. He had undergone a complete makeover; the straggly, unkempt appearance had vanished. He was now smartly dressed in a slightly worn, but nevertheless adequate two piece suit and was wearing a nice gold watch on one wrist with a matching gold bracelet on the other. He appeared to have also managed to recently locate a bar of soap, shampoo, barber and a razor and possibly even a toothbrush.

At long last he had finally managed to stand up in a court of law outside the dock. Doing his utmost to present himself as quite the country gentleman and proudly stated, almost boasted in fact, that his occupation was as a utilities officer and once more described his duties as "having to take care of the day to day health and safety of the building site". Johnny was left ever so disappointed when he failed to elaborate as to the detail of what his duties actually entailed.

Mr. Westerman then went on to give a comprehensive list of his extensive qualifications and the extent of his experience in the haulage industry. Then the court was treated to his amazing powers for estimating the apparent weight of wagons with a mere glimpse of the clearance between the arches of the mud flaps and the tyres below. In precise accordance with his police witness statement, he informed the court that he clearly remembered that the wagon's wheels had a very high clearance[2]

---

[2] Three inches, to be exact. What a memory! Eh?

thus indicating to him that the trailer was in fact empty. This view was reinforced because as the wagon driver had reversed, he noticed that both the trailer and tractor unit wheels were skidding on the road surface as the driver reversed into the entrance to the building site. He continued suggesting that only a loaded trailer would have sufficient weight to prevent skidding when reversing. During his meetings with the barrister, Johnny had informed him that even an unloaded wagon and trailer would have had a combined weight of over fourteen tons. Small cars weighed a little over one ton. So here the Crown had a notorious petty criminal giving expert evidence that could never have been substantiated. Johnny often pondered the legitimacy of the evidence he was allowed to give.

When Tom Watson confronted Adrian Westerman with the video of the loaded, sheeted wagon, which the entire court could see that despite it's being loaded, the trailer and tractor unit's wheel clearance appeared to be even more than the three inches that he himself had described as being on the wagon he had seen in Holme Lane, Bradford, two years previously. From the video you could actually see right through to beyond the other side of the wagon, past the hard shoulder and onto the luscious green countryside.

The barrister then said to Adrian Westerman, "In light of the video evidence that we have just viewed, I put it to you that when a trailer is loaded the clearance between the wheels and the wheel arches remains the same as an unloaded wagon due to the self-levelling air suspension".

Mr. Westerman was now quite severely disconcerted by Mr. Watson's apparently superior technical knowledge which far outweighed his own fantasy version of technical knowledge. He paused to consider his reply, for what seemed to Johnny to be an extremely long time, before answering in the most affectedly posh and haughty tone, he could possibly muster, with, "Sir, I do beg to differ with you".

Following yet another pause, the Judge came to his rescue, by asking Mr. Watson if he intended asking the witness any further questions. When he replied that he did not, Adrian Westerman was informed that he was free to leave the court. As he stood down he seemed to be quite severely displeased that he was not invited to stay and watch the proceedings. After all it would have been a real treat for him to have watched any court proceedings from his newfound safety of the public gallery, instead of from his usual position behind the dock.

To Johnny's surprise he had adhered to his police witness statements throughout, almost *verbatim*, answering all questions so correctly and so precisely that Johnny was left with the distinct impression that he was sticking to a well planned and rehearsed script. Tom Watson, the barrister for the defence, was unable to find any fault in his answers to his questions.

At the end of Mr. Westerman's stint, Johnny comforted himself with both the barrister's and Adrian, alias Andrew's, performance. Believing that surely the jury would be able to see through Adrian Westerman's testimony just as easily as they had seen through the MAN diesel's wheel arches in Frances' video.

Next up was Ms. Brough, who was about five foot two tall and it was obvious that she had been quite good looking ten or fifteen years ago. She was dressed in a very smart office type suit and had obviously made the effort to make the most of her fading looks and figure. In an almost word perfect recital of her police witness statement, she recounted her version of the telephone conversation with Johnny as he drove along the M58 almost two years earlier to the day.

The police witness statement had stated that he (Chesney) had said "something like" "companies like Heinz lose millions every day". Now two years later her memory had improved to the extent that she was absolutely 100% certain that Johnny had indeed said "companies like Heinz lose millions every day", the something like from the police witness statement had now vanished. As she repeatedly and emphatically stressed that it had been such an unusual comment and he had appeared to be so unusually unconcerned that it stuck in her mind. That she felt the need to repeatedly and emphatically stress the part of the conversation where the alleged damning statement had taken place.

For some unknown reason, the hearsay rule had disappeared into thin air and worse still, the barrister exacerbated (albeit probably unintentionally) said hearsay by encouraging her to repeat her quote a staggering five times in total. This was the one thing she kept repeating time and time again. Not before the lunch break did Johnny get a chance to question the barrister over this. Tom Watson's reply was that the judge can allow any evidence he sees fit, whenever he sees fit.

Her evidence was followed by four different witnesses, each of whom gave short statements to the court in rapid succession. One of these was Mr. N. Robinson, from a company called Watts Tyres, located directly opposite the unit where Johnny had been unloaded by the two young Asian men. According to the police witness statement he had said that Watts Tyres and Watts Tyres alone owned a fork lift truck in Square Street Industrial Estate. Any other company that required the use of a fork lift would come and borrow theirs. The statement continued that no-one from Watts Tyres either remembered having lent the fork lift on that day or had seen a wagon being unloaded in the unit opposite their premises.

When Johnny and Frances had visited Square Street on the day that they went to Bradford with the video camera, they counted another fourteen small firms within the small industrial estate. Both thought it extremely unlikely that anyone would be prepared to lend such a valuable piece of equipment such as a fork lift to quite so many other firms.

However, despite the police witness statement that Mr. N. Robinson had made and presumably put his signature to, two years earlier his position had now altered a very great deal, to the extent that now in the court he said that there were indeed other fork lifts owned by various other companies on the small industrial estate and that Watts Tyres only lent their fork lift to one or two choice, friendly firms. When questioned as to whether he had seen a wagon load of goods being unloaded in the unit opposite he now said that it was indeed very likely that a full trailer load of goods could have been unloaded without him noticing; especially, as was often the case, if he had been busy with his own work at the time.

Between the end of Mr. Robinson's testimony and the intervening time until the next witness was called, Johnny cast his mind back to the time when the police had tried to trick him into an admission during the interrogation, when they had pretended that they had video evidence of the United Carriers wagon being loaded. He thought to himself, *I could have been sitting in a prison cell, right at this very moment, if I had been stupid enough, or did not have the strength of character to stick to my guns and allow them to coerce me* into *saying something that wasn't true.* Continuing on a very similar train of thought, he was beginning to see a pattern emerging in the witnesses against him, a pattern that was to continue throughout the course of the entire trial.

There were a group of witnesses like Mr. N. Robinson who had said something to the police that had either been misinterpreted or deliberately distorted to such an extent that it only resembled what the police wanted it to sound like. The Mr. N. Robinsons of this world had complete trust in the police and had signed whatever they had put in front of them. When in due course it had come to the trial, these honest citizens had given their own true interpretation of what was actually said to the police.

The other group were a great deal nastier and more malicious, these had meticulously rehearsed what they were going to say to the police. Probably going to the extreme of ensuring that their version of events was backed up by someone else who like themselves had a vested interest in ensuring that the blame be put onto someone else. Once the deal had been struck as to what the story was to be and agreed upon and then said story recited to the police, then they too had inadvertently caught themselves in a trap. If they changed their story back to the truth, it would mean they had earlier lied. If they'd admitted lying once, then who would believe that their second version was true. So they would have to keep up the pretence no matter what, even if it meant adding other lies to the original one in order to save their own skin. So the old adage that *one lie leads to another* held its own water and was indeed completely true.

***

So following Mr. N. Robinson's evidence, and without further delay, the court proceed onto count two which concerned the forty one bicycles from United Carriers. In accordance with Johnny's experience with the actual company itself, the six United Carriers employees were every bit the complete and utter shambles in court as well as in their workplace. This gave credence to Johnny's assertion that this charge was added purely in order to create a detrimental impression of the jury from the outset of the trial, by giving the impression that his loads never reached their final destination.

In the police witness statements given some twenty months earlier, all six witnesses had been almost entirely consistent with each other, each corroborating the other five United Carriers' employees statements. Now that it had actually come to the trial however, all of them were now contradicting each other on just about everything they were being questioned about.

One witness in particular was to prove to be Johnny's redeemer, at least for the United Carriers case, albeit not by his own design. He was to stand out from all the others as giving particularly dishonest, inaccurate and inconsistent evidence. Enter count two's raconteur, Mr. Derek Hughes, a thick set man with a swarthy appearance, square jaw and wide penetrating, staring eyes. Only now, some eighteen months after the event, did Johnny realise why he had been chosen to confront him on the day of the incident in the United Carriers transport office, as this guy did indeed look quite intimidating. Twenty months previously had made up the final third of the pantomime-like, three way argument in the transport office at United Carriers. He had apparently been responsible for the loading of the wagons during the night shift. In the dock he had completely altered his original statement to include claiming that he was absolutely certain that there were indeed bikes on that specific wagon, as he had watched Mr. Chesney open up the back of the wagon and put a hand held cargo truck into the rear of the vehicle. Johnny certainly couldn't remember any such event, but now Mr. Hughes was emphatically stressing this and made a point of further emphasising just how important this (new) piece of evidence was.

What followed next was to be Tom Watson's one and only glorious moment throughout the entire course of the trial. At long last he had actually managed to read a police witness statement and discover such a serious discrepancy. He asked Mr. Derek Hughes if he thought that the fact that he had actually seen Johnny open up the back was important as to proving his guilt. To which he answered that in his opinion it was of the utmost importance and unequivocally proved beyond a shadow of a doubt that Johnny must have had the bikes on his vehicle when he had left the yard that morning.

"Then why didn't you bother to tell the police this crucial piece of information when they initially interviewed you"?asked the defence barrister.

A long pause followed, as he considered his reply; unable to think of anything better he replied, "They didn't ask, so I didn't tell them".

"They didn't ask, so you didn't tell them…in which case why did you decide to tell the prosecution barrister, Mr. Lewis-Jones? He didn't ask you either, did he"?

Another even longer and more painful pause followed, eventually the silence was broken when he stammered out.

"Well I must have forgotten at the time that I gave the statement! That's what I seen that day and that's that".

"Mr Hughes, most people's memories tend to wane with time. Yours on the other hand seems to have improved, doesn't it"? stated the barrister.

His mind must have gone a complete and utter blank, as he was unable to think of any kind of reply, Derek Hughes stared vacantly back at Tom Watson for an agonisingly long time, until the judge came to his rescue, asking, "Mr. Watson, do have any further questions for the witness"?

"I don't believe so, your honour"

"Thank you Mr. Hughes you may now step down. You are free to leave the court",said the judge.

The relief on Derek Hughes' face was clearly visible. The wild, wide staring eyes had suddenly been replaced by a much softer demure, even sheepish countenance. The intimidating look had vanished to reveal a much gentler person concealed behind the rough exterior. Grateful to be relieved from what had become an ordeal for him, he stood down from the witness box and hastily left the court room. By now it must have been glaringly obvious to the entire court that he was lying to the point of giving the impression that he himself may very well have had involvement in the theft of the bikes.

Although all the other five witness from count two fared considerably better than Derek Hughes, each of them nevertheless managed to give entirely different accounts of the events surrounding the apparently missing cycles, both from each other and from their own police witness statements. So by the end of the second day, everything was still nice and rosy and going favourably for Johnny, as he watched the prosecution's case disintegrate before his very eyes. There was still nothing so far that could possibly have given him any cause to lose any sleep, as the Crown still didn't have a snowball's chance in hell of getting any kind of conviction.

Wednesday the third of July, day three had arrived and still no problems of any description. Two of the final witnesses from count two gave their evidence, one of whom was Mr. Mulley, a scientific officer, who worked for the police forensic laboratory in Chorley, Lancashire. His field of professional expertise was the analysis of tachograph charts. He had analysed the tachograph chart taken from the wagon on the day in question and despite noting the odd small inconsistency; which could easily be explained, was of the opinion that the recordings were entirely consistent with the route that Johnny had described as having taken on the day in question. Leaving Johnny with the impression that perhaps Mr. Mulley had not fulfilled his intended function. Thus ended the evidence for count two.

***

Proceedings then moved swiftly on to count three: the Nottingham wagon. Jenny Callahan from Hexagon's statement was read to the court, as was the statement of Mr. A. Price, a TNT employee, in yet another seemingly pointless exercise.

Next up was Stuart Rimmer, a bespectacled and perfectly respectable looking young man who appeared to be in his late twenties and just a tad overweight. He also gave the appearance of being the epitome of the young family man. He was the traffic manager, to whom Johnny had handed the keys to when he had returned from Nottingham to TNT's yard in Looters Lane, Warrington. He was to give his initial stint of evidence between 11.51 and 12.26, thirty five minutes in total, which was about the average time for most of the witnesses on the stand. As with all the other police witness statements Johnny had been given, he had taken a great deal of time and trouble to scrutinise in minute detail, S. Rimmer's statement. Before each witness was due to be called, Johnny and Frances would go over each police witness statement time and time again, so both of them knew each statement practically off by heart.

The prosecution began by asking Stuart Rimmer questions on the forms Johnny had completed on the morning in question, including the fact that the driver (Johnny) had been given a map of the suggested route. A few other questions about security procedures at TNT followed. Which were in turn were followed by a question about the location of an immobiliser fob, which was answered by "it is kept on the keys". Immediately something clicked inside Johnny's head, that something wasn't right here. As he wasn't quite able to put his finger on exactly what was bothering him so much, he made a concise mental note of what Mr. Rimmer had said. The prosecution barrister finished off by asking him what had occurred when Johnny had arrived back in the office on that fateful night.

Mr. Richard Johnston, the head of security, had also been on the witness list Johnny received as part of the disclosed material he had been given. However, he was the only witness from said list that was never called as a witness, nor had his statement read to the court.

At thirty one minutes past twelve the next witness to be called was Mr. D. Stanley, a man who was probably in his late fifties. Johnny did not recognise this man on the stand, however, from his police witness statement and the evidence he gave, it was clear that he must be *Mr. Thrust the Mobile in Your Face*. Again with this witness, Johnny recognised he had answered one specific question with something else that wasn't right again. As one of his answers to one of the prosecution barrister's questions was that the driver (Johnny) had seemed annoyed because he had to return on the train. Whereas in reality, Johnny had been enraged because of the way he was treated, in addition to the insinuation that he had stolen the load by Mr. Richard Johnston, the head of security at TNT's Warrington yard. His apparent *annoyance* had nothing whatsoever to do with the train. Again Johnny made a mental note of this, intending as with the other problematic answers given by S. Rimmer, to examine the police witness statements of these two witnesses and then discuss any discrepancies with the barrister, afterwards.

After twenty eight minutes of questioning, Mr. D. Stanley was duly dismissed from the witness stand at one minute before one o'clock, the jury left the room and Johnny was told by the barrister that he needn't stay for any longer and he would speak to him when he was ready; meaning, you leave the court now and I'll catch you up shortly! So Johnny and Frances left the courtroom and went out for lunch as usual. During which both of them carefully read through Mr. Rimmer's and Mr. Stanley's police witness statements. The discrepancies soon became very obvious, even to the untrained eyes of Johnny and Frances. Which begged the question, why was it only Mr. and Mrs Chesney, who were both non professionals, that had noticed this, completely independently to each other? Both agreed that said discrepancies should be discussed with the barrister before the afternoon session began, and so they curtailed their lunch break so that they would have plenty of time to discuss the discrepancies with the barrister. However, both Johnny and Frances were left with the niggling question of why hadn't these two professionals who were after all supposed to be acting in Johnny's best interests noticed said discrepancies? Especially the much more serious one?

On returning from lunch, the barrister and solicitor were nowhere to be seen; neither Johnny nor Frances thought too much of this, as they presumed that they were having a longer than usual lunch break, which would not have seemed too unusual in itself. As a result they had a considerably much shorter than usual meeting with the barrister and solicitor before the afternoon session began; and so could only hurriedly inform them about the discrepancies, that both had noticed earlier. The barrister answered with, "That's not too important don't go worrying yourself about it".

However, the barrister placed much more emphasis on a warning that he himself had never given to either Johnny or Frances, but a warning that had previously been given to them by the solicitor on at least one other previous occasion during the course of the trial, which was: "Do not to go shouting out in court; if you hear something you do not like, wait until we're back out of the courtroom and ask me then. Otherwise the judge will be only to happy to give either one of you, or indeed both of you, a jail sentence, even if you don't get found guilty on anything else! He finished off by robustly asking "DO YOU UNDERSTAND"? A question to which they both answered in the affirmative. He repeated this warning and reminded Johnny that Judge Farmer had specifically asked for Johnny's case to be put aside in order that he could preside over the case and added that he (the judge) has definitely got it in for you!

The afternoon session began as normal, with Johnny sitting in the dock awaiting the judge's arrival before the bog standard "all rise", Judge enters and then everyone sits back down again.

The next two witnesses that Johnny had on his list were two policemen. So when Johnny heard the judge initiating a conversation between himself and both the prosecution and defence barristers about locks and keys, he naturally assumed that it was something to do with the two police witnesses on the list. As they spoke, Johnny's thoughts wandered back off to his by now distressing concerns he had over the evidence given by the two witnesses (Messieurs Rimmer and Stanley), but especially Mr. Rimmer's from the morning's session. Yes, Mr. Rimmer's questions, those were the ones that were really beginning to wind him up! Johnny focussed his mind on the questions that he had never got round to asking, due to the late arrival of the solicitor and barrister back at court after lunch. The location of the immobiliser fob and the reference to Johnny being annoyed at having to return by train being his predominating thoughts at this exact moment in time. Had such mistakes been accidental or deliberate? It seemed odd that these mistakes had been made by two different people, in quick succession.

Johnny thought to himself, *Something that fucking twat of a barrister has said just isn't right at all.* By now he was quite seriously piqued, as he went over and over the conversation in his mind, but he just couldn't put his finger on it! The barrister had seemed unusually strange during their extremely short lunchtime meeting. There it was again, that thought, that very same thought, but what was it? His head was beginning to spin with a multitude of questions rattling about in his mind. It had to be something to do with the questions Stuart Rimmer had been asked, yet it wasn't the actual question that had freaked Johnny out. It was the answer, not the question. Yes, of course! Yes, that's it—the answer, not the question! Well if it's not the question, then just what the fuck was it? Johnny tried desperately to find an answer to the recurring question, only taking the most rudimentary fleeting notice of the conversation between the two barristers and the judge, most of which was just sheer legal gobbledygook to Johnny anyway. They were all were messing about with big legal books, with those little yellow sticky markers protruding from various pages, which were obviously there to act as reminders.

***

Little did poor, old, beleaguered Johnny realise that at this very moment in time, what was unfolding just a few meters away from his very own nose was about to change the entire course of, and ultimately the outcome, of the trial. This would have repercussions way beyond the trial and ultimately would affect the rest of both Johnny's and his entire family's lives.

Despite the fact that all of this was going on right in front of his very own eyes, his mind was so preoccupied that he could only later remember the odd reference being made to expert witnesses and knowledge of the subject matter of the layman, etc. The next reliable memory that he could claim to have was of a Mr. Geoffrey Robert Travis being sworn in. Johnny could imagine Chubby Brown's response to this undisclosed witness being sworn in; TRAVIS! TRAVIS!—WHO THE FUCK IS TRAVIS?

Although Johnny did not have his list of witnesses in front of him whilst he was in the dock, the name seemed to be at the very most, only vaguely familiar to him. The name Travis certainly didn't ring any bells with the two police witnesses that he was expecting to be called. Unsure as to what was going on, he told himself to wake up and sat in astonished silence and listened with the keenest of interest!

Mr. Travis was sworn in. Johnny couldn't quite guess his age, he could have been an extremely battered forty year old or an extremely youthful sixty year old. He wore a black or dark brown leather jacket, which could hardly be described as being new, but not old either, with an open necked shirt beneath it. He gave his full name and his occupation as a commercial vehicle engineer and a company director. He went on to say that he owned a company called Ashbrook Motors, located on the Sankey Bridge Industrial Estate in Warrington and that he had been a vehicle engineer for the past thirty eight years. He stated that his job entailed "every mortal last thing" to do with commercial vehicles. From his opening few words, you could tell that despite his very moderate appearance, he was nevertheless an extremely confident man. The type of person that when he spoke, people would generally stop and listen to him. He would turn out to give the most glib performance of the entire trial.

He went on to say that his company employed eight people and had a link with the vehicles belonging to TNT for the past fourteen years, which was maintaining all of TNT's vehicles in the Warrington area, currently something like 130 vehicles. Right at that exact moment in time, on top of all Johnny's other concerns was an entirely new one. Both the barrister and solicitor had strongly urged Johnny in the strongest possible terms to retain his shield and not to harass Adrian Westerman, a.k.a. Scrooge, a.k.a. Walter Mitty, the apparently reformed petty criminal, compulsive liar and romancer from count one, with the amazing abilities to estimate the load and weight of wagons without the aid of any equipment. He remembered that they had advised him that Mr. Westerman "was not connected to the complainants and that it would therefore be difficult to find a motive for him to lie". He could now clearly see that Mr. Westerman had been one of the very few witnesses throughout the entire trial who had no apparent "axe to grind" and "was not connected to the complainants".

So what about all of the other witnesses throughout the trial, that in all probability did have an "axe to grind" and were without a doubt connected to the complainants? Even without including the police witnesses, (from whom we could not expect get a dispassionate from view anyway). If we discount Adrian Westerman from the calculation, there were twelve others in total. From count one— Lythgoe, Lesley Brough and the security guard from Family Hampers. From Count two—there were six in total, but especially Mr. D. Hughes, in particular. From count three—Stuart Rimmer, *Mr. Thrust the Mobile in Your Face,* Mr. D. Stanley and now Mr. Travis. Thus giving a grand total of thirteen witnesses with a ratio of 12:1, or twelve out of thirteen, or 93% against, that did have an "axe to grind" and were definitely "connected to the complainants". On that basis alone, retention of the shield had hardly been good advice, had it? Especially when Travis had deliberately been kept a secret until the last possible minute!

Johnny was absolutely 110% certain, if not more, that the man on the stand was about to lie his head off. Not only had Mr. Travis been kept a secret from Johnny, but he had just said that he was joined at the hip to the complainants. He personally, as well as his company, were completely and utterly dependant on TNT for the bulk of their business, as were the livelihoods of his employees. Now Johnny could clearly remember what the barrister had said. When he had been so insistent that it would be wrong to harass Mr. Adrian Westerman because the prosecution would portray him as "having no axe to grind" and that he was not connected to the complainants, it would therefore be difficult to find a motive for him to lie and "preferred to question his accuracy; rather than his honesty". However, whilst giving this advice, Tom Watson had made no mention of Travis when he had insisted on the retention of the shield.

Johnny had also taken care to remember the explicit warning that the barrister had given to both he and Frances immediately prior to the beginning of the afternoon session, so what else could either of them do? Other than merely sit in stunned silence like a rabbit entranced by the oncoming headlights, and listen intently to what Mr. Travis was encouraged to say to the jury, that must have presumed throughout the entire course of his evidence, that said evidence had been thoroughly checked and verified for truthfulness and accuracy. After all this was a British court of law, wasn't it?

It would be this very same jury that would ultimately determine the outcome of the trial. Yes, this jury that must have been informed that what they were about to hear from Mr. Travis was to be the truth and nothing but the truth!

The man in the witness box was already emerging as by far the strongest and most convincing witness of the entire trial, and Johnny instinctively knew that it would be he, Mr. Travis, who was going to make or break the trial. He was indeed the kind of man who could convince a jury. The thought which immediately sprung into Johnny's mind was, how much experience had this guy had at this kind of thing?

The prosecution barrister started Mr. Travis off by informing the jury that he was the person that had travelled to Nottingham on the evening of the theft, in order to retrieve the abandoned vehicle. Mr. Travis was then encouraged to claim that it was locked when he examined it and continued stating that the vehicle could not possibly be locked without the use of it's own unique key. Johnny was later to see that this was a contradiction of P.C. Harris-Briston, who was the policeman who had originally found the abandoned vehicle. He was also the police witness that Johnny had on his list and had expected him to be called at the beginning of the afternoon session. However, unbeknown to Johnny or Frances, Travis had secretly been inserted into his place. In addition, the jury were informed that there had been no apparent damage whatsoever to any of the locks on the vehicle. He went on to say that he had with him a set of keys, consisting of two door lock keys, one ignition key, one immobiliser and one rear padlock key. At his point the judge interceded asking these two questions: [13G - 14A]

HIS HONOUR JUDGE FARMER:

Q. "There were two immobilisers altogether, were there"?
A. "No, one".
Q. "One immobiliser"?
A. "One immobiliser".

Thus the judge had implanted into the jury's mind that there was only one immobiliser fob for M316 XLV. A point that Travis was only too eager to try and reassert at a later stage of the trial.

The next line of questioning again focussed on keys and the apparently undamaged locks on the wagon, in what was to become a prelude to a later devastating blow to Johnny's defence, but for now the questioning returned to the issue of the immobiliser fob. The jury were informed that before the vehicle could be moved, the immobiliser had to be deactivated by placing the fob into an electronic contact located on the dashboard, that then releases the immobiliser system.

Something intriguing followed; the secret undisclosed witness was not only an expert in the field of all aspects of vehicle maintenance, especially when it came to locks and immobilisers, but he also had a hidden talent. He must have done a bit of moonlighting on his days off as a clairvoyant because he managed to answer the next question without the need for the prosecution barrister to finish it.

Referring to the immobiliser fob, the prosecutor asked: [15C]

Mr. LEWIS-JONES:

Q. "Help us if you can, is that then left in the—"

Low and behold, Mr. Travis interrupted Mr. Lewis-Jones, the barrister for the prosecution, saying, with a distinct emphasis: [15C]

A. "**No, no.** It's attached to the keys".

Thus the statement given earlier by Mr. S. Rimmer that the immobiliser fob for that wagon is kept on the keys, had been reaffirmed, despite the fact that it had contradicted his police witness statement.

Johnny's mind was now well and truly spinning into a frenzy, but he had to slam the anchors on to stop his mind from spinning any further, because now the jury were being informed that the immobiliser and fob system could be bypassed and there was apparently no need for any specialised equipment to carry out this task. However, according to the secret undisclosed witness, in order to do so expert knowledge would be essential as the immobiliser system was an extremely high-tech and complicated system. Travis was encouraged to claim that in such systems there were no fewer than ten wires, all of which were the same colour, black in this case. Each black wire had a different function, so presumably a manual, or some kind of high-tech equipment would have been required in order to decipher the function of each wire. He informed the jury that the slightest mistake in this procedure left the immobiliser defunct, with the ignition system permanently switched off. In which case an entirely brand new immobiliser system would have to be fitted, in order to bypass the old, defunct one. Mr. Travis assured the jury that this procedure would have been "a massive, massive operation", but practically in the next breath he was stating that he was not a qualified alarm engineer. In fact the job would take him " the best part of half a day 'cause the dashboard has got to come out, all the fuse boxes have got to come out, there's loads of connections to be made, it's not a two minute job, not a two minute job at all". Now that last sentence surely has to beg the question…if he is not an expert, then what in the name of fuck is he doing giving supposedly expert evidence?

Johnny's already beleaguered and battered brain raced and whirled even more furiously than before as he tried his utmost to integrate all this false information as best he could. All the time whilst this was going on around him, he thought to himself, *None of this can be right because these types of immobiliser systems were only in existence for a couple of years during the early to mid 1990's. By the late 90's they had become obsolete.* He distinctly remembered that in 1996 or perhaps 1997 he had owned a British Leyland Rover 213, with such an immobiliser fitted. That immobiliser system had been so fantastic that he'd only had that car for about three months when it had been stolen, from right outside his own front door. It had been either an D or a E registration, probably a D, he couldn't remember which as he had plenty of old rust buckets in his time and he never got the car back after it had been stolen.

True enough Johnny couldn't start the car without the fob, but it had been an old banger at the time, probably not even worth the £100 he paid for it. So neither the technological knowledge, or the equipment involved in it's theft could have been too advanced, as it was probably only kids that had stolen it anyway.

After giving a sufficient pause in order to allow all this blag information to be assimilated by the jury, some of whom were now furiously scribbling away in their note pads and had obviously lapped up every word that the undisclosed witness had said, Mr. Lewis-Jones then returned to the subject of keys. He almost, yes almost but not quite, got the chance to ask another full question as to the location of where spare keys are kept in TNT's transport office when he asked: [16E]

Q. "and so in the office you will find a box or a series of hooks on the wall or—"

However, Mr. Lewis-Jones was denied the chance to finish off the question, when the seemingly clairvoyant Mr. Travis interrupted him yet again. [16E]

A. "**No, no.** They're kept in a filing cabinet away from—"

Q. "In a filing cabinet"?
A. "Yes. In a box in a filing cabinet locked away".

From there the questioning went on to cover the apparent procedures involved in the duplication of spare or extra sets of keys. Travis informed the jury that the procedure for obtaining door keys for ERF wagons was every bit as simple as just going to the key cutting shop that everyone is so familiar with[3], when His Honour Judge Farmer interrupted Mr. Lewis-Jones' questioning; by asking: [18B - C]

Q. "Can you have it (a spare door key) cut in a shop, take it to a shop and have one cut? Suppose you had another key, a spare key"?
A. "Yes".

Q. "Could you go to a locksmith and have one cut"?
A. "You could have the door keys cut that way, yes".

Q. "What about the ignition"?
A. "No, not at all".

Q. "Why not"?

---

[3] However, he later contradicted himself back and forth, several times, on this issue.

In order to answer that question, Mr. Travis was more than willing to expound the apparent procedures involved in the duplication of spare or extra sets of ignition keys for an ERF wagon, which according to him were not anywhere near as simple as the door locks.

Oh no, these were very special keys that could not be duplicated by anyone other than the lock manufacturer via an astonishingly agonising, protracted official procedure. Even this official route for obtaining spare keys was to be the most extraordinarily complicated matter, involving "letters of authority from the owners of the vehicle". Said letter was useless without it having been franked by the ERF garage.

Verbatim Geoffrey Travis: "I've got to get a letter from the manager stating that the vehicle belongs to them, I then go to ERF at Manchester, present the letter, they then ring up the firm who does the keys in Bolton to say that I'm on my way and then they frank that letter to allow me to go to Bolton to get the key. When I arrive at the shop, I've got to give them the letter before they'll do me a key. So in other words, only the rightful person, the rightful owner can get a key, nobody else can get a key…you must go through that procedure". [18D - G]

On answering the next question put to him he once again reiterated that you must go through that procedure. He was to reiterate the importance of the "authorising letter" later, during questioning by Johnny's barrister.

After a couple of more mundane questions Mr. Lewis-Jones asked his final question for this stint: [19C]

Q. "As a matter of interest, which keys did you use to drive it (the stolen wagon) back"?

A. "The original keys that the driver gave to me".

Johnny's brain was working at full speed now and he immediately understood the importance of that last question, because now Mr. Lewis-Jones had informed the jury that the locks could not have been damaged during the theft of the vehicle, because if they had been then the original keys would not have worked, would they? Johnny suddenly thought to himself, *Hold on, wait a minute I never gave this man the keys, besides didn't Stuart Rimmer already say that I'd given them to him? I couldn't have given them to two people, let alone one that I've never previously laid eyes on before this afternoon.*

It was now Mr. Watson's turn with the secret witness. His first question to him was on the subject of the Eaton gearbox that Johnny had described to him during the meetings with him and the solicitor. It was the same

Eaton gearbox that had influenced Johnny's decision as to what route should be taken to Nottingham.

Only at a much later point in time, just a couple of weeks over a year later in fact, was poor old Johnny to realise the importance of the first two questions that his own barrister put to Geoffrey Robert Travis! [16E - G]

Q. "Does the vehicle have an Eaton gearbox"?
A. "Yes".

Q. "The older type, the pre P registration type"?
A. "P registration"?

Q. "Yes"
A. "It's got an RT601 [inaudible] box. **It's in my notes…"**

Something struck Frances' mind that there was something just not right at all in the answer to that specific question. There was something particularly nasty and not right at all, that Johnny himself had missed. However, for the moment, in addition to all the other hoards of demons running around inside both Johnny's and Frances' heads, right now they had to try and concentrate on the fact that Travis was saying that the vehicle had some other type of gearbox to that which had helped to influence his decision not to take the computer's suggested route. Johnny interpreted this as meaning the prosecution would make a song and dance over the time it had taken him to get to Nottingham. He felt sure that they would suggest that the vehicle was emptied well before it ever reached Nottingham, which caused him to skip over a much more important point.

The next line of questioning returned back to the issue of keys. Johnny thought, *Why do these fuckers keep on rattling on about keys? Especially as I've never made any suggestion that a spare key had been involved in the theft.* His position on any theories as to how the vehicle was stolen remained the same as during the interrogations by D.C. Johnston and from which he never deviated. If he was not present at the time when the wagon was stolen, then it would be utterly impossible for him to make any kind of conjecture as to how it was stolen, or by whom. The questions on keys continued relentlessly, with Travis emphatically stating and reiterating that there were no spare keys, either obtained or kept, by TNT[4]. Something stirred in Johnny's brain, wait a minute, didn't he say earlier: [16E]

"**No, no.** They're kept in a filing cabinet away from—"

---

[4] Travis seemed to know a hell of a lot about TNT, especially considering that he wasn't even a TNT employee!

When Travis had so eagerly interrupted Mr. Lewis-Jones, denying him the chance to finish his question. The seemingly clairvoyant Mr. Travis was getting a wee bit beyond himself here and was getting his lines mixed up! Either there are or there aren't spare keys. It can only be one or the other, not both.

An incredible amount of pussyfooting around the issue of keys ensued, with Mr. Travis 'going all around the world' in order to avoid the issue of whether or not you could or could not get door keys cut in a key cutting shop. Johnny sat and silently willed Tom Watson to ask him the question, either you can or can't get keys cut, a few seconds later and the barrister acquiesced to Johnny's wishes. When he reminded Travis of what he had previously stated: [22C]

Q. "I misunderstood. I thought you said earlier that (when asked by the judge) you were asked could you get keys cut"?

A. "Yes, you could probably get keys cut, yes".

More pussyfooting ensued and Mr. Watson moved onto something else, back to the issue of the immobiliser fob. At last the barrister seemed as if he just might make a little headway with Travis on this subject. He had managed to get him to change his story on the numbers of fobs. When Travis had been previously asked by the judge as to how many immobilisers were in existence he had replied that there was only one. Now Travis was pussyfooting and his amazing memory was failing him. The fluency that was apparent in his previous answers was missing, now there were several pauses and flicking between one subject to another in an attempt to avoid giving a direct answer to Mr. Watson's question. Perhaps this was a question that he hadn't been prepared for? At the beginning of his protracted answer, he conceded that, "—there probably is (another spare fob). If there is another one, it'll be with the spare keys". From there he rattled on about the cost of replacing the immobiliser system and finished with, "You cannot get a spare immobiliser fob". [23B] Travis then answered a few other questions which centred around the impossibility of locking the vehicle without any keys, much more fluently, as if these were questions he had been prepared for. At this point Johnny cast his mind back to eighteen months previous when he'd had the four and a half hour (30 minute) *chat* with D.C. Jimmy Johnston. Only now, after all this time, had the conversation going on in front of him reminded him that during said chat, D.C. Johnston had vaguely mentioned something in passing about you couldn't lock an ERF wagon without any keys. Up until this moment, Johnny had completely forgotten all about it, as he knew that the policeman had been talking complete and utter rubbish. Now however, such rubbish was being presented to a jury as a fact that Johnny was sure that the jury must surely have believed had been thoroughly checked and verified, before it would have been allowed to be given as evidence in a British Court of law.

After *much ado about nothing*, the issue of the locked or unlocked wagon seemed to merely fizzle out, but not before the judge kept repeatedly interrupting Tom Watson each time he appeared to be getting the upper hand with the secret undisclosed witness[5]. All of this would have served no purpose other than to leave the jury in an totally confused state, equalled only by Johnny's state of mental confusion.

Right at the very end of Mr. Watson's stint with Travis, the undisclosed witnesses managed to make his *coup de grace* statement. When on yet another instance of the judge interrupting Tom Watson, as he was about to trip the secret witness up, coming to Travis' rescue, the judge asked him: [25C - D]

HIS HONOUR JUDGE FARMER (interrupting):

Q. "Now if the police had locked the vehicle, does it make any difference to your conclusions"?

A. "Not really. It's not the locking of the vehicle that worries me, it's the opening of the vehicle without any sign of—I mean as I say, I've been on breakdowns where vehicles have been outside shops where the driver has lost his key, damaged his key and I've never got in a vehicle by unpicking the lock or then better still, a really good trick, *picking them back on again. Now that would be a very good trick"*.

Johnny could now clearly see the point of sneaking in Travis, without his knowledge. The prosecution were trying, nay actually succeeding quite convincingly in fact, to make it look as if it was Johnny himself that had come up with some kind of hypotheses involving previously made keys that had been involved in the wagon's theft. Which would explain why Travis needed to say that the wagon's locks had somehow been picked. There was however a fundamental and fatal flaw in the lock picking theory, after all hadn't he already said that you can get a key made for the door locks. In which case there would be no need to go picking the locks. Throughout Travis' testimony Johnny had noticed that he appeared to be repeating some very well rehearsed answers. Especially those that he began with **No, no.**

---

[5] DON'T JUST TAKE THE AUTHOR'S WORD FOR THIS. READ THE TRAVIS TRANSCRIPT AND DECIDE FOR YOURSELF!

After one more insignificant question Mr. Watson asked the judge: [25F]

Q. "May I just take instructions, please, your Honour"?
A. "Yes".

Up until the point when Travis suddenly appeared unannounced in the trial, Mr. Watson would make a point of occasionally popping round to the dock to ask Johnny if he had anything he wanted him to add, with respect to the questioning of witnesses. Not that he ever took the slightest bit of notice as to what Johnny had suggested on these occasions anyway. But he never once popped round to ask any questions with this witness, as during the entire time from Travis stepping onto the stand, right up until when he left the courtroom, Mr. Watson and the solicitor both kept their eyes trained forward. Never once making the slightest turn, thus denying Johnny any kind of chance to communicate with either of them. The instant Johnny heard that last request to the judge he thought for one single fleeting moment, *Now this is my chance, at last to ask what the fuck is going on here?* However, his hopes were immediately dashed when Tom Watson merely slid along the bench, no more than a couple of feet and whispered a few words into Mr. Lewis-Jones' ear. Then slid back the two feet he had already travelled, still with his eyes fixed firmly to the front and said to the judge:

"No further questions, thank you, your Honour". [25F]

Travis was then re-examined by Mr. Lewis-Jones, who *went all around the world* via a ludicrously complicated route in order to allow Travis to explain that despite his giving the impression that the wagon could not be locked without the use of keys, that it could in fact be locked, simply by the technique that we are all so familiar with i.e. pressing the button down whilst simultaneously keeping the handle button pressed at the same time. So ended Travis' stint in the witness box throughout which neither Tom Watson or Gordon Spofforth's eyes looked anywhere other than directly forwards, as if they'd both been on a military parade.

At the end of all of this Johnny was utterly dumbfounded, his brain was quite literally in bits as he knew the jury's brains would be also. As if the inconsistencies in Travis' testimony weren't going to be enough for Johnny to contend with, he was also going to have to get some answers as to why this one single witness had not been disclosed to him. The issue of the non-disclosure was in the future to become the bane of Johnny's life.

Travis had given evidence that even now Johnny knew was going to be his downfall. Without being able to verify this himself, even at this exact moment, he could say with 100% certainty that the whole lot of this evidence had been completely false. Not only that, but Travis had been encouraged to say it without his having to show the slightest shred of proof to substantiate whatever lies he choose to tell. He might not have given any proof, but Johnny was determined to get hold of some and make sure that someday, someway, somehow, somebody was going to be shown exactly what lies the secret undisclosed witness, Geoffrey Robert Travis, had been encouraged to tell the jury. Johnny was absolutely certain that the prosecution also knew that everything Travis had said was a lie, **for the simplest of all possible reasons :**

If Mr. Geoffrey Robert Travis had been a genuinely impartial witness "with no axe to grind" and who "was not connected to the complainants", if the Crown knew that he would give *bona fide* evidence that was truthful, accurate and reliable, then there would have been no reason whatsoever to have held him back as an ADDITIONAL witness who remained undisclosed to the defendant.

***

Next came an extremely short statement from a D.C. Brahman, which was read to the court, in a process that took up only one single minute of the court's time, from beginning to end.

Next came P.C. Harris-Briston who stated that he found the vehicle unlocked and he himself locked the vehicle. He made no mention of whether or not any damage had been done to any of the wagon's locks. Therefore all information regarding locks, whether damaged or not, and immobilisers could only have originated purely from Travis himself.

After P.C. Harris-Briston came the Thyssen video, from which there was no possibility of identifying the driver of the abandoned vehicle, in addition the timers were still absent. Despite the fact that Johnny had pointed out to the barrister all of the locations of the other cameras within the immediate vicinity of the where the wagon had been dumped, Mr. Watson made no attempt at introducing this information.

Another much less significant witness' statement was read to the court and Mr. Mulley, the tachograph expert, was recalled in order to make a very minor correction to part of his previous testimony, which brought that day's proceedings to an end. Only then was Johnny able to ask the extremely obvious question; how could it be that he was not told about Travis?

The answer he got was that the judge could call any witness, any time he wished, including any additional witness that he saw fit to call. Mr. Watson said that he had a lot to do before tomorrow morning and that any questions Johnny had about the day's events would have to wait until the following morning.

Johnny and Frances went home, well aware that he had been well and truly stitched up. There was nothing else for them to do but to return home. Neither could get a wink of sleep that night, so both did their level best to prepare a multitude of questions, ready for Mr Watson on the next morning.

The fourth day arrived. Johnny and Frances were there extremely early, as neither had been to sleep at all, not for a single minute, throughout the entire night. Predictably, the instant they laid eyes on Tom Watson they both began bombarding him with the questions that he must surely have been expecting.

Who the fuck was this guy Travis? Why in the name of fuck wasn't Johnny given any disclosure on him? These were questions that Johnny didn't really need an answer for, because in his heart of hearts he knew that Mr. Tom Watson, the barrister for the defence must have been in on it himself, right from the very start.

Amongst the multitude of questions and comments that Tom Watson now found himself being bombarded with was Stuart Rimmer's deviation from his police witness statement. During their all night analysis of the third day's events Johnny and Frances had both come to the conclusion that not only had he altered his position in relation to the location of the immobiliser fob, but in addition to this Mr. Lewis-Jones had been asking Rimmer several questions as to the location of the shop where the ale should have been delivered to. He had got the shop's address as being in Water Street and the location of the abandoned vehicle as Manvers Street, which of course was wrong. Manvers Street was where Johnny had parked the wagon and Water Street was where the Thyssen building was where the abandoned wagon had been found.

A major point that Johnny made to the barrister concerning these two mistakes was that *apparently* only Johnny and Frances, who had lost 60% of her hearing as a consequence of her childhood illness, and not the solicitor present, defence barrister, prosecution barrister nor the judge had managed to spot either of these two mistakes. Which was of course poignantly indicative of Mr. Watson's level of enthusiasm and professionalism throughout the bulk of the entire trial.

Purely as a matter of expediency had Johnny become an extremely eager and willing student of the underhand techniques employed by Warrington Crown Court. All of a sudden he had learnt to become every bit as cunning and devious as those who sought to destroy him. So under the pretence of not being fully aware as to the importance of Rimmer's changed testimony on the issue of the location of the immobiliser fob, he insisted that Rimmer be recalled with respect to the wrong address as being the more important of the two 'mistakes'. Only upon Johnny's utmost and persistent insistence and his very real threat to dismiss him in the middle of the trial, did the barrister agree to ask the judge if Rimmer could be recalled to rectify these two mistakes.

Even with the barrister's agreement to ask if Rimmer could be recalled, the solicitor present still kept trying to get Johnny to desist from this course of action saying, "Don't do it! Don't make the judge recall him. The judge will go apeshit if he's got to recall somebody that he doesn't want to. You're only going to hang yourself if you insist on having him recalled"!

Undaunted Johnny did indeed maintain his insistence that Rimmer be recalled. Answering the solicitor with, "Well I'm fucking hung anyway, aren't I"?

Although Johnny did not dare relate this to either the solicitor or barrister, he fully understood the implications and ramifications of Rimmer's changed testimony. Which in unison with Travis' assertion that he believed there was only one immobiliser, despite the fact that Travis had already altered his position on this point and had insisted that it could not be duplicated, would according to the prosecution mean that only the set of keys that Johnny had handed back into the TNT yard in Looters Lane in Warrington could have been used to move the wagon from Manvers Street to Water Street.

It turned out that the rest of the day in court was called off, as one of the jurors had become ill. So Johnny would have to wait until Friday to see if Rimmer would be recalled. If so and everything went to plan, he would then insist that Travis be recalled also. For the rest of Thursday Johnny did his level best to calm Frances' nerves, which were clearly beginning to fray. After the sleepless night on Wednesday, she at least managed to get a good nights sleep, even if Johnny wasn't quite so fortunate.

The relentless march of time continued and Friday morning duly arrived. Once again the Chesneys were in court before anyone else, anxiously awaiting the outcome of Johnny's insistence on Rimmer being recalled.

Each morning and before the start of the afternoon session, Johnny would meet with the barrister. Today he was told that Rimmer would indeed be recalled, but not before Mr. Mulley, the tachograph expert, was to go over some minor point on yet another occasion. And so the morning session began with Mr Mulley repeating what he had already gone over on the previous occasion when he'd been initially recalled, practically word for word. Johnny thought to himself that this was obviously done to prime the jury and make it appear that a witness being recalled was not such a big deal, in readiness for Rimmer's return. When he did return to the witness box, Johnny instantly noticed that same look that had so bothered him on the first occasion Mr. Rimmer stood in the witness box. He distinctly remembered that it wasn't the question, but at the same time it had to be something to do with the questions Stuart Rimmer had been asked, yet it still wasn't the actual question that had freaked Johnny out. It was the answer, not the question. Yes of course! Yes that's it, the answer! Not the question! Well if it's not the question, it must be that stupid look he's got on his face right now, yes that look, the one he knew so well. He's seen it many dozens, nay hundreds, possibly even thousands of times before. Johnny was now thirty nine years old and had brought up three kids of his own. He had seen that look many hundreds of times on his children's faces especially throughout their earlier childhood. But when they got to about seven or eight, they had learned to conceal that look from him. Now he recognised that same look, that he saw more often than not on a daily basis, if not several times a day.

The one they had when you'd asked them who'd ate all the strawberries? Who drew on the wallpaper? What one of you horrible little shits poured the orange juice down the back of the telly? When all of them replied it wasn't me, Johnny instinctively knew exactly who the culprit was. He could spot the culprit a mile away. Dead easy! The naughty little boy look gave the game away every time! That look where they couldn't look you in the eye and lie.

So here was Stuart Rimmer, a traffic manager for a big logistics company, even now in his late twenties, perhaps possibly in his early thirties. He'd obviously managed to make it all the way through his school years and presumably gain some kind of qualifications. He then entered the employment world and became at the very least reasonably successful by gaining a promotion to the status of manager. But for all that, he still hadn't got the hang of concealing the odd little porky pie from his peers, simply because the expression on his face gave it away. And here he was back in the witness box and true enough the naughty little boy look was there, in an even more obvious form, but so too was another expression. One of fear, dread, trepidation, sheer terror even, however you chose to describe it, there it was as plain as the nose right on the front of his face. After all if he'd lied during the course of an *ordinary trial* he would have put himself in a position where he could go down for perjury, but then again this was no *ordinary trial*, was it?

Mr. Lewis-Jones eased Stuart Rimmer gently into the questioning procedure, by informing him of the mistake that had been made over the two addresses. Next Mr. Watson, initially went over some previously well tread ground with respect to the security procedures at TNT, then asked, "With reference to the location of the immobiliser fob, can you just remind us where the fob is kept"?

Stuart Rimmer paused for a moment; before giving his well rehearsed reply. "It is kept on the key ring".

"Mr. Rimmer, may I ask that you look at the police witness statement you have there in front of you? Is that your statement that you gave to the police on the 8th of January 2000 and is that your signature at the bottom of it? "

"Yes".

"Mr. Rimmer, perhaps you'd like to read through it for a moment or two, just to make sure that everything in there is correct".

After a short pause, in which time he could not possibly have had enough time to read through it properly, he replied, "Yes".

"So Mr. Rimmer, perhaps you could read through it once more and tell the ladies and gentlemen of the jury what your statement says in relation to the location of the immobiliser fob"?

Johnny watched and listened more intently than he's ever done throughout the entire course of the trial, as he looked for the tell tale signs of that naughty little boy look. Yes! Definitely; absolutely 100%, there it was, his head began to bow and he lowered his eyelids in an attempt to avoid his inquisitors peering eyes and gulped down that big piece of nothing that was stuck in his throat. Yes—defo! Defo! There it was—he's fucked it up!

Stuart Rimmer looked back down towards the pieces of paper in front of him for just long enough to make it look as if he'd actually read it. He knew fine well exactly what it said. "The fobs are left in the wagon, as they get damaged (presumably by the keys) if they are left on the keys".

Johnny imagined that at this moment Stuart Rimmer must have been asking himself the questions. Was what he had gotten himself involved in really worth sticking his neck out for? Was it going to be worth risking loosing not only his entire career, but perhaps even his family as well? Johnny hoped that he would realise that whoever had coerced him into lying, would leave him to take the rap alone. If it were to 'come on top', they'd deny all knowledge and Stuart Rimmer and Stuart Rimmer alone would be the one to go to jail! If TNT weren't impressed by his performance today, he could always go and get another job, but not if he were to get himself a criminal record for perjury. Johnny sat and silently willed him to think! Do go and allow these bastards to leave you to carry the can! When suddenly his thoughts were interrupted, as Stuart Rimmer demurely stammered out his reply. “It’s in the wagon”.

“Yes, thank you Mr. Rimmer; it’s in the wagon”!

Johnny sighed an enormous sigh of relief, equalled only to King Darius’ sigh of relief. It wasn’t just for himself, from the dock he could almost feel Stuart Rimmer’s tension. Had his thoughts been his thoughts? Had Johnny somehow managed to hypnotise Mr. Rimmer? Had Johnny just acquired some magical form of mind control? No not really; Stuart Rimmer just shit his knickers, that’s all!

Thus ended Mr. Stuart Rimmer’s horrifying ordeal. He must have known that he had not only contradicted his own evidence, but also that of his buddy, Travis. So at last Mr. Rimmer was permitted to leave the court, in what must have been an extremely relieved state, and needless to say, must have visited the toilet before even attempting to leave the building.

At last Tom Watson had regained something of his former glorifying moment, during count two when he’s questioned Derek Hughes so successfully and with such panache. Still less than 100%, never mind 50%, never mind 10% satisfied with his performance, Johnny thought to himself, *I wonder if that wanker would have been quite so zealous in his approach to his questioning of Rimmer if I hadn’t forced him to recall him*?

The question most prominent in Johnny’s mind now was that, despite the fact that he knew the significance of this altered testimony, he wondered if the jury would take it into consideration, when they retired to consider their verdicts? In addition to this, believe it or not Johnny actually had some sympathy for *poor Stuart Rimmer*. To his way of thinking, although he had allowed himself to become embroiled in the conspiracy to attempt to commit an act of perjury; he had nevertheless not been a willing accomplice. Or at least so it seemed to Johnny, as he believed that such a poor liar would have had to known his own limitations. So Johnny eventually came to the conclusion that Stuart Rimmer must have undergone possibly some quite severe form of coercion to have forced him into firstly agreeing to and secondly actually trying to perform such a dangerous mission, that quite frankly the poor guy just wasn’t up to.

***

The final witness against Johnny was D.C. Tomalin, who was the policeman that along with Mr. Deliberate Mistake had tried to trick him with the non existent video of the bikes being put onto the United Carriers wagon. D.C. Tomalin’s function was to read out some choice parts of various interrogation notes, but managed to omit the part about the United Carriers video.

The day ended abruptly, as there was no afternoon session, so as soon as Johnny was permitted to leave the court, he demanded that Travis be recalled also because if Rimmer had changed his story then so too might Travis. However, despite Johnny's strongest entreaties to the barrister, he refused outright to have anything to do with Travis being recalled and Johnny demanded to know why not. The best answer the barrister could come up with was, "well he's gone now anyway". Johnny was well aware that he was flogging a dead horse, after all the barrister must surely have been in on the stitch up, albeit probably under duress, but regardless, he wasn't going to stand up to the judge and risk jeopardizing his career for a penniless gob-shite that had been stupid enough to put his future in his hands, was he? Johnny had already come to the conclusion that the reason they knew they could get away with not disclosing a witness with Johnny was specifically because he was indeed a penniless gob-shite. It had to be a hell of a lot easier to abuse the rights of someone without the financial clout to get a proper defence. <u>Had this been the reason for Gordon Spofforth's home visit</u>? Was it a reconnoitre patrol, to see how much money he had? After all you can tell a hell of a lot about someone's income by the house they live in. At the time of the visit they'd been living in a run down area, their house had been valued at less than a fifth of the national average house price.

In addition to the Chesney family's obvious lack of funds they must have known that it would be easy to get away with stitching up the defendant in this case, by virtue of the fact that it was such an insignificant trial and nobody in the media would ever have given it a second glance. True enough, Johnny's life was ebbing away, right in front of him, but he hadn't murdered anybody, it was only a relatively small amount of money involved, so it would never make the headlines and go completely unnoticed. What neither Warrington Crown Court nor Gordon Spofforth hadn't counted on, was that this time, out of Christ knows how many other times they'd gotten away with it, they had inadvertently picked on someone who was in possession of more than just two brain cells to rub together and someone who had an inexhaustible amount of determination.

Johnny and Frances consoled themselves with the knowledge that they could have at least one more weekend together, all of which was spent partying as hard as they could, with bucket loads of sex and the kids got to go to Blackpool on the Sunday.

Monday arrived and Johnny spent the entire day in the witness box. As he entered the box he had the most God-awful feeling of dread, the like of which he'd never known. He knew he should be in tip-top condition right now, but he also knew that he wasn't. Nobody had warned of this nauseous sickly feeling he was to experience as he took the Bible in his right hand and repeated the oath. His head thumped, chest ached, he felt sick to the bottom of his stomach as he asked himself, *What happened to all the moisture in my mouth and throat?* The months of fear, anxiety, stress, the countless sleepless nights and the ten million thoughts of what had gone on during the previous week were only now beginning to tell on him. Right now just when he really needed his brain to be in fully operational order, it had decided to go on strike.

Throughout the previous week, Johnny had actually been looking forward to this moment, because it meant that he would have his chance to have his say, but now that the moment had arrived, he dreaded every single second of it. He'd never experienced anything even remotely like it in his entire life. Possibly the best analogy to describe it was when you'd stood and waited in the queue for almost an entire hour, paid four quid of your hard earned cash, got in, sat down, then heard the big foam covered steel harness click into place. All you wanted to do was get back off, but to do so would mean you'd be the laughing stock with your mates for months to come. So what did you do? You sat and waited, until you'd felt the first jolt as it moved off. By now your heart was well and truly lodged in your throat as it began to gather speed through the first of several nasty twists and turns at break neck speed. Then all of a sudden, it slowed, almost to a halt. Within a second you began to hear that same repetitive, big industrial noise of the mechanical ratchet clicking that you'd heard the whole afternoon and well into the early evening.

The track in front of you looked like a perfectly good piece of track, but it wasn't supposed to be pointing in that direction, not at 45 degrees up into the sky. No it was supposed to be flat, at 180 degrees along the ground, wasn't it? Your heart began to fill with the anticipation of the horror that lay ahead as you were being dragged further and further upwards. Now you could see the moon and the stars, without having to bend your neck. Now your head was filled with what ifs. What if a coupling snapped? What if the breaks don't work? What if a bolt comes loose? The big brave hero was now a crumbling, shivering wreck and there was absolutely sweet fuck all you could do a bout it, was there? You came almost to the very top and all the others started screaming with their hands up in the air while you clung to the harness with all the strength you could muster. Just that instant before the industrial mechanical clicking changed to a supersonic whiz…that feeling, just then didn't even come within a million miles of what Johnny was feeling now!

This was much worse that any of that and now poor old Johnny was stuck on this particularly nasty roller coaster. He hadn't paid the fare for this ride because he had never wanted to get on in the first place, but he was going to have pay the price regardless.

The Warrington Crown Court theme park's roller coaster was owned and controlled by none other than His Honour Judge Farmer and operated by his own little group of highly paid lackeys. A ménage à trios consisting of Mr. Lewis-Jones, Mr. Tom Watson and sandwiched in between the two of them was Gordon Spofforth, *gaily* getting a bit of both push and shove and lapping up every minute of it. Once this roller coaster had got moving there was no going back and Johnny was trapped on it and had no choice but to stay on it until the very end.

So now the questions started. The prosecution barrister didn't make any attempt to ease him into the ordeal. No chance! Straight in at the deep end, for Johnny! He didn't start as he'd expected, with the Bradford wagon, not even in reverse order. No, he began with the United Carriers. Johnny correctly assumed that this was a deliberate attempt to disconcert him and more importantly to get the weakest of the three counts out of the way as soon as possible, because the next one he questioned him on was the Bradford and then finally the Nottingham wagon. This was done in more or less the same way that D.C. Tomalin and Mr. Deliberate Mistake had interrogated him in Northwich police station; they'd obviously gone to the same school of tactics. He too was chopping and changing the subject by switching form, one count to another; lingering on what he obviously felt were his strongest points and then switched back again, to something completely different, whenever he felt that he wasn't getting anywhere. The chopping and changing continued throughout the entire morning. In the afternoon session it was exactly the same routine but some questions seemed to have more significance than others, one of these was when the prosecuting Barrister reminded Johnny that he had parked the wagon in Manvers Street, despite the fact that Johnny couldn't have possibly remembered the address of the shop where he was supposed to have delivered. Mr. Lewis-Jones informed him that it was Woodborough[6] Road. He then showed Johnny an enlarged page from his own *A to Z* and asked him to point to roughly where the wagon was left; so Johnny pointed to the location and said the grid reference out loud. Then Mr. Lewis-Jones asked:

Q. "Can you now show us the location of Woodborough Road, where the delivery address was"?

---

[6] The author could not remember the name of the road, but has taken the liberty of assuming it was Woodborough Road, because David Stanley mentions it on continuation sheet number two of his police witness statement.

A. “No”.

Q. “It’s on the same page”.
A. “Well, where”?

Q. “Look at the top right hand corner of the page”.

Johnny stared in stunned amazement, he couldn’t believe it. He had parked the wagon one and a half grid squares away from the road, or at least a section of the road where the shop was. He quickly guessed that he could possibly have been less than 200 meters away from the shop when he’d parked the wagon. Now there were several questions running around inside his head as to what was this twat trying to make of this?

So it had been extremely close to where he was supposed to have delivered on the day, so what? He noted that both Mr. Lewis-Jones and his own barrister had used this tactic of asking a question followed by a long deliberate pause. Tom Watson had used it with particular success with Derek Hughes from United Carriers. Now it was Johnny’s turn to be on the receiving end of this tactic and he didn’t like it, not one little bit. Johnny was intelligent enough to know that right here and now he was stuck in an awful ‘catch 22’ situation, just as Derek Hughes had been previously.

The first option he had was to answer with whatever he could think of, but quickly, however, an answer made in haste could easily be the wrong one and Mr. Lewis-Jones wouldn’t have bothered to ask the question if he hadn’t already anticipated several possible answers that he could in turn throw back in Johnny’s face.

The second option being to say nothing, but this would only be construed by the jury as being stunned silence. In which case they would interpret it as meaning that just like Mr. D. Hughes, he had somehow been caught out at something.

Mr. Lewis-Jones certainly knew his trade well. His Honour Judge Farmer had chosen his prosecution barrister well. Now that Mr. Lewis-Jones had the upper hand, he was going to use his advantage to crush this stupid penniless gob-shite that he had in his sights.

Johnny’s thoughts were: *Either way he wins! Either way I’m fucked*!

Bearing in mind what he thought the function of the Travis testimony had been both to lie and to make it appear as if his evidence had been a counter to what Johnny knew to be, a non-existent hypothesis on how the wagon had been stolen and by whom. Yes, therein lay his dilemma. He knew that he hadn’t made up a story involving duplicated keys. Johnny could now clearly see that if anybody had been lying in wait for the wagon to arrive at the shop then he had given them a fantastic bonus by not parking directly outside the shop. But somewhere incredibly close by, from which any plans could be executed in direct accordance with the original plans. Should he say this out loud and take the risk of Mr. Lewis-Jones having a reply ready, or just sit there like the stupid dumb fuck that he knew he must surely have looked like in the jury's eyes?

In the end he never had to make the decision as by now Mr. Lewis-Jones had already moved onto something concerning the Bradford wagon. While Johnny just sat and silently stared into the abyss.

Another of the questions stuck in Johnny's mind as being particularly significant, for a number of reasons. The question itself was:"Do you agree that within the space of six months, you managed to lose three separate loads"?

"No, two".

"Nevertheless within a very short period of time you had *problems* concerning three loads, with which the police became involved. You must be the unluckiest lorry driver on the road. Has this ever happened to you before"?

It was these last two sentences that troubled Johnny; these two questions had caused yet another half a dozen different thoughts to start spinning around in his head, on top of the half million thoughts already causing a vortex of confusion inside his brain. Now he had the added problem of having to answer in a very short time otherwise the jury would see he was struggling and Christ only knew what they would make of that. But right at this moment, his mind went directly back firstly to "you must be the unluckiest lorry driver on the road". These had been exactly the same words Tom Watson had used in his chambers, as part of a different sentence, but still in exactly the same context. The barrister's words had been our defence will have to be... The quotes resembled each other too closely for comfort. There had to have been plenty of collusion between them as to who was going to say what at the trial. Only half way through that thought and another thought jumped into his head. Has this ever happened to you before? He had heard somebody else say that somewhere before. Now at the worst possible moment, his brain had decided to recall something from the murky depths of his mind. It was big time important, but not now! For the love of Christ, not now! But still he couldn't budge that thought from his head. It was stuck there, he tried to shake it off as the questions kept coming, but to no avail. He struggled to concentrate on the current more pressing problem of trying to answer not only the prosecution barrister's questions, but now the judge was butting in as well; all of which just flew right over the top of his head. Both must have known that they had their quarry beaten. When all of a sudden that part of the ordeal was over, now it was Tom Watson's turn but Johnny couldn't even manage to remember as much as a third of the entire ordeal. *At last surely I'll get some respite from this twat*, he thought to himself, as he tried to gather his thoughts. Well in theory at least, in practice it was to prove to be an entirely different matter. Mr. Watson bombarded Johnny with a multitude of questions that he hadn't taken the care to prepare him for. What was the point anyway? Every single person in the court knew that the undisclosed witness had already sealed Johnny's fate on the previous Wednesday. A bit of damage limitation was the very best that Johnny could now hope for. Finally the ordeal ended and Johnny went back to sit in the dock until the court had finished for the day.

Tuesday the 9th arrived, which was supposed to be the judge's summing up, but it was cancelled due to another ill juror, perhaps it could have been the same one as before. Or maybe they were all getting sick of the trial, either way they weren't half as fucking sick of the trial as poor old Johnny!

On the morning of Wednesday the 10th there was a seemingly meaningless, endless pissing about by the court officials, followed by a short seemingly meaningless video, followed by the judge's summing up. The knife was already inserted, now it was time to give it a good twist and watch Jock writhe in agony. The entire summing up took up just shy of two hours to complete, with the judge's finishing words being that he wanted a unanimous verdict and that it was quite permissible for them to leave any decision making until the following morning, as these things shouldn't be rushed.

The following morning there was still no sign of a verdict being reached on any count. So at ten past ten, the judge called them back into the court to ask them if they were anywhere near a verdict yet. He reminded them that if possible, he'd still prefer a unanimous verdict; eight minutes later they retied to consider their verdicts.

At half past two the judge again called the jury back into the court and went 'all round the world' to tell them that in order to save time, he would now accept a majority verdict.

At twenty past four came the dreaded moment; they had reached a verdict on count three (Nottingham), but not on the other two counts. Even the greatest amount of wishful thinking wasn't going to help now. The instant Johnny heard that a verdict had been reached only on count three, he was absolutely 100% certain that it would be guilty. Alas he was proved right; Travis had indeed served his purpose well. The jury had assumed that his evidence had been checked, leading them to believe his story on the "essential letter of authority", the "picking back on of the locks", the "ten black wires", the "three hours at least and that's with a qualified alarm engineer", "the dashboard having to come out, all the fuse boxes had to come out", "the massive, massive operation" involved in the whole process. Besides why shouldn't they have believed him? Johnny had been unable to counter any of his false evidence, simply because he had no idea that a man called Travis was going to be called against him as a witness, nor what he was gong to say, nor that what he was going to say was to be completely false!

Soon after the court finished for the day, and Johnny and Frances went back home to Liverpool. Almost certain that it might well be their last night together for a long time to come because they were certain that the jury would make up their minds either way the next day. As Frances reminded Johnny that at the beginning of the trial, the judge had apologised to the jury because they had been waiting 'on standby' for an entire week before being allocated a trial. Which meant that this was now nearing the end of their third week in Warrington Crown Court. Johnny imagined to himself how disappointed they must have been after waiting around for a whole week only to be allocated a shitty insignificant little trial like this. They'd have been wanting something a hell of a lot more juicy that this—like bank robbers, serial killers, ten million pound fraudsters...anything except some stupid cunt that had got two wagons stolen. Not only that, but it was also Friday tomorrow. If they didn't decide tomorrow, then they'd have to take another week off work; so tomorrow was definitely crunch time.

Friday morning duly arrived. Before leaving home they both tried their best to eat something, anything that would see them through the day ahead. A bacon butty each was the best they could manage; until a few minutes later and Frances was vomiting the butty back up, into the kitchen sink.

On the motorway driving to the court, Frances said that it all seemed so surreal and she couldn't actually believe that this was really happening to them. It all just seemed like a bad dream.

"I wish to Christ you were right Frances and this really was just a nightmare", replied Johnny.

By half past ten in court there was apparently still no verdict in sight. 'No news is good news'. At a quarter to eleven, everybody was called back into court for a jury question. They wanted to see the Family Hampers video. Johnny could now vaguely remember something that the judge had asked him, during one of his well timed interruptions, when he had been in the witness box. It referred to Johnny's statement that he had given to the police on the night, when he'd gone back with Ian Lythgoe. Now he could remember that the statement had apparently said that "I drove past the Family Hampers yard because the entrance had been blocked". Which returns to the issue of people having too much trust in the police and signing whatever a policeman puts in front of them. Johnny now realised that he too wasn't perfect and hadn't been alert enough and had been gullible enough to sign the statement without reading through it properly. However, the fact was that, in this case there actually had been a wagon in the Family Hampers yard, which was right up close to the gate and facing towards the gate. So given the view from the wagon that Johnny was driving as he had driven up towards the entrance, it would have appeared as if that wagon was about to leave the yard. Johnny now recalled that the judge had interrupted the questioning in order to put his own spoke in. He had asked Johnny the question, "In the video, is there anything blocking the entrance to the gates"? To which Johnny had been stupid enough to give an honestly reply, which was of course no. At the time his head was well and truly battered with the "you must be the unluckiest lorry driver on the road", quote that was so similar to what Tom Watson had said to him, months earlier. Consequently he never gave it quite enough thought, so now was Johnny's last chance to watch the video to try to discern what they were looking for in the video. So it certainly now appeared to Johnny that the intensive pressure that Mr. Lewis-Jones had brought to bear on him had paid dividends for him. The video was duly played to the jury which confirmed that the view from his cab was entirely different from that as seen on the CCTV. Well had he said so or hadn't he? He couldn't remember. Either way it was staring him right in the face now, if he hadn't said it he'd be sure to be berated by people saying that he should have said so at the time. These very same people that had never been in front of a jury themselves and who were in no way qualified to comment on the pressures of being in the witness box, when your life was hanging by a thread.

After the video was played, the jury left the court. The first chance he got, Johnny immediately asked the barrister if he'd explained to the jury about the view from the cab being different to the one that they were watching on the CCTV. When the barrister replied that he didn't think so, Johnny said, "Well don't you think they should be told of the difference"!

The reply he got was that the judge would not allow additional evidence to be given. To which Johnny replied, "Well why the fuck not, he (the judge) had no problem whatsoever in allowing 'additional' evidence to be given by the undisclosed witness, did he"?

"Well it's too late to do anything about it now and I'm telling you, I am absolutely certain that he will not allow YOU to enter any additional evidence".

Although it could never do any possible good now, a thought was firmly entrenched in Johnny's mind that anybody; including himself that had a forthcoming trial should go to at least a couple of other trials first and just sit in the public gallery, watch, listen and take notes. It just might give you that tiny little bit of an edge.

Less than half an hour later, the jury returned a guilty verdict on count three (Bradford) and a not guilty on count two (United Carriers). The judge found it extremely difficult to conceal his glee, as he insisted on Johnny's previous convictions being read out to the court, so as to help justify (or de-justify if there is such a word) any pangs of conscience that they might have felt for him. Judge Farmer's glee was plain; he was basking in his glorious power at being able to destroy yet another life. What kind of horrific, tormented, tortured childhood must this old man have had to endure that created this warped, twisted, damaged, sadistic, monster whose greatest, depraved, pleasure in life was to gloat as he watched others suffer? He'd gone out of his way to manipulate the trial so that an undisclosed witness could furtively sneak into the trial, without the defendants knowledge and the only reason for doing so could have been simply because he was well aware that all the evidence that the undisclosed witness gave was completely false! His machinations had succeeded, all his wicked plans had come to fruition. As he gloated he could feel comfortable in Gordon Spofforth's assesment of Johnny as being a penniless gob-shite who would never in a million years be able to raise the money that would be necessary to get himself a decent lawyer and fund either a proper trial or appeal. Gloat on Judge Farmer! But, and yes—there's always those niggling little buts, isn't there? Wait a minute, you're reading this book, aren't you? You've paid just short of twenty dollars for this book! Twelve and a half percent of which will go to Johnny, some of which he'll spend towards completely normal things like food, clothes, a decent home for his children and all the rest, but not before he's allocated a good whack of his earnings from the book directly to his appeal fund. Gloat on Judge Farmer!

Just to add insult to injury; or perhaps visa versa, in what seemed like less than thirty seconds after the first guilty verdict, Tom Watson informed Johnny that Mr. Lewis-Jones intended enforcing a compensation order for the value of the missing goods. Now he too was basking in his own glorious success, reminding the judge that he now intended to add the Bradford goods, bringing the total to £65,000. A sum of money that Johnny had absolutely no danger of being able to raise.

The judge interceded, spoiling Mr. Lewis-Jones' moment of glory by saying that he didn't see the point in such an exercise. Johnny knew the exact reason why he was so unwilling to adopt this approach. The only way they could have hoped to get away with not disclosing a witness, especially one they knew would give completely false evidence, was specifically because he was a penniless gob-shite. Anyone else would have had the financial clout to get a proper defence. His house had been less than a fifth of the national average house price, valued at a paltry £33,000, even in 2002 that was buttons for a house; so there was no point in trying to take that off him. Besides, the threat of taking the family home away from him might just serve to encourage Johnny to appeal against the convictions and bring some unwanted attention to the *activities* of Warrington Crown Court and that would surely have been the last thing that Judge Farmer would have wanted! He was much more content, merely to sit back and gloat as he told Johnny that he was releasing him on bail, pending a sentencing report, telling him that if he failed to turn up for sentence, the inevitable prison sentence he could expect to receive would be greatly increased. The date for sentencing was set for Friday the 6th of September, a staggering eight weeks away and an extraordinarily long time between verdict and sentence that Johnny had never heard of before or since. The eight week gap did however very conveniently greatly exceed the twenty eight day time limit by which an appeal may be lodged.

Johnny was then permitted to leave the court, before the jury were discharged, quickly followed by both the solicitor and barrister who reiterated the judge's warning. But they couldn't get a word in edge ways, because both Johnny and Frances were demanding an immediate appeal, but both the solicitor and barrister immediately began writhing and trying to dissuade him. When that failed, they launched a counter offensive, saying that an appeal would never succeed, he had been found guilty and that was that. Not only that but Messieurs Watson and Spofforth began haranguing him, telling him that under no circumstances whatsoever should he attempt to appeal against the convictions. Both were in perfect unison with this advice, even when Frances offered to sell her house for whatever little she could get for it and pay for an appeal unsupported by legal aid. Neither would relent and kept insisting that if he were to appeal the appeal court would deem his grounds as being frivolous and would make him restart his sentence from the point when his appeal was heard.

All of this was too much for poor Frances, she ran (hobbled) as best she could from the building, completely and utterly distraught, with tears streaming down her face and muttering incoherently. Johnny was but a few paces behind her. Try as he might, there was no consoling her. That was the last that either Johnny or Frances were to see of either the barrister or solicitor before the date of the sentence.

Chapter IX
½ V

For a painfully long time Johnny pondered the extremely vexing question as to the extent of his own Barrister's involvement in everything surrounding Travis. Reading through the first six pages of the Travis transcript, it was clear that he did indeed make an attempt to prevent Travis being called as an expert witness, which he clearly wasn't, but the judge said it was up to him to decide on who was or wasn't an expert and that was that.

In latter parts of the transcript Johnny could also see that Mr. Watson did indeed try on several occasions to try and trip up Travis. However, on each and every one of these occasions, the judge interceded on Travis' behalf. Thus preventing Mr. Watson from questioning Travis properly. Thereby giving Johnny the impression that the stitching up of himself had nothing to do with his own barrister.

However, these positive thoughts towards Mr. Watson were contradicted by several other factors, including the fact that he didn't ask for any extra time to go through Travis' evidence with Johnny. Something that was well and truly within his rights to do. Not only for his own benefit, but also for Johnny's. It was also well within his rights to request extra time to have a proper *bona fide* expert to give evidence for the defence that would surely have put Travis' evidence into touch.

Then there was the question surrounding his extreme reluctance to recall Rimmer, in addition to his vehement refusal to recall Travis and his even more vehement opposition to even the slightest mention of an appeal from which he and the solicitor could have made yet another bucket load of money.

At the end of the day, either way it made no difference whatsoever to either Johnny or his family. Whether or not Mr. Watson had been involved from the start, or whether he'd been coerced into going along with the stitch up, Johnny was still gong to rot in jail for something he didn't do, regardless.

FORMIDABLE, COMPELLING AND OVERWHELMING EVIDENCE

During the long, lonely nights in his cell, Johnny came up with an extremely good analogy of the consequences of Mr. Watson's refusal to follow his instructions during the trial and make even the slightest attempt to recall Travis. Consequently he left the job half done. If he'd insisted in finishing the job off properly you wouldn't be sitting there reading this book, because there wouldn't be a story to tell, because Johnny would never have gone to jail, because he wouldn't have been found guilty, because Travis' lies would have been uncovered, right in front of the jury's eyes!

Could you imagine going to your doctor, Dr. Snipit, and telling him that under no circumstances whatsoever can you allow your wife to become pregnant, stressing that it's a life and death matter and asking him for a vasectomy and he answers you with, "Yes, sure; I'll book you in for an appointment. It will cost you two grand".

"Oh doctor, two grand is more than I've got in the whole world. But if that's how much it costs, then for the sake of my wife, I'll need to pay it, won't I"?

So you go ahead and break your bank. You beg, borrow and steal, maybe even prostitute yourself and somehow manage to find the money. You turn up at the appointed time and place and pay your money up front, but the doctor's in a hurry. He's got much better things to be doing than sorting your life out for you, despite the fact that he is being extremely well paid for doing so. He knows only too well that this matter really is life and death for you and your family, but regardless he's still unconcerned and wants to get onto doing something else. Something that will be a lot more lucrative for him than your pissing little two grand.

So you get your kit off and lie down on the table, spread your legs and feel the needle going in and wait for ten minutes or so. After which it's time to do the deed, but thankfully you can't feel a thing; well not yet anyway. In the meantime he's busying himself hacking away for a few minutes and you're ever so grateful that you can't see what he's doing underneath that apron thingy, until a nurse comes into the room and whispers something into this ear.

"I'll be back in two shakes of a lamb's tail", he tells you as he disappears out of the room.

Sure enough he's back within a minute or two, three at the most and he's back chuckling away to himself, underneath the apron. Now he's in an altogether much happier mood.

"Nurse! Pass me the hammer, drill, ten mill spanner, hacksaw. No, no, the big one"!

Then the doctor pops his head up over the apron, smiles and gives you a wink and pops his head back down again and in an over exaggerated loud voice, shouts, "Superglue and the nine inch nails, please"!A minute or so later he pops back up, claps his hands, smiles and cheerfully tells you, "All done and dusted! I'll see you in ten or fifteen minutes when you've been cleaned up".

Fifteen minutes later you're sat down, just that little bit uncomfortably, in his office and he's telling you to get yourself home because the pain will be here soon. But don't panic, because it'll go within a week to ten days. After which you should still keep using contraceptives for the next month, until it's time for the next check up.

Sure enough, as promised the pain comes right on cue and you wish to Christ that you'd sent her to go and get done instead, but thankfully, less than ten days later the pain has completely disappeared and you wonder to yourself what all the fuss was about?

The month passes and you have to force yourself to put on one of those videos that you keep hidden, well out of reach for the kids, because you've got to fill up (or at least put a little dreg into the bottom of) another one of those little bottle thingies. Luckily enough, you're not alone and as always the missus is there to lend a hand.

Next day you take the little bottle into the surgery and wait for another two days, before returning for the final check up.

When you do so you're extremely relieved that the tests are all negative and you don't need to return. The doctor assures you that you can safely lash the contraceptives into the bin and just keep shagging away! Happily ever after.

Nine months later you're either suing for divorce, or you've believed the missus' story and you're back down at Mother World, forking out for a new perambulator. To those that are *in the know*, by now you must have realised that the title of this chapter has nothing whatsoever to do with chemical reaction rates.

In which case Johnny's barrister, Mr. Watson, must have had a twin brother who preferred to study medicine over law.

Conclusion: By the time Dr. Snipit came back into the operating theatre in order to continue the operation, his mind was somewhere else entirely. Perhaps something bigger and better was looming on the horizon. He was so preoccupied by whatever had taken him out of the room in the first place, that he'd forgotten all about the left bollock, so thinking it had already been done, he stitched the patient back up.

Which is of course analogous to Tom Watson's failure to carry out the initial part of his job properly and inform Johnny of even the slightest possibility that a man called Travis could be called to give evidence against him. Worse still, he failed to get proper technical (and accurate) advice on the disabling of immobilisers and the duplication of their fobs, in addition to failing to get accurate information on the ease with which ERF door AND IGNITION keys could be obtained.

In an attempt to reduce costs, Dr. Snipit decide to cut corners, instead of the little tubes that he should have been cutting and didn't bother to send the little bottle off to the laboratory that the patient had tried so hard to fill for him.

Which in turn is analogous to Tom Watson's failure to recall Travis!

Now there are plenty who'll say that there are also analogies in Johnny's little story about the doctor who didn't pay attention to the job in hand and that if only Johnny had taken the care to phone Heinz and tell them about the new delivery address, or if he'd just kept the Nottingham wagon within eyesight and not wandered off when he'd gone to buy the *A to Z*, then all this could have been avoided and that effectively he was just getting a taste of his own medicine.

He'd agree wholeheartedly, but in that case he would have only have been guilty of neglecting his duties, but nobody ever lost a daddy through his inactions, nobody ever lost a husband. No husband or father was ever torn away from his family. Nobody ever had to face complete and total financial ruin, through his inactions. Anything that he did, or failed to do, had all been done whilst he remained within the bounds of the law. Which is more than likely why, in Gordon Spofforth's own words, "You'd never have got charged with anything at all, if it hadn't been for Nottingham".

But now the problem with Nottingham was that the court was relying on what they must have known to be completely false evidence. Otherwise they would have disclosed him in the first place, now wouldn't they?

Chapter X
Prison

Prison, according to the government's spin, was supposed to rehabilitate; in reality, for most prisoners including Johnny himself, it had exactly the opposite effect. Like most people who have suffered at the hands of the British legal system, he became increasingly embittered towards anything to do with any form of law enforcement and ultimately the British government, which ultimately has control over the British legal system.

As part of the farcical show, called rehabilitation, that the government put on, Johnny had allowed himself to become a pawn in their game. Whilst in prison he made every conceivable attempt to make the very best of an extremely bad situation, by going on as many educational courses as possible despite the fact that he was only too painfully well aware that no matter how many courses he did whilst in prison, he was destined to leave there completely and utterly unemployable. The prospect of gaining employment placed Johnny in an entirely new quandary. From several conversations with ex-convicts and later upon his release from his probation officer, he learnt that on well over 99% of all employment application forms there's a section called the declaration. Which is the declaration of whether or not you have had a criminal conviction within the past five years. The knowledge that Johnny had gained on the subject was that if he was to fill in the form falsely, claiming he had no criminal convictions to declare, he would stupidly leave himself wide open to the possibility of yet another conviction for *fraud*. Which he knew he would have deserved if he had indeed filled in the form fraudulently.

He'd also heard from other sources that you could always leave the space blank, as if you'd forgotten to fill it in. However, this carried the same risk, as that left you wide open to being charged with *gaining advantage by deception*. In plain English, it was just another form of fraud, which would ultimately bring about exactly the same consequences as filling in the declaration falsely. However, there was no immediate need for him to worry about all that. In the meantime he wanted to overcome the problem of being forced into going to work every day in one of the prison's several workshops, which would just help make the government even more money, with which they would be only too happy to build even more prisons and buy even more bombs.

So what was he to do then? Sit around bitching all day? Or get his arse into gear and do something positive? If he could do something positive whilst in jail, then Gordon Spofforth and Judge Farmer would have failed. Well maybe not completely failed, but at least they wouldn't have completely gotten the better of him.

Whilst in prison, you've got very similar choices to make as on the outside. You can either *sit on the dock of the bay and watch your life drift away*. Or you can at least attempt to constructively utilise the vast amount of spare time available to yourself. So he threw himself into education, regardless. It would keep his mind occupied and stop him from giving Tony Blair even more money.

There was no shortage of proper shite teachers in Kirkham prison, that were only there because they lacked the dedication, enthusiasm and professionalism that would be required in any other better paid teaching job other than in a prison. Besides the majority of society, including these shite teachers, would consider the prison only to be filled with scum bags who didn't deserve a proper education in the first place.

However, most of the people who worked within the prison's education department were only too happy to encourage anybody that was willing to do something constructive with their ample amount of free time. Amongst the most notable of these that Johnny came across during his time in Kirkham, was Dave, the maths teacher. Who was just one these people that just couldn't do enough for you, provided that he had seen that you were trying in some way to advance yourself.

Although Johnny wasn't the greatest mathematician in the world, he had a perfect attendance record at Dave's classes. Most of the prison's educational courses were only for a very basic level. However, maths was one of the few areas of the prison's education department that gave Johnny the opportunity to expand his knowledge. In addition to the maths, Johnny did courses in English, but got himself threw out of the class because he was too advanced for the class; and it was only supposed to be there to help those with a very poor standard of English. Johnny didn't have any such experience with Dave, the maths teacher, because when he saw that the class work was too easy for you, he'd get you to help the others that were struggling a bit. Dave had the good common sense to kill two birds with one stone, by keeping the more capable pupils occupied and getting himself a classroom assistant, *pro gratis*. For some strange reason neither the English or Information Technology teachers could see the sense in such an approach.

So in addition to the courses in maths, English and IT, which even at Johnny's very basic level of knowledge on the subjects, were far too basic for him. There was also the guitar lessons, which he eagerly attended each week without fail. He had his own guitar at home and when they were having a drink in the house, once Johnny was sufficiently *fou an unco happy with the nappy*, out came the guitar and his audience would duly put their fingers into their ears. But now was his big chance to put that right! After a few weeks at his lessons he'd already learnt to read music properly and Frances sent him in his own guitar. Which in turn gave him plenty of opportunity to keep on practicing. After a couple of months he'd progressed from being absolutely abysmal to being merely atrocious and by the end of his nine months inside, he'd advanced himself to the dizzy heights of being fairly shite, which was indeed a phenomenal improvement from the previous September.

Johnny's enthusiasm for staying in the education department and keeping out of work didn't end there, he volunteered for practically every course that was on the go within the jail. In addition to the maths, English, music and IT, he also did Health and Safety, Food Hygiene, First Aid, an art project which involved painting a mural on the wall of the kids play area in the visiting room and a Fork Lift Truck course, which he passed dead easy because he'd had plenty of practice over the years. Especially at a transport company that carried paper products and with whom he nearly always had to load and unload himself anyway. Johnny had no real intention of ever getting a job as a fork lift driver, mainly because it was to closely related to lorry driving, but at least the course got him out of work for a whole week. Besides you never know when it just might come in handy anyway.

In addition to his educational pursuits Johnny did, as a hell of a lot of other inmates did, and used the gym much more often than he would have done on the outside, which partly helped to greatly reduce the size of his waistline. The reduction of his waistline was also *aided* by the *quality* of food available in Kirkham, on a good day it reached the dizzy heights of being tasteless, on an average day it was revolting and on a bad day you just didn't bother with it and did without. On the 6th of September 2002, he weighed 90kg (14stone) and by the time of his release on 6th of June 2003 his weight had fallen to a frighteningly all time low of 63kg (10 stone). Who needs to pay for weight watchers; when you can go to Kirkham for free, eh?

So when a course for a Community Sports Leader Award (CSLA) came up, he dived onto it. Amongst other things, the course involved helping disabled people that came to the prison in order to use it's physiotherapy facilities. These included stroke victims and car accident victims that were learning to use new prosthetics[7]. Johnny was painfully well aware that the skills he was learning, albeit very basic skills, just might be needed one day with Frances, if her condition were to deteriorate any further. The course also involved teaching skills for all sports activities, which was sure to come in handy when Johnny returned to the real world and started back at the Ju-Jitsu club.

Despite all these various attempts at keeping himself as busy as possible, every single minute in the jail seemed like an month. Doing all these courses was fine, but they couldn't come even remotely anywhere near compensating for him being so near and yet so far away from his family. No matter how hard he tried, his thoughts were never inside Kirkham jail, but always thirty six miles away, back in good old sunny Bootle.

***

So here was Johnny sitting rotting away in jail, with every minute seeming like a month. No matter what he tried he just couldn't manage to adequately fill the time. Back out in the real world he'd only very rarely watched TV; 99.9% of what was broadcast on it was complete and utter shite and as for the news, well that was either filed with yesterday's tragedies or was just part of the government's propaganda machinery, wasn't it? But Johnny's going out of his mind with boredom and so the dreaded television that he spent so much time and effort trying to avoid whilst out in the real world was slowly but surely creeping into and becoming part of his everyday prison life.

He liked comedies, but mainly only the old ones; proper old, like Laurel and Hardy, Jerry Lewis and some more modern stuff like the Monty Python films and *Fawlty Towers*, which never became dated. But he even liked shows like *The Young Ones* and *Bottom* that had become very dated, very quickly. He never tired of good old cartoons neither, among his favourites were Beep Beep, the Roadrunner, *Wacky Races* and *Tom and Jerry*. As for films, he liked the Clint Eastwood spaghetti westerns and most cowboy films in general. He was also a fan of the typical action blockbusters, with the likes of Arnold Schwartzenegger and Nicholas Cage starring in them, but apart from those Johnny wasn't much of a TV man at all.

But when you're bored to tears, you're bored to tears; and like anybody that's really bored to tears, Johnny ended up like all the other sad twats,

---

[7] Artificial limbs.

prepared to watch any old shite on the television just in order to pass the time of day. It got to the point where he was getting so sad that he even started watching the news.

From about October or November 2002 to March or April 2003 the two worst low-life pieces of shit[8]on the face of the entire planet were plastered all over the television and papers putting their hands on their hearts and giving a multitude of glorious rallying speeches proclaiming how much justice, democracy, freedom, human dignity and human rights meant to them. All these things meant so much to these two vermin that they intended spending something like £87,000,000 a day each[9], as well as forfeiting countless lives[10] including soldiers from both their countries to ensure that the inhabitants of a country that nobody had even heard of since 1991 were going to get more justice, democracy, freedom and human dignity and human rights than they knew what to do with, whether they wanted it or not.

But for all their proclamations about justice, democracy, and freedom and all that shite, both had apparently completely forgotten to make even one single mention of the word OIL.

If there is such a thing as a syndrome for *selective* memory loss, Johnny thought that these two must have had the worst cases in medical history; however, he was to find out that it wasn't only these two that suffered from this terrible newly discovered medical condition.

---

[8] At least one of whom had been a lawyer in a previous life.
[9]Not of their own money of course, just the gob-shite tax payers money, in each of their respective countries.
[10]Not their own lives though!

Chapter XI
Appeal # 1

Well before Johnny was sentenced on the sixth of September 2002, he had made a resolute commitment to appeal against both convictions. Following the convictions, Johnny had been released on bail for sentencing reports. One month before the sentencing was due to take place he went to a local scrap-yard that specialised in wagon spares. Purchased an ignition system, with a key for an ERF wagon of a similar age and model to M 316 XLV, which he had to remove from the scrapped wagon himself, he then went to an ordinary key cutting shop—i.e. not a specialised locksmith—who took all of 30 seconds to cut a new key. So despite Mr. Travis' assertion that to obtain ERF keys was a difficult task, to say the least Johnny had by now proved this not to be the case.

Knowing that both barrister and solicitor would be at the sentencing hearing, first he went in person to the barrister's offices in an attempt to contact the barrister directly so as to inform him of his *discovery*. However, the secretary at the barrister's chambers informed Johnny that he would not be permitted an audience with the barrister without first going through the solicitor. So he made the next obvious move and tried to contact Gordon Spofforth, firstly by telephone, but despite making repeated phone calls to his office, no return call was ever made or received. Undaunted he tried calling in person at the solicitor's offices on three separate occasions, but Mr. Spofforth had become somewhat elusive since the trial and Johnny was told on each occasion that he was not in his office each time that he called at the office in person.

So Johnny had no real option but to wait until the day of the sentencing before presenting his *discovery* to the barrister, with only the faintest of hopes that he could somehow abort the impending prison sentence. The barrister's reaction to the newfound discovery was that it did not constitute strong enough evidence to support grounds for an appeal. He added that the jury had made their decision and that was that, end of!

So Johnny was duly sentenced to two years for each offence, to run concurrently. After being taken down to the cells below the court. A court screw informed him that his legal advisors wanted to speak to him and so he was led to a small room where Watson and Spofforth awaited him. Once alone, they immediately began haranguing him, telling him that under no circumstances whatsoever should he attempt to appeal against the convictions. Neither could be dissuaded from offering this advice, even when Johnny once more offered to sell his house and pay for an appeal unsupported by legal aid. Neither would relent and kept insisting that if he were to appeal the appeal court would deem his grounds as being frivolous and would make him restart his sentence form the point when his appeal was heard.

Gordon Spofforth's parting words to Johnny were: Do not appeal Johnny; don't entertain the thought, not even for a single moment. I'm telling you, you will be made to restart your sentence. I have a lot of experience in these cases and I've seen it happen. So take my advice; DO NOT APPEAL!

Tom Watson's parting words, as he walked away and just before disappearing behind a closing door were: If you appeal the judge will say this guy is really taking the piss here, and take my word for it, he will give you more time, I promise you, because you are taking the piss especially with the ridiculous story that you made up for the Nottingham charge!

Johnny's immediate thought as he watched Watson disappear behind the closing door was, what story? I've never had neither a story nor a defence to the Nottingham charge. I've insisted from day one that if I wasn't there at the time of the theft, then I couldn't possibly say how or by whom it was stolen. As he remembered how many times that these two had tried to embroil him into postulating on how the wagon had been stolen in the first place.

These parting words by Tom Watson helped make up Johnny's mind right there and then, that come what may, his days of taking advice from Messieurs Watson and Spofforth were well and truly over. And before the end of September Johnny had initiated his own do it yourself (DIY) appeal. DIY for two main reasons, first and foremost was the knowledge that all lawyers stick together and if these two were going to be involved in stitching him up then so too would every other lawyer in the country. The second and far more obvious reason was lack of money; pure and simple!

Knowing full well that the appeal judges had it well in their considerable power to restart his sentence if they so chose, on the twenty fourth of September 2002, Johnny posted his first appeal letter and completed Form NG to the appeal court in London, with an explanation as to why he had exceed the twenty eight day time limit. In part of the application form there was a section called grounds for appeal in which you were to write your grounds for appeal, in your own words. So Johnny clearly stated that he had no prior knowledge that Travis was to be called as a witness against him, nor, as to what his evidence against him was to be either. He also made it perfectly crystal clear that he now had, in his possession, evidence to counter Travis' assertion that ERF ignition keys were nigh on impossible to duplicate, other than via '*his own protracted official route*' which Johnny could prove only existed in Travis' blag world. He also made several references to Mr. Adrian Westerman, regarding his expert knowledge and references to Ms. Lesley Brough's hearsay, in addition to the extreme bias that Ian Lythgoe had shown towards him.

By mid October Johnny had received confirmation of receipt of his appeal application. By now he had spoken to several various other prisoners about what had happened to him during his trial, in particular the non-disclosure of and the apocryphal evidence given by Travis. Two main points began to emerge. One was then as it still is to this very day, that Johnny was to be the one and only person that he had ever heard of that DID NOT get disclosure on a witness. The second was why was a jury so willing to believe that these keys were so impossible to duplicate? The only conclusion that he could come to on this point, was that the jury must have thought it utterly inconceivable that the Travis testimony had not somehow been verified and it must have therefore have been true.

The keys! Yes, the keys! Johnny realised that there had to be something more to them than he had previously thought. By pure chance, one of Johnny's fellow lags on the same block, who had never been an HGV mechanic, but who had gone from stealing cars in his youth and then progressed onto lorries and plant machinery in later life, now found himself caught and in the same prison as Johnny. He was able to inform Johnny that immobilisers systems on M registration ERF wagons could easily be bypassed, by an extraordinarily simple method.

Apparently these immobilisers worked by breaking a circuit to an essential component of the ignition system within the wagon's engine; the starter motor was apparently one of the favourite immobilising points. So if you didn't turn off the immobiliser by inserting the electronic key to re-establish the circuit between the wagon's battery and the starter motor, it would remain broken and the wagon wouldn't start. The circuit could be re-established by running a wire from the battery's positive terminal to the positive terminal on the starter motor. Then use a big plastic handled screwdriver to cross the starter and—Hey Presto!—the wagon would start. The only problem with such a system for stealing any vehicle was that if you stalled the vehicle you would need to repeat the process in order to restart the vehicle, but said process would only take up to two minutes at the very most. So now Johnny had an extra bit of information to counter

Travis' assertion that to bypass the immobiliser system would be "a massive, massive operation" which in the hands of someone who was not a qualified alarm engineer, like himself, would "take the best part of half a day 'cause the dashboard has got to come out, all the fuse boxes have got to come out, there's loads of connections to be made, it's not a two minute job, not a two minute job at all".

His wayward but extremely informative new friend went on to inform him of what would eventually become much more fruitful and useful information regarding the duplication of ERF keys. As the registration number of M 316 XLV suggests, it was quite obviously an M registration and more than likely manufactured in 1994 and as such would have been fitted with the old type of keys that Johnny had previously obtained. However, after P or R registration 1996 or 1997, a newer more sophisticated type of ignition key had been installed into that particular make of wagon. They didn't have teeth, like the old type, but instead had holes drilled into the sides of the keys. A system of ball bearings within the ignition lock slotted into said holes and thereby operated the lock, thus allowing the engine to be started just like with the normal keys. He told Johnny that if the ignition lock had been replaced after 1997, then it would more than likely have this new type of ignition lock fitted.

His foremost thought was Travis' repeated assertion that an official letter of authority was essential to obtain a duplicate key. Johnny knew exactly what Travis had said in the witness box, simply because of his non-disclosure, Johnny had taken the time and trouble to make very careful notes of what Travis had said that same evening when he'd returned home. Travis had said that these were keys that could not be duplicated by anyone other than the lock manufacturer, via an agonisingly protracted official procedure. Even this official route for obtaining spare keys was the most extraordinarily complicated matter, involving "letters of authority from the owners of the vehicle"and said letter was completely useless without it firstly being franked by the ERF garage.

Verbatim Geoffrey Travis: [18D - F] "I've got to get a letter from the manager stating that the vehicle belongs to them, I then go to ERF at Manchester, present the letter, they then ring up the firm who does the keys in Bolton to say that I'm on my way and then they frank the letter to allow me to go to Bolton to get the key. When I arrive at the shop, I've got to give them the letter before they'll do me a key. So in other words, only the rightful person, the rightful owner can get a key, nobody else can get a key"... "you must go through that procedure".

Mr. Travis had reiterated that "you must go through that procedure" and had again repeated the importance of the "authorising letter" during the questioning by Johnny's barrister, when the judge had again interrupted.

Bearing in mind that Travis had made such great play about the procedure involved in obtaining an official key from the ERF company. So both Johnny and Frances decided that it would be much better if he could obtain a key directly from the manufacturer; rather than via an 'unauthorised' route. So as an extra precautionary measure Johnny himself phoned the ERF main dealer (in Widnes and not in Manchester) ordered and paid for a post 1997 ignition lock system, using Frances' debit card numbers.

Another thought began to materialise inside Johnny's head, regarding Travis' assertion that you would need to travel all the way to Manchester for the nearest ERF garage. He pondered that when someone wants to conceal something from you, or simply just lie to you, they often rely on making whatever they are trying to conceal from you appear to be far away; as if in the hope that by increasing the distance, whether it be in time or miles, it somehow forces you into relying on their version, because what they are talking about is too remote for you to be able to verify it for yourself.

Although Johnny had no direct access to the newly acquired ignition lock, Frances informed him that the keys were exactly like his new mate had described to him. So using the prisoner's telephone, Johnny then ordered a duplicate key. This time however, he insisted that the key must be paid for by cash, knowing that if he could obtain the key without the supposedly essential "authorising letter" and pay by cash, someone that had just walked in off the street could do the same. Then surely that would blow Travis' testimony right out of the water? The plan was duly put into action and lo and behold no "letter of authority from the owners of the vehicle" was required. Which obviated the need for the ERF garage to frank a non-existent letter. Nor did Johnny have to go to Bolton either. How could he? After all, wasn't he sitting inside a prison cell, in Kirkham, Lancashire? Mrs. Chesney certainly didn't need to go to Bolton, she just went to the garage in Widnes, ordered the key and picked it up at the same garage which was less than five miles away from Warrington. So despite the dissimilarities in the two different types of keys he had yet again obtained a duplicate key, without any real effort. Johnny would be sure to emphasise this point, when writing his next letter to the appeal court, that he had achieved this from within a prison cell, over the phone. All conversations regarding the ordering of said duplicate were done over the phone. All phone calls made by prisoners (using their own individual pin numbers) were monitored and recorded. Prisoners ordering bits of wagons, especially bits that were concerned with vehicle security, must have been an extremely uncommon conversation for the eavesdropping screws to listen in to. So such a conversation could not possibly have gone unnoticed by the prison authorities. Therefore, if there had been anything whatsoever illegal or even slightly underhand about this transaction, firstly it would have come to the attention of the police, and secondly Johnny would have been prevented from obtaining the duplicate.

Johnny now felt absolutely sure that the appeal court could not possibly deny that something was seriously amiss with the evidence that the 'additional' witness, Mr. Travis had given at his trial. However, he was learning fast, and his previous experience with judges, barristers and solicitors, lead him to believe that these people very definitely do stick together and it was extremely likely, if not an absolute *dead cert* that a cover up loomed ahead. Time would indeed tell if he would be proved right on that point.

In an attempt to deny the appeal court even the slightest chance of covering up, it would be better if Johnny could gather further evidence to counter Travis' false evidence, otherwise they might use the excuse not to grant him leave to appeal because this was only one single point that he was confident that he could prove beyond a doubt and a *single point doth not a trial make*. So the obvious thing to do was gather more than one point with which to launch his appeal. Yes, that was it! Get more dirt on Travis!

Johnny sent another letter to the court of appeal in London, entitled the 'first Judge letter' which was intended for the single judge who would decide if Johnny was going to get past the first hurdle and be granted leave to appeal. For the benefit of the uniformed in Britain there is no such thing as an **automatic right to an appeal**. You might think that such a right exists, but poor old Johnny found out the hard way that it doesn't. In order to get anywhere even remotely close to an appeal, you first have to be granted **leave to appeal.** If you don't have untold bucket loads of money to throw about, then you have got absolutely no fucking danger of getting past this first crucial stage. This doesn't just apply to Johnny, it applies to every single poor person in the whole of Britain. The appeal court's most favoured tactic for denying anyone wrongly convicted any chance of an appeal is simply to prevent them from getting past the first stage. Thus effectively denying them a *proper appeal*. Furthermore, anyone foolhardy enough to persist and attempt to further an appeal without first being granted leave to appeal runs the very real risk of having their sentence increased, should the appeal court decide that the initial appeal was frivolous and groundless. This tactic usually deters the vast majority of people from trying to take their appeal any further; regardless of how justifiable their case for appealing was in the first place.

As with the form NG, the latest letter also clearly stated that he was not given disclosure on the Mr. Travis, nor his evidence. In addition he pointed out several discrepancies in his testimony. Including the fact that he contradicted P.C. Harris-Briston who had found the abandoned vehicle and in the absence of any expert training had somehow managed to lock what Warrington Crown Court had tried to lead the jury into believing was an apparently unlockable wagon. At this point Johnny too was under the impression that Travis had stated that the wagon could not be locked without the use of it's own keys. Only at a much later stage, when Johnny had bought the Travis transcript, was he to find out otherwise.

He pointed out that when Rimmer had been induced into changing his story on the location of the immobiliser fob, then surely it must have become all the more imperative to also recall Travis to see if he could stand up to a little closer scrutiny. He added that he had implored Tom Watson to recall Travis, but that his entreaties had been ignored.

He continued by asking for a re-trial and pointing out that even if you were to dilute Travis' and Rimmer's lies down 1000 fold, you would still be left with grossly inaccurate and extremely misleading evidence and asked the judge to make note of just how partial, to the point of being extremely biased, these two had been against him at the trial. As well as how easy it had been for him to obtain duplicate keys. He specifically asked the judge to take note of the vital point that prior to July 2002, he himself (as would the jury) would have expected that any evidence given at the Crown Court must have been thoroughly checked for truthfulness and accuracy. Despite the fact that this was apparently not the case at Warrington Crown Court, he went on to reiterate his position that he had never made any suggestion that duplicate keys had been involved in the theft of the Nottingham wagon.

To ensure that the single judge was well aware of the point that he was trying to make as to how easy it had been to obtain duplicate ERF keys, he reiterated just how easy it had been to obtain the older type keys. And in anticipation of Travis being able to say that the wagon in question was fitted with the older type, but was perhaps fitted with the newer type, he set out the following text (boxed), *verbatim* and in exactly the same format.

As an extra 'precautionary measure' I have 'invested' in the ignition lock system which is fitted to the more modern type of ERF wagons. The keys used in this type, are dissimilar to the older type. However, despite the dissimilarity, I have yet again succeeded in obtaining a duplicate key; without great difficulty! I have achieved this from within a prison cell. All conversations regarding the ordering

of said duplicate were done over the phone from jail. All phone calls made by prisoners in this jail are monitored and recorded. If there had been anything whatsoever illegal or even slightly underhand about this transaction, I'm absolutely certain that:

A/ It would have come to the attention of the police.

B/ I would have been prevented from obtaining the duplicate.

In which case the Travis sentiments on the 'high security' afforded, even by the newer type of ERF keys has to be totally incorrect and perhaps a complete and utter prevarication.

In addition to this, due to the absence of proper legal advice, he requested relevant details of the appeals procedure, information on the British legal system's own rules governing the pre-disclosure procedures and on the rules governing the production of 'expert' witnesses. However, none of these requests were ever to be fulfilled.

Instead Johnny had to rely upon information that he derived either from other prisoners or Mr. H from the prison's legal aid department. Mr. H stressed to Johnny that he was only trained to a very basic level in legal matters and that he was not a qualified solicitor. Furthermore any information given to Johnny by him should be treated as such.

Despite this advice, Johnny fully trusted Mr. H to give him the best possible advice he was capable of giving him. He advised him that he was not automatically entitled to a full appeal. In order to get to the full appeal stage he had to get over the first hurdle, which was the single judge. Only if he granted Johnny leave to appeal, could he then get to three judge stage and from there onto the full appeal stage and even then, nothing was guaranteed.

Johnny also made several well founded complaints concerning the use of Mr. Adrian Westerman as an 'expert' witness and ended his letter by saying that in the event of a re-trial, there would be a vast array of other issues that would need to be dealt with in much greater detail.

The letter was duly sent off and Johnny began what can only be described as a pestering campaign on Mrs. Mary Soskin, who was the manger of the lawyers in the appeal court and had been given the unenviable task of dealing with Johnny's case. He deliberately, relentlessly bombarded her with numerous phone calls and letters as to the likely date of the first judge appeal hearing to see if was to be given leave to appeal or not.

She in turn wrote back asking (practically pleading) Johnny not to keep harassing her, as she had a vast workload to contend with and that such an approach would not get his appeal dealt with any quicker. She tried to appease him by telling him that his application would be dealt with in approximately three weeks. At the end of the three week period—surprise! surprise!—nothing happened and so Johnny restarted his letter writing and phoning campaign. Again she assured him that it would only take at the very most another three weeks before the application for leave to appeal hearing would be heard. Yet another three week period elapsed and the cycle again recommenced. During this time one of the appeal court's letters stated that because Johnny had made complaints about his former legal representatives, his complaints would be put forward to both the barrister and solicitor and that he could expect to receive a copy of their reply to his complaints.

The reply to his complaints duly arrived, which Johnny in turn scrutinised in fine detail. Reading into the reply, a pattern of ***selectivity*** began to emerge. In the reply it was clear that both the barrister and solicitor had only bothered to reply to the points that they felt were their stronger ones for failing to represent Johnny properly and had either *misinterpreted* or chosen to omit anything that they felt the slightest bit uncomfortable with. From the reply there was also a detectable degree of panicking by the barrister and solicitor. By far the most important of these uncomfortable points was of course the non-disclosure of Travis. Despite the fact that Johnny has in every single piece of correspondence connected to his appeal, he had made a point of deliberately, repeatedly mentioning and elaborating his complaints in very great detail, especially as to the non-disclosure. It was then and still remains to this very day one single point that has never on any occasion been tackled by either Gordon Spofforth, Tom Watson, the single judge, the Honourable Mr. Justice Langley, the appeal court's outside lawyer, any of the three appeal court judges or the Criminal Cases Review Commission. The ignoring tactic by the appeal courts has been entirely consistent throughout Johnny's appeal efforts since day one! Johnny soon came to the conclusion that they must obviously think that just by ignoring the issue, it will somehow just go away.

Chinese whispering (distortion of facts) was another favoured tactic that Johnny had to contend with. Both The barrister's and solicitor's versions of what had happened at the trial, in addition to both Johnny's testimony and that of the various witnesses, were riddled throughout with said Chinese whispers. Which were not used only by Johnny's former solicitor and barrister. Throughout the entire course of ALL of his appeal efforts, he had to endure what for want of a better expression, Johnny could only describe as being **a *process of multi-layered* Chinese**

whispering.

The extent of these Chinese whispers were to multiply through each and every single stage of the appeal process, by each and every person involved, as the points for appeal were *handled* by ever increasing numbers of judges and lawyers who were vehemently opposed to a successful appeal, up to the point where any given original statement or piece of evidence was to be rendered barely recognisable, if not completely unrecognisable, to the original.

Johnny easily detected a stupendously vast array of extremely serious discrepancies within the replies to his complaints. There was also an easily discernable degree of panicking in both the solicitor's and barrister's replies to the complaints.

So in turn, Johnny retorted with another letter in *reply to the reply.* Making a point of elucidating exactly what and where the discrepancies were.

One (of several, if not dozens) of the major discrepancies was where Gordon Spofforth really cocked up big time when he made an attempt at claiming that Johnny had been given disclosure on Travis. On the fifth paragraph of the second page of his reply to Johnny's complaints, Gordon Spofforth stated:"We can advise the court that Mr. Travis' statement was served upon the defence a long time before[11] Mr. Chesney's case came to trial. Instructions were taken off Mr. Chesney in relation to Mr. Travis' statement in particular".

Regarding the above statement Johnny made it absolutely clear in his *reply to the reply* that **Travis was an ADDITIONAL witness. MEANING HE WAS 'EXTRA' or 'SUPPLEMENTARY' and brought into the trail at the very end of the trial.**

So there would be no need whatsoever to discuss a statement that was presumably to be left out of the trial. Which in turn has to beg the question, why go to the bother of taking statements that should never be used?

Unless of course it was planned well in advance that it was to be used in exactly the undisclosed manner in which it was used!

Even taking into consideration his previous disastrous, if not catastrophic, experiences with his former solicitor, Johnny was still taken aback by the blatantly obvious desperation in Gordon Spofforth's claim; he

---

[11] Travis' police witness statement was dated **11/12/01,** some eleven months after his buddy, David William Stanley, had given his statement. **[Why the delay?]** Some seven months before the trial! So it would seem that there would indeed be ample time for Mr. Travis' statement to be served upon the defence a long time before Mr. Chesney's case came to trial. **[So why didn't Gordon Spofforth inform his client, about this new *so called evidence*?]**

was clearly clutching at straws.

Surely to Christ any fool would know that an undisclosed witness would not be discussed with the intended victim and besides Gordon Spofforth hadn't made even the slightest attempt to specify just what these *supposed* instructions were. Well how could he? No instructions had ever been given!

Even if the illegal non-disclosure of Travis was dressed up as him being an ADDITIONAL WITNESS! It would have to be completely obvious, if indeed not absolutely essential that in order to properly defend his actions, Gordon Spofforth would and indeed should have been more than willing to expound exactly what these mysterious *instructions* supposedly were. Isn't that what you'd expect anyone else to have done under those circumstances?

But he didn't expound exactly what these mysterious *instructions* were and the reason he didn't was because no instructions were ever taken and the reason that no instructions were ever taken is quite simply because Johnny was never made aware of the existence of Travis or his false evidence prior to him being sworn in!

Johnny was well aware that Gordon Spofforth's claim could well be his *redeeming factor* as well as Gordon Spofforth's downfall. So he took what seemed like a sensible precaution at the time of making several copies of the replies and ensured that they were distributed far and wide. This making of multiple copies and the care in their ensuring their distribution, was to become a prevalent feature with anything that he felt was of significant importance throughout his appeal efforts. *Just because you accept that you are paranoid doesn't mean that they're not out to get you! Sometimes it pays to be a little paranoid!*

Johnny then went on to ask the appeal court for a copy of these apparent 'instructions' that were given in relation to Mr. Travis' statement. The reader won't be too surprised to learn that **Johnny never received a copy of these apparent *instructions* and doubtless never will!**

Also in the in the *reply to the reply*, letter Johnny made it clear that he himself had taken the time and trouble to make the video for the loaded moving wagon in order to counter Adrian Westerman's ludicrous, so-called evidence. He had done so because he had actually been given disclosure on said ludicrous evidence and that IF! YES, IF! he'd known about Travis at any point before he was sprung on him out of the blue then he'd have done the same kind of thing—i.e. gone out and bought all the locks, etc.—BEFORE the trial!

Eventually his relentless pressure on Mrs. Soskin paid off, well in a fashion, at least. The date for the first judge to 'consider' his application for leave to appeal was set for 25/11/02. By this time he had been in jail for over three months and had discussed the appeals procedure with several other prisoners on many occasions and he was now beginning to become familiar with the techniques employed by the appeal court used to discourage anybody from appealing.

By far the most commonly used techniques were a combination of preventing you from getting past the first stage in the appeal process—i.e. denying you leave to appeal, used in conjunction with the threat of extending your sentence. Which was exactly the same threat that both Messieurs Watson and Spofforth had used on the day of the sentencing. Johnny had become well versed in each stage of the appeal process and the apparent dangers involved in each step. The first judge stage that he was now at, was completely safe, a point that Messieurs Watson and Spofforth had neglected to point out to him; they had led him to believe that it was at this first stage that his sentence could be increased. However, from Johnny's own inquiries he had learned that this was not the case.

However, the downside was that if this first judge refused him leave to appeal and he persisted to go over his head and continued onto the three judge stage without the first judge's *blessing,* then it was at that stage the sentence could be increased, if they deemed his case for appeal to be frivolous. During the preceding three months whilst in prison he had heard many 'horror' stories whereby sentences had been increased on various prisoners. However, at no time during the entire nine months that he spent in prison did he actually ever, not even on one single occasion, manage to personally come across one of these unfortunate people. These unsubstantiated stories were like a great deal of many of the vast majority of prison folklore that he was to hear during his nine moths inside.

The twenty fifth of November duly came and went. A few days after which Johnny received a form from the appeal court, notifying him that his application for leave to appeal had been refused. By now he was becoming increasingly sceptical about anything to do with the legal system and was not in the slightest bit surprised by the refusal. The form stated that the Honourable Mr. Justice Langley had 'considered' his grounds for appeal and had refused his application for the following reasons: "The reality was that you were convicted on compelling if not overwhelming evidence after a full and fair summing up because the jury were sure of your guilt and that you were not telling the truth. Your solicitor's counsel has dealt clearly and convincingly with what you say. I see nothing at all unsafe in the jury's verdicts".

Johnny agreed that the evidence was indeed both compelling and overwhelming, but only in the same sense as Tony Blair's compelling evidence as to Saddam Hussein's huge stockpiles of weapons of mass destruction, and every bit as overwhelming as Tony Blair's evidence that

Saddam was about to launch a nuclear attack on either Britain or America, within the next forty five minutes. Johnny could clearly see the parallels between the two statements and the calibre of the evidence that both Tony Blair and Mr. Justice Langley had based their statements upon. Mr. Justice Langley had merely skimmed over his application and had been extremely one-sided in his approach to Johnny's application. The compelling and overwhelming evidence had in fact been both confusing and blag evidence given by the secret, undisclosed witness who had biased the jury with what they must have presumed to be verified and accurate evidence. Mr. Justice Langley had seemingly caught a dose of Messieurs Bush and Blair's *selective memory loss* and had now inadvertently added himself to the growing list of court officials who were refusing to acknowledge the issue of the non-disclosure.

Chapter XII
Appeal # 2

Johnny considered his options for an entire two and a half milli seconds before deciding to soldier on regardless. On the back of the form which contained the refusal was a section to renew the application for leave to appeal which was duly filled in and was in the post and back on its return journey the following morning. Which was followed in quick succession by the by now usual accompaniment of persistent letters to Mrs. Soskin, which followed the same three week cycle as before. In each and every one of these letters, Johnny made reference to Mr. Travis and on several occasions he requested the police witness statements and trial transcripts and audio tapes for the entire trial, and as always, placed a special emphasis on those for Geoffrey Robert Travis.

The initial feedback that Johnny got from these letters was that the appeal court would under no circumstances allow him access to the audio tapes, heaven forbid them ever getting into the public domain and that he would need to pay for the police witness statements and trial transcripts at his own expense. Although he couldn't get an exact figure as to the cost of these items, Mrs. Soskin assured him that it was a very substantial amount of money. She also informed him that it was extremely unlikely that he would be allowed to attend the application hearing, so in each of the letters, he also repeatedly requested to attend the application hearing, in order to gat a fair crack at the appeal whip. He felt that he could better explain his reasons for appealing in person and show the court the two sets of ignition locks with their easily obtained duplicated keys.

Eventually his persistence paid dividends, but not quite in the way he had expected. At last on the 7th of February, he had a real breakthrough. On several occasions Johnny had asked for a list of all the witnesses that had given evidence against him at his trial. Mrs. Soskin had sent him what was supposed to be the list he'd been requesting. However, there were two absolutely crucial names, both of whom gave evidence in court, for count three, that became all the more conspicuous by their absence from the list.

So at last, the plot begins to thicken. **You ain't gonna get no prizes for guessing the name of at least one of them!**

Throughout his life Johnny had always been an extremely resourceful person and when it suited him, he could also prove to be extremely determined as well. He obtained the phone number for the clerk of Warrington Crown Court. Throughout his appeal efforts, using a combination of the prison's education department and the prison's legal aid department photocopiers, he had taken the precaution of making a seemingly ludicrously vast amount of copies of every single piece of correspondence form day one and ensured that they were distributed far and wide in the outside world. So he already had the trial's case number - T2002 0028 from a copy of the NG form, with which he had made his original application for leave to appeal.

The next step was to make the call to the clerk of the court, introducing himself as being the defendant's legal representative. Which after all wasn't exactly a lie, now was it? He requested a copy of the court's log (which gave the full and hopefully the correct details of every witness at the trial and the times and dates, that they were called to give evidence) and informed the clerk that he urgently required the details contained within the log and so he requested that she read him the details of the log over the phone. The clerk was more than willing to comply with the request made by Mr. Chesney's legal representative and ten minutes later he was in possession of all the witnesses details. Hey Presto! Johnny found that Messieurs Stanley and Travis had miraculously reappeared.

In the list originally supplied by the appeal court, the time and date for Mr. Travis had been replaced by P.C. Harris-Briston and Mr. Stanley had simply been omitted from the list, with no corresponding time or date.

So Johnny then wrote another letter to Mrs. Soskin in which he informed her that on Tuesday 18/2/03 he had obtained the **full and correct details of ALL** the witnesses, directly from Warrington Crown Court's clerk. He also informed her that he had already been given all but one police witness statement as part of the depositions that he'd received from his former solicitor, prior to the trial. He continued to tell her that the only police witness statement that he now required, was that for Mr. J. Travis, which he had never received either before, during or since the trial. He then stated that he would be only too happy to pay for the cost of Mr. Travis' police witness statement and finished his letter with a copy of the list, in table format that he had made from the dates and times that he had received from the clerk of the court. The letter was dated 18/2/03 and written on the same day that he had obtained the details of the court log and was posted to London on the following morning.

On March 4th he received both Mr. Geoffrey Robert Travis' and Mr.

David William Stanley's police witness statements in addition to the transcript of the Judge's summing up, which he had asked for on many previous occasions. For some strange reason the costs involved had apparently been wavered and these were all supplied to Johnny free of charge.

***

Almost immediately after Johnny had been sentenced (which by this time seemed like a million years ago—back in the middle of September of 2002) and started to get his appeal up and running, Frances had started to send him some of the documents that he had in his possession from the regular supply of the **pre-disclosed** deposition material, that his former solicitor, Gordon Spofforth, had assured him was the sum total of material that the Crown intended using against him at his trial.

Johnny had each of the twenty five police witness statements catalogued and filed in clip folders according to each count: Bradford, United Carriers and Nottingham. Needless to say, no matter how diligently either Johnny or Frances searched amongst this material, neither could ever find anything relating to somebody called Travis, with one notable exception, which was in the police witness statement by David William Stanley; a.k.a. *Mr. Thrust the Mobile in Your Face.* Which was dated **8/1/01** and consisted of some four pages. As with all of the pre-disclosed police witness statements, it had hand written numbers on the top right hand corners of each page, from number one through to just under two hundred. The numbers for his statement were numbers 74 through to number 77. His statement mainly covered his own version of events when Johnny had returned the keys to TNT. He continued that he had gone to Nottingham to "collect the vehicle with another driver" and gave a valuation of the goods that were stolen. The final sentence of the third to last paragraph of his statement which contained of only ten words, read as follows:"The person who drove the vehicle back was Jeff TRAVERS".

Despite the misspelling, presumably by the policeman who took the statement, it was clear that this must have meant Geoffrey Robert Travis.

So the two names that had been missing from the list supplied by the court of appeal were of course Geoffrey Robert Travis and the only person that had made any mention of him in the pre-disclosed material.

So on 4/3/03 for the very first time, Johnny now had some type of documentation on Mr. Geoffrey Robert Travis and his evidence. His police witness statement was dated **11/12/01** some eleven months after his buddy, David William Stanley, had given his statement. It consisted of just over two pages. However, unlike the pre-disclosed police witness statements, it did not have hand written numbers on the top right hand corners of each page. The statement mainly covered his business, place of work and the fact that he had 38 years experience as a mechanic. It stated that he would class himself as an expert in the field of repairing commercial vehicles. He continued to say that he owned the company that was responsible for the maintenance of all of TNT's vehicles and that he had done so for the past 14 years.

The first thing that immediately sprung into Johnny's mind was his recollection of the barrister's insistence on the retention of the shield. He clearly remembered Tom Watson's reluctance to harass the one and only witnesses that he could describe as "having no axe to grind" and that "was not connected to the complainants"; it would therefore be difficult to find a motive for such a witness to lie. However, the statement before Johnny's own eyes clearly indicated that this witness was *joined at the hip* to the complainants.

Travis then went on to say that he and David Stanley had travelled to Nottingham in order to retrieve the wagon and among some other less important points, he then went on to state that he could not detect any damage to the locks of the vehicle and finished his statement by stating, "In my opinion, it would be impossible for a driver to obtain another set of keys, the only way anyone would be able to obtain another set would be by authorised letter from the vehicle owner to ERF. I can say that this was never authorised".

He knew that with this police witness statement and the fact that he had already obtained duplicated keys very easily, then no honest court of appeal could possibly refuse him his appeal, on the grounds that the *inaccuracies* that formed the overwhelming majority of Travis' evidence undermined the integrity of the entire trial. But as always, Johnny wanted just that little bit more evidence, so as to deny the appeal court the slightest chance of wriggling out of giving him access to a full and proper appeal, which would have put the activities of Warrington Crown Court into the public domain.

Right from the very first time Johnny had laid eyes on Travis during the trial, he had noticed a striking similarity to his demeanour and that of Adrian Westerman. So striking in fact that because he knew Mr. Westerman did have a particularly nasty previous record, he had also always assumed that regarding Mr. Travis, Warrington Crown Court had more to hide than just his false evidence.

Johnny sent off another letter asking for, as he had done on many occasions, details of Travis' previous convictions. When he received no reply to this letter he phoned Mrs. Soskin and asked her for these details. She in turn informed him that a defendant should not have access to the witness' previous convictions. There was however, a major problem with Mrs. Soskin's latest assertion, as Johnny already had the details of the previous convictions for four of the witnesses against him. Adrian Thomas Westerman from count one, had by far the most extensive record, with an *impressive* nineteen previous convictions, covering almost the entire spectrum of criminality. This included burglary and theft, arson, with another three offences taken into consideration, theft, obtaining property by deception, making false representation to obtain benefit from national insurance fund (Benefit Fraud), forgery, driving without a licence or insurance and impersonating a police officer, with another three offences taken into consideration. This blackguard was of course the man that Warrington Crown Court had seen fit to present to the jury as being an 'expert' in the field of weighing wagons without the use of weighing equipment. However, Johnny will never be able to get away from the fact that he himself was inadvertently responsible for *introducing* Mr. Westerman to the police!

As for the three other witnesses with previous convictions, all were from count three (United Carriers), none of which could be described as being in any way severe. So the upshot of Johnny's possession of these details of the witnesses' previous convictions was that there were only two possibilities as to Mrs. Soskin's information on defendants having these details, which was that either he really shouldn't have possession, or that she'd misinformed him.

***

As for the rest of the remainder of the twenty five police witness statements that were catalogued and filed in clip folders, after weeks of picking out and sending off to prison the various documents that Johnny had been requesting, she had eventually got sick of falling over the trial's documents and decided to store all of them in the garden shed, sealed in a cardboard box. A few weeks after that, Jack's bicycle got a puncture. Unable to locate the bicycle pump, Jack had decided to remove the entire contents of the shed, in search of the elusive pump. With the seemingly unimportant bits of paper being strewn all over the back yard, Jack and his mates duly fixed the puncture. But with all the usual consideration and attention associated with your average ten-year-old, the trial's documents were not put back into the shed but left open to the elements. An hour or so later, there was a sudden downpour. Eventually the soaked documents were returned to the shed in a crumpled pile; every other day Frances would unravel a few pages and place them so that they could dry out. This continued for a few weeks until most of the pile had been dried out. By now it was early November and Jack returned to the shed, this time in search of bonfire fuel for Guy Fawkes night on the 5th of November. Amongst some of the other old shite, he found some old papers in an old cardboard box that he had long since forgotten about.

The next time Frances went into the shed looking for one of the documents that Johnny had asked to be sent into him, she couldn't find the old battered cardboard box. So now their eldest son had gone full circle and *Jack, the nice little boy!* regained his former title.

***

Johnny now felt increasingly confident that the could disprove all Travis' so called evidence every bit as easily as he had been able to disprove his assertions as to the impossibility of procuring duplicated keys. He was painfully well aware that his wife was by now in severe financial straits. However, he was also well aware that Mrs. Soskin had not actually denied that Travis had a criminal record, that had also never been disclosed to him. The more he thought about it, he came to realise that the appeal court were now ignoring the *criminal record issue* in exactly the same way as they had been ignoring the non-disclosure issue, all along; thus strengthening his belief that they were playing a waiting game with him. After all they could just let him rot in jail for as long as they pleased; by now he had seen plenty of examples of other prisoners that this had happened to. There were plenty of guys in Kirkham that had gone well over their tariffs. In the odd particularly severe case, some had done twenty two years out of a nine year sentence; he always shuddered to think of what they had done in order to deserve such treatment and often wondered, if these were such bad people, then what were they doing in an open prison?

Johnny knew that if he could find such discrepancies with Travis' police witness statement, then surely he could discover more from the court transcripts. He obtained the phone number for a company which specialised in providing transcripts. During his very first phone call to this company he was absolutely horrified to discover that the cost of obtaining the full trial transcripts would be a staggering £5287.50, a sum of money that he knew to be totally beyond Frances' means. Next he asked for the cost of just the Travis transcript, which although it was still very expensive, at least it was an attainable £146.88, which he knew would almost certainly deprive his already impoverished family of much needed money. Despite this knowledge, during one of Frances' weekly visits, he forced himself to ask her if she could come up with some money for transcripts.

As always, she was prepared to do whatever she could for him and much to his relief her immediate reaction was to say, "Forget the fucking money; you know I'd never manage to find five grand, but I'd do anything to have you back home, the kids need you home every bit as much as I do. You know as well as I do, you shouldn't even be here in the first place. Just leave it to Super Fran"!

When she returned home that evening, her friend called round to visit and the conversation eventually turned to Johnny's appeal efforts and the cost of the Travis transcript. Her friend apparently left for home about ten o'clock. By twenty past she was knocking on the door again, when Frances opened the door her friend didn't bother to come back into the house, but instead passed her a small wad of cash containing the £150 Frances needed. She told her that she'd been to the cash machine and insisted that Frances need not worry about repaying her, finishing the conversation with, "Just give me it back when you've got it".

The following morning the transcript was ordered with a special emphasis on Johnny's requirement that he needed every mention of Travis from the first to the last.

On the 12th of March 2002 Johnny received a big brown envelope. On opening it he found what the transcript company claimed to be what he'd asked for. However, on reading the very first page of the transcript, he immediately noticed that Travis had been discussed in the absence of the jury and much more importantly, that according to the transcript Mr. Watson was the person who initiated the dialogue concerning Travis. Which couldn't possibly be correct, because even Johnny's faith in Mr Watson hadn't been so utterly depleted for him to believe that he had 'invited' Travis to give evidence. [1A - D]

[In the absence of the jury]

MR WATSON: Your Honour, I wonder if your honour would have a look at the statement of Mr. Travis in the additional evidence. My submission is that he is not really an expert in that much of what he said he should not be allowed to say but—

HIS HONOUR JUDGE FARMER: So there is an issue about admissibility?

MR WATSON: Yes.

HIS HONOUR JUDGE FARMER: Shall we deal with that straight after lunch then?

MR WATSON: Your Honour, yes.

HIS HONOUR JUDGE FARMER: Is that the one you were calling next?

MR. LEWIS-JONES: That would be the next witness, your Honour.

-Mid-day adjournment-

Johnny pondered this opening to the Travis transcript long and hard, until he remembered what had happened at the end of the questioning of D. Stanley, who had been dismissed from the witness stand at one minute before one o'clock and was followed after lunch by Travis. Yes, that was it! Now he could remember... the jury left the room and Johnny was told by the barrister that he needn't stay for any longer and he would speak to him when he was ready—meaning you leave the court now and I'll catch you up shortly! So the missing part before Mr. Watson began speaking must have also included the part where Johnny had been asked to leave the court. So the transcript should have began—In the absence of the jury ***and the defendant***. Johnny knew that in order to substantiate his suspicions, he would need the transcripts for the entire trial and he would never be able to afford them without the aid of a lottery win, so he had to soldier on and make do with the *part* transcript that had been purchased with money borrowed from Frances' friend, which would in due course need to be repaid.

It didn't take Johnny very long to notice several interesting comments and inconsistencies within the transcript. All of which he tried time and time again to bring to the attention of the appeal court, who in turn, time and time again consistently ignored them and **all of which he would be able to disprove, if the appeal court gave him the opportunity to do so!**

The missing part at the beginning.

The fact that Mr. Watson's advice about the retention of the shield (which was supposedly purely for the *benefit* of Mr. Adrian Westerman) and on not harassing witnesses "that had no axe to grind" was well and truly the worst possible advice he could have given. Here was a man that was clearly *joined at the hip* to the complainants. [8F - G]

MR LEWIS-JONES:

Q. "Now, has your company had a link with the vehicles belonging to TNT"?

A. "Yes, about 14 years".
Q. "And what link has that been"?
A. "We maintain all the vehicles belonging to TNT in the Warrington area, currently something like 130 vehicles".

The well rehearsed script did not help when he was asked by the Judge about the number of immobiliser fobs in existence, which later on he wasn't to be too sure about. [13G - 14A]

HIS HONOUR JUDGE FARMER:

Q. "There were two immobilisers altogether, were there"?
A. "No, one"
Q. "One immobiliser"?
A. "One immobiliser".

Although here he was very certain as to the number of immobiliser fobs, when being asked by the Judge, at a later point he wasn't quite so sure when cross-examined by the defence barrister. [22G - 23B]

MR. WATSON:

Q. "Now with the immobiliser fob"?
A. "Yes"?
Q. "I think your evidence is there is one"?
A. "I think there's only one for that vehicle".
Q. "You think"?
A. "Yes".
Q. "So again, we are in the area of you can't say there isn't a second one"?
A. "I can't remember whether—there probably is. If there is another one, it'll be with the spare keys. I cannot recollect whether there was one with it or not, because of the same reason I spoke of before, they're quite delicate, drivers throw them about, they break and when one goes missing—when one gets broken they usually pinch the spare one because once the spare one has gone, in other words, you've got two fobs, one spare, one in use, if you break the one in use then you have to use the spare one. Once that's gone, it's another £800 for a new system. <u>You cannot get a new immobiliser fob</u>".

Try a nice easy exercise; write out a copy of the above answer to Mr. Watson's question that he wasn't prepared for and then compare it against any safe similar answer to one of Mr. Lewis-Jones' questions of a similar size, e.g. when Travis is being asked a question he is well prepared for e.g. by Mr. Lewis-Jones about the level of expert knowledge required to disable the immobiliser system. One reason for this exercise is to see just how much, or indeed how little sense Travis' answer makes to the reader. [15F - H]

MR. LEWIS-JONES:

Q. "Do you need specialised equipment to do it"?
A. "No, but you do need specialised knowledge for one simple reason: that these alarms system come with 10 black wires and when they're fitted they have instructions on the end of each wire what the wire is to go to, like positive, negative, attempting start, attempting this. When you fit the system, you then rip them tags off and you're left with ten black wires, they could go anywhere and they could do anything so unless you know which ones they are, cutting them all would do nothing for you. They've got to be taken off in sequence and if you do cut them all or you tamper with it you can cut the wrong one so the immobiliser becomes defunct and you have to have a brand new one put on".

The Judge was clearly so eager that Travis reinforce his assertions as to the huge degree of security that this supposedly high-tech immobiliser afforded, that he couldn't help himself but to intercede, asking Travis these three questions. [16A - C]

HIS HONOUR JUDGE FARMER:

Q. "You can't start the lorry in those circumstances if it becomes defunct"?
A. "No, if you take it all off completely you could start it but it means a massive, massive operation".
Q. "It means you have to replace it"?
A. "Yes. A massive operation".
Q. "How long would that take"?
A. "Three hours at least and that's with a qualified alarm engineer. I mean, **I'm not a qualified alarm engineer** but I have fitted them and it probably takes me the best part of half a day 'cause the dashboard has got to come out, all the fuse boxes have got to come out, there's loads of connections to be made, it's not a two minute job, not a two minute job at all".

In the above answer Travis stated that he was "**not a qualified alarm engineer**". From part of the transcript prior to Travis' giving evidence, Mr. Watson had protested against Travis being used as an expert witness several times. However, the Judge completely ignored all of Mr. Watson's feeble attempts at protesting; he made sure that his undisclosed witness was going to give his false evidence, no matter what. This was his court in which he was the *BIG CHEESE* and that was that!

This second answer is much more fluent, every thing is definite, here he can remember—no probably, no pauses, no going over the same ground, no need to stray off the subject when he feels he's on shaky ground.

Johnny informed the appeal court that provided they gave him the opportunity to do so, he could easily disprove, "with real physical evidence", every single lie that Travis had told in both the first and the second answers. In the first answer he could not only show that Rimmer had gone back on his word and changed his testimony as to the location of the fob, which would mean that there had to be two fobs and not one. Which of course contradicted Travis' previous testimony in which he had confidently told the Judge that there was only "one immobiliser" but Johnny was now also in a position to prove that not only were the immobiliser fobs very easy to duplicate, but were routinely legally duplicated for anyone that had either lost or broken a fob.

As for the second answer the "real physical evidence" would show without a shadow of a doubt that there was no such thing as ten black wires in these immobiliser systems. There was in fact only five wires, all of which were colour coded. There was a black (negative) and a red (positive) which provided the power for the immobiliser and only three wires—a red, a white and a blue wire, which were actually involved in the immobiliser's function. This would of course negate the necessity of removing the wires in sequence.

In addition to this; still regarding Travis' testimony on the "massive, massive operation" involved in disabling the immobiliser. For those who are unaware most, if not all offenders who are nearing the end of their prison sentence, are released on temporary licence for home leave, which is intended as a means of gently re-integrating the offender back into society. Home leaves usually last for between four and six days. As Johnny was only serving a relatively short sentence, he only ever had one home leave, during which he done all the normal things like getting a decent feed, getting drunk and shagging himself (or rather Frances) to death (but not before she done a war dance over his weight loss). In addition to all these normal activities, he also took the time and trouble to pay another visit to the wagon scrap yard from whom he had initially bought the old type ERF ignition system. This time he was looking for door locks, with the intention of proving that the keys for them were every bit as easy to have duplicated as normal car keys.

On arrival at the scrap yard, Johnny stressed to the owner that he needed a lock specifically for an M registered ERF, so the guy led him to one of his M registered ERFs that still had it's door locks fitted. And as he, some seven or eight months previously, told him that he was a very busy man, Johnny removed the door locks by himself. He then handed Johnny the relevant set of keys. On receipt of the set, Johnny could hardly believe his luck. There were three keys on the key ring, one for the ignition, one door lock key and another that was probably for the fuel cap. But in addition to these was an immobiliser fob of exactly the same type that had been on M 316 XLV. As he approached the wagon, two thoughts were foremost in his mind: was this type of immobiliser fitted as standard in M registered ERFs, and much more importantly; was the receptacle and wiring loom still going to be fitted intact? He prayed that today was going to be his lucky day! For once in his life was Lady Luck about to smile upon him and bless him with a bit of good fortune? Even a total looser like Johnny deserved a bit of luck now and again.

By the time he opened the door and entered the cab, the door locks he'd initially gone there for were the last thing on his mind. On inspecting the dashboard area, he was overjoyed, if not completely ecstatic to find that the fob's receptacle and wiring loom were still intact. But in addition, he found that the receptacle could be removed by an incredibly simple and quick method, which was simply to put a sharp object, such as a screwdriver behind the lip of the receptacle and prise it out of the socket. This could be done without causing any damage to either the dashboard, receptacle, socket or the wiring loom. His good fortune continued; when he inspected the wiring loom, he was unable to find the ten black wires that Travis had assured the jury were fitted to the immobilisers in ERF wagons.

There were in fact only five wires protruding from the inner and usually unseen part of the receptacle, all of which were colour coded. A black (negative) and a red (positive) which Johnny assumed were to provide the power for the immobiliser and only three wires, a red, a white and a blue wire, which he assumed were actually involved in the immobiliser's function. Providing that this immobiliser system was the standard type and the same as Travis had supposedly been going on about to the jury, then Johnny would obviously now be in a position to show without a doubt that far from taking "three hours at least" or the "best part of half a day", in reality it would actually take no more than 30 seconds to remove the receptacle and gain access to five colour coded wires and not the “10 black wires“ that Travis had described to the jury.

The obvious next move for Johnny was to remove, pay for and keep the part of the dashboard with the receptacle fitted, with the fob, in order to double check that it would have been the same type as that fitted to M 316 XLV. He had no real way of checking, quite simply because Travis had never needed to produce one single piece of evidence to back up any of his claims. Why should he need to? After all, he had never been disclosed to Johnny in the first place. Needless to say the jury had just assumed, as would anyone including Johnny himself prior to July 2002, that his evidence would have been checked and verified before being allowed to be given. The prosecution must have known that this evidence could so easily have been disproved, which would have formed **part** of their reasons for withholding the false evidence from Johnny.

Regardless Johnny was going to double check anyway. Over the years Johnny had various electrical problems with his cars. Whenever these occurred, he always phoned the same auto electrician to come and sort out the problem. He recalled that this guy also fixed car alarms and immobilisers. So instead of paying him to come to his house, Johnny chose to call him on the phone and then arranged to meet him in his local pub. He bought him a couple of pints and explained his *predicament* in detail. This included showing him the fob from the scrapped wagon and explaining that as far as he could remember, it looked exactly like the one in M 316 XLV.

The auto electrician said that the fob was probably for a Bison immobiliser and that he had never heard of a Bison being fitted with ten black wires; the only ones he was familiar with was the type with the red, white and blue wires. He went on to explain that, just as Johnny had himself suspected, with access to the wires, the immobiliser could be disabled in a matter of seconds, by very simple means. The auto electrician agreed to write out a letter for Johnny explaining how the immobiliser could be disabled and explained an extremely simple method by which the immobiliser fob could be duplicated at a very low cost (under a tenner). He added that he would be only too happy to appear before a court, in the event of an appeal hearing in order to give evidence to this effect and to provide the court with genuine evidence of his qualifications on Johnny’s behalf.

So now Johnny could show even more lies coming from the undisclosed witness. He was beginning to wonder if Travis had told even one single piece of honest evidence?

As for the door keys, Johnny had also obtained the door lock and had then gone to an ordinary key cutting shop and had a duplicate key made in less than a minute. In which case why— following yet another interruption of Mr. Watson's questioning of Travis by the judge, at a crucial point where he was beginning to get on top of Travis—why did Travis feel the need to say the following? [25B - D]

MR. WATSON:

"Well it was put in opening that the police found the vehicle open and when these gentlemen attended it was locked, so I—

HIS HONOUR JUDGE FARMER (interrupting):

Q. "Now if the police had locked the vehicle, does it make any difference to your conclusions"?

TRAVIS:

A. "Not really. It's not the locking of the vehicle that particularly worries me, it's the opening of the vehicle without any sign of—I mean, as I say, I've been on breakdowns where vehicles have been left outside shops where the driver has lost his key, damaged his key and I've never got in a vehicle by unpicking the lock or then better still, a really good trick, picking them back on again. Now that would be a good trick".

Johnny's only conclusion had to be that Travis was sticking to a well rehearsed script, for numerous reasons. At the beginning of the answer above Travis says "It's not the locking of the vehicle that particularly worries me", meaning that a duplicate key would easily do the job. So why the need to contradict himself by finishing off the answer with "a really good trick, picking them back on again. Now that would be a good trick"?

Which tied in perfectly with another reason that Johnny suspected something was seriously amiss with the Travis evidence, because earlier in one breath he was claiming that you could not get door keys, but when prompted, in another of the Judge's interruptions, in practically the very next breath Travis stated that you could easily get a duplicated door key. [17G - 18F]

MR. LEWIS-JONES:

Q. "Now, keys go missing"?
A. "Yes".
Q. "Let us assume for the purpose of this question that a set of keys has

gone missing. Is there a procedure whereby another set can be obtained"?

A. "Yes. The door locks are **not** readily available, you just buy a new door lock which come with a key. The ignition key is—"

Note how eager he is to get into his "essential letter of authority" routine!

Q. "Sorry to interrupt you, but how would you go about getting one of those"?

A. "You would have to ring up the agent and he'd just send you a box with a door lock and the key attached to it. That's for the—"

HIS HONOUR JUDGE FARMER (interrupting):

Q. "Can you get it in a shop, take it to a shop and have one cut? Suppose you had another key, a spare key"?

A. "Yes".

Q. "Could you go to a locksmith and have one cut"?

A. "You could have the door keys cut that way, yes".

Giving the opportunity for the judge, during the same interruption, to lead Travis into the following well rehearsed questions, which he knew would be answered untruthfully.

Q. "What about the ignition"?

A. "No, not at all".

Q. "Why not"?

A. "Because ERF have a policy, the blanks for ERF vehicles are only kept by two companies, one in the south and one in Bolton. If you want a spare key, the operator of the vehicle, i.e. TNT, I mean I would be the person who would have to go and get the key, <u>I've got to get a letter from the manager stating that the vehicle belongs to them,</u> I then go to ERF at Manchester, present the letter, they then ring up the firm who does the keys in Bolton to say that I'm on my way and then they frank that letter to allow me to go to Bolton to get the key. When I arrive at the shop, I've got to give them the letter before they'll do me a key. So in other words, only the rightful person, the rightful owner can get a key, nobody else can get a key. I found this out to my… er… thingy because originally I tried to get keys and they said no, you know. That you had to go through that procedure".

Johnny took note of the fact that Travis reiterated the need for this 'essential letter' and the procedure involved in it's use **five times** in total, but he already had 100% concrete proof that there was no such need for any kind of letter to obtain a duplicate ERF ignition key! Johnny then went on to elucidate even more evidence of the suspected well rehearsed script that Travis tried his best to adhere to during his stint in the witness box, whilst at the same time pointing out that such contradictory evidence given by Travis could only have led to a great deal of confusion in the jury's mind. So the jury would have been left with no alternative but to assume that as his evidence had been permitted to be given in a court of law, then it must somehow have been valid and truthful.

Johnny even managed to show where Travis had put Mr. Lewis-Jones back on track and back to the script, when Mr. Lewis-Jones was asking about how many times the locks had been changed on M 316 XLV. [14F - 15A]

MR. LEWIS-JONES:

Q. "Have you yourself carried out such an operation"?

A. "Probably fifty or sixty times. Maybe more, I don't know. I've done that many".

Q. "Can you tell us whether you have done any such work on this particular lorry prior to that"?

A. "Not off hand. Not off hand. I mean, if I'd been asked about that, I mean, I could have brought it".

Q. "I have asked it out of the blue"?

A. "I could have brought everything to support it one way or the other".

Which ties in nicely with Travis' apparent clairvoyance, of which there were a few examples, but by far the most crucial example of Travis' ability to answer a question before it had been finished was during his initial stint with Mr. Lewis-Jones, when being questioned about the location of the immobiliser fob. [15C]

MR. LEWIS-JONES:

Q. "Help us on this if you can. Is that then left in the—"

A. "**No, no**. It's attached to the keys".

From as far back as during the trial, Johnny had noticed that the above answer had been *spoken with a distinct emphasis,* with the obvious intention of reinforcing the statement that had been given earlier by Mr. S. Rimmer—i.e. that the immobiliser fob for that wagon "is kept on the keys", despite the fact that it had contradicted Stuart Rimmer's police witness statement.

Returning to the issue of the well rehearsed script, on reading the transcript Johnny now noticed for the first time another extremely interesting quote from Travis, which was again stirring Johnny's mind into a frenzy regarding Tom Watson's role in the stitch up! Up until now, Johnny couldn't be too sure as to his former barrister's role because from the transcripts he could see that Mr. Watson had tried on at least a few occasions to try and trip up Travis, but on each occasion the Judge had interceded and prevented him from doing so. Also in Tom Watson's favour as far as Johnny was concerned, was the fact that during the first six pages of the transcript, it was clear that Mr. Watson had tried, albeit in vain, to prevent Travis from being introduced as an additional witness.

However, as Johnny read into the very first half dozen or so questions that Tom Watson had put to Travis, he began to see that during the meetings at the barrister's chambers, the barrister had actually listened to at least part of what Johnny had told him as to the reasons for the route he had chosen to take to Nottingham. Or perhaps he hadn't listened at all and the solicitor, Gordon Spofforth, with whom Johnny had by far the most contact over the preceding months, had filled him in on the details. [19D - 20B]

<u>Cross-examined by MR. WATSON</u>:

Q. "Does the vehicle have a *Heaton* gearbox"? (*misspell; should say Eaton)*

A. "Yes".

Q. "The older type, the re-P registration type"?

A. "P registration"?

Q. "Yes".

A. "It's got an RT601 [inaudible] box. **IT'S IN MY NOTES…"**

Q. "Well, that doesn't mean a lot to me but let me see if this makes any sense to you. A gearbox, semi-automatic"?

A. "No, manual. Six speed manual".

Q. Does it involve changing gear without clutching"?

A. "No".

Q. "Or double clutching"?

A. "No".

Q. "How do you change the gear"?

A. "Just like you would normally change gear in a car. It's a fully synchronised gear box and double clutching isn't required. It's not a range box, not a multi speed box, just a straightforward six speed gear box".

Q. "It's like a car"?

A. "Basically, yeah".

All of this caused a complexity of contradictions and unanswered questions in Johnny's own mind, because Tom Watson's first two questions that he put to Travis must have meant that he'd taken in precisely what Johnny had told him as to the reasons for the route he had chosen to take to Nottingham. In which case he must have taken the time and trouble to prepare these questions for Travis. Which in turn meant that he knew Travis was going to be called as a witness. Which in turn led to the second question. **In which case why didn't he inform Johnny about Travis?**

The third question was even more interesting, because Mr. Travis knew the exact model number of the gearbox, "an RT601". He had previously stated that his company was responsible for maintaining "all the vehicles belonging to TNT in the Warrington area, currently something like 130 vehicles". A very substantial amount of vehicles; surely there must have been a couple of dozen different types of vehicles among them. You could be persuaded into thinking that the guy just had a terrific memory, but for the fact that Travis had "notes". [19F]

"NOTES"—yes, Travis had notes on Johnny, but Johnny didn't have any notes on him! More importantly; why do you need notes? Nobody else throughout the entire trial mentioned the need of having to rely upon notes; it only added credence to Johnny's suspicion that he had been reciting a well rehearsed script! After all, anyone relying on a real memory and not just what someone had told them to say, wouldn't require notes, would they?

The other questions at the beginning of Mr. Watson's examination just served to reaffirm that he had indeed taken a great deal of care to listen to exactly what Johnny had told him as to the gear box fitted in M 316 XLV. Johnny recalled that he hadn't taken quite so much care to take note of what other witnesses such as Adrian Westerman were going to say; so he must have known about Travis well in advance of the trial!

In addition to all that Johnny made clear his complaint that because he had no disclosure on Travis then he was also denied access to the details of Travis' criminal record, which he had no option but to assume must have been a particularly nasty criminal record, which would also have formed part of Warrington Crown Court's reason for withholding his disclosure, as Mr. Watson's advice, the retention of the shield, was supposedly purely for *benefit* of Adrian Westerman.

Even more lies emanated from Travis when he claimed that *for some strange reason* Johnny had given him the keys. [19C]

Q. "As a matter of interest which keys did you use to drive it back"?
A. "The original keys that the driver gave to me".

Johnny was only too painfully well aware that he'd never given this man the keys; he had given them to Stuart Rimmer when he'd returned to the TNT office on the evening in question. He couldn't possibly have given them to two people, let alone one of whom that he'd never laid eyes on before.

The transcript ended with *much ado about nothing* over the issue of the locked versus unlocked abandoned wagon, either with or without the keys. Johnny took great note of this part of the transcript. Firstly, because this must have been extremely confusing to the jury, forcing them to rely on the assumption that because it had been allowed to be said in a court of law, then it must somehow have been pertinent to the case before them.

However, there was a far much more important reason for Johnny's interest in each and single every line of the last five pages of the transcript, because ever since the day of the trial, right up until during the writing of this book, Johnny, both barristers and even the judge and presumably the jury, had been led to believe that Travis had inferred that the wagon could not be locked without using the vehicle's own door key. Otherwise why else would there be the need to go over the issue, for so long, or in such detail?

Only from the murkiest depths of his memory, could Johnny only very vaguely recall that during the four and a half hour (30 minute) chat with D.C. Johnston, way back in January 2001, had the police mentioned something about the impossibility of locking the vehicle without any keys. It was complete and utter shite then and still remains so, to this day and forever. However, the thing that really bothered Johnny about all the *much ado about nothing* was the issue of the locked or unlocked wagon and the fact that the subject had taken up almost six pages worth of the transcript.

The initial seven pages of the transcript were taken up by Mr. Watson's attempts to prevent Travis being called as an expert witness. The part of the transcript which actually dealt with Travis' questions and answers was only nineteen pages long. So therefore the amount of time and effort that was spent on the issue of the apparent impossibility of locking the wagon without it's own keys represented about a third of the entire questioning of Travis.

BUT! B-U-T, BUT! At absolutely no point whatsoever, throughout either the entire transcript or even his police witness statement did Travis ever actually say that the wagon was not able to be locked without it's own keys. It was insinuated on a great many occasions, but never actually said out loud.

So what conclusion can you draw from that? Other than that, the judge, both barristers and presumably Gordon Spofforth had access to some other secret information, presumably originating from Travis, to the effect that you needed the wagon's own door keys in order to lock it. Which if true would mean that either a duplicate set of keys had been involved in the theft, or that Johnny had used the original keys to leave the wagon where it was found.

***

So now Johnny could attempt to further his appeal efforts which even to those who were completely sceptical as to his innocence must clearly have been able to see that the Travis transcript could only serve to strengthen his case for appeal.

Johnny informed the appeal court of the inconsistencies that he found within the Travis transcript and those within the judge's summing up, which he had been sent to him free of charge, after he had obtained the full and correct details of ALL the witnesses, including Travis despite the fact that the appeal court had omitted his name from *their* list of witnesses.

It didn't take Johnny long to start finding fault with the judge's summing up. He discerned that the judge was already anticipating an appeal. [4B - D]

Summing Up:

"The law is my responsibility, procedure in the court is my responsibility and I have to preside over the proceedings *so that a fair trial is held and a fair trial within the law.* I give you directions as to the law. *If I get them wrong, nevertheless you must apply them because another court will put my mistake right if counsel in this case do not put it right".*

He then went on to say… [4E] (SU)

"Part of my job is to remind you of the prominent features of the case, not to go over it but *remind you of what is important…*"

He made damn sure that Johnny didn't get a *fair trial.* He made sure to remind them only of what he wanted them to remember. He went on to tell the jury only to concentrate on the (blag) evidence that he seen fit to put before them. Telling them… [5A - D] (SU)

"*You must not speculate about what evidence there might have been, about what evidence there wasn't that you would have liked to have heard which was not called in front of you. You must not speculate about what evidence there might have been or allow yourself to be drawn into speculation at all".*

Meaning the evidence that I've allowed you to see, is exactly what I wanted you to see.

Later he told the jury that the defendant was entitled to know exactly what the charges were. [6F] (SU)

"*Our law requires that the defendant who comes before a Crown Court knows precisely what he is charged with...*"

However, he conveniently managed to omit that Johnny should also have known about ALL witnesses that he intended calling against him.

When referring to the Bradford lorry, the judge insinuated that Johnny had been unwilling to supply the tachograph chart for the day in question. [11G] (SU)

"The lorry was equipped with a tachograph and the defendant *eventually* supplied the tachograph (chart)..."

In reality Johnny had offered the tachograph chart to Ian Lythgoe on the day of the incident and willingly supplied it the day after the agency had asked for it.

The judge then repeated Walter Mitty's, a.k.a. Adrian Westerman's, supposedly expert evidence as to the apparent weight of the wagon, as if his evidence had somehow been true and accurate. Where Mr. Westerman expounded his expert knowledge and fantastic memory in great detail for the benefit of the jury... [16A - B] (SU)

"There were two drums underneath the back axle and if the lorry had been loaded, those would have been compressed and not quite so high so that you could see them and the trailer would not be quite so high so that you could see the drums clearly as I could that day".

His Honour Judge Farmer was actually presenting this as expert evidence to the jury and astonishingly from a man that the Judge knew to be a "Walter Mitty" character himself, with a shed load of convictions for dishonesty. Johnny knew that as the judge was well aware of Adrian Westerman's convictions, then he must surely also be aware of whatever convictions the undisclosed Travis would almost certainly must have had.

Johnny's thoughts returned to Adrian Westerman's previous

convictions, he knew that it would be only too easy for the police to coerce this man into saying whatever they desired. It would be so easy for them to threaten him, by saying that due to his extensive list of convictions, they thought he was involved in the theft. Unless of course he could come up with something that would point the finger of blame as far away as possible from himself.

The Judge finished off his recital of Adrian Westerman's evidence reminding the jury that when challenged about the accuracy of his evidence relating to self levelling suspension, Mr. Westerman maintained his stance on the issue and again he reminded them to consider the importance of Mr. Westerman's evidence. Then he dealt with the (unbeknown to the jury) hearsay evidence of Ms. Brough, by reiterating said hearsay and repeatedly using one of his favourite words (eventually) to reinforce exactly what he wanted the jury to believe about Johnny's apparent reluctance to help either Ian Lythgoe, or the agency and his having to be forced into going back to Bradford. Whereas in reality, Johnny had gone back quite willingly.

Next the judge dealt with count two, for the bikes from United Carriers. The more Johnny read through this part of the summing up, the more confused and bewildered he became. Well why shouldn't he? The entire charge had only been used by the prosecution in order to reinforce what the prosecution wanted to implant into the jury's mind, which was that this guy (Johnny) was constantly tampering with the loads that he carried whilst he was at work. In reality the prosecution knew that neither this nor any of the other charges could possibly have stood up in court in their own right, so they had to create a coincidence factor. So why not throw in an added extra in order to create a detrimental impression on the jury from the outset?

When the judge moved onto count three, he was careful to imply that the recalling of Stuart Rimmer was nothing out of the ordinary; by making a short reference to his return to the courtroom. [29A] (SU)

"Came back twice didn't he"?

He then contorted the fact that Rimmer had been caught out lying about the location of the immobiliser fob (which in essence was also part of Travis' well rehearsed script) by distorting what Stuart Rimmer had actually said. [29F] (SU)

"It is usually on a key ring but sometimes comes off and is kept in the vehicle".

Going over David Stanley's evidence, he again reiterated what he wanted the jury to believe. [32F] (SU)

"He was a bit agitated because he had to come back on the train".

Whereas in reality Johnny had actually been enraged because of the way he was treated in addition to the insinuation that he had stolen the load by Richard Johnston, head of security at TNT's Warrington yard. His apparent *annoyance* had nothing whatsoever to do with his train journey.

When dealing with (unbeknown to the jury) the false evidence given by the undisclosed witness that the Judge had been responsible for sneaking him into the trial the first place, he was more than happy to reiterate the false evidence. Not only on the supposed impossibility of getting a spare immobiliser fob, but especially on Travis' part of the pre-arranged script containing his *coup de grace* statement. The judge reminded the jury that it was his final piece of evidence when he was cross examined. [35D - E] (SU)

"Remember it was his final piece of evidence when he was cross examined. It's how they got in, in the first place that puzzles me. Remember him saying that and that is what the prosecution says, whoever got in in the first place without damaging the lorry could only be the defendant".

He repeated the same statement yet again, only a few lines down the same page. He obviously placed a great deal of importance on the (false) evidence given by his secret witness. The judge's insistence on constantly repeating this part of the script that he'd obviously been so very proud of, most certainly served it's purpose well in prejudicing the jury against Johnny. However, now reading into the transcript, something else had dawned on Johnny after all this time. The judge's eagerness to repeat that part of Travis' testimony stirred something inside Johnny's memory; it helped Johnny to recall something that had been troubling him for absolutely ages. The judge's relentless banging on about the importance of Travis' blag evidence had suddenly helped something else jump back into his head, just when he least expected it to.

On the second paragraph, on continuation sheet number two of Mr. Stanley's police witness statement he stated, "I also tried the key in the padlock several times and it operated very easily". Which was a total contradiction to of the Travis transcript which said [13A] "I had to use the key that was on the spare key ring to undo it". Well they'd obviously got that part of the script a mixed up! Hadn't they?

However, that wasn't the part that had been bugging Johnny for ages that he'd now remembered. It was on the next paragraph on the same page of David Stanley's police witness statement, where Mr. Stanley had said, "The vehicle was taken back to Warrington *WITHOUT* being examined forensically by the police".

Well so what? You might ask.

First and foremost, there surely to Christ has to be some kind of procedure that both the police and courts have to follow in which evidence cannot be compromised. So surely you'd expect the vehicle to be examined forensically <u>before</u> someone that was so closely connected to the complainants was allowed access to it. Especially one that the prosecution had seen fit to keep a secret from the defendant. Which in turn leads onto the second point, which has to be also of equal importance, and that is all of the information relating to the apparently undamaged locks had came from the undisclosed witness who's other evidence Johnny was now in a position to 100% prove was a complete and utter fabrication. Well he could prove it, COULD being the operative word and very easily so if, YES, IF he had been given the opportunity to do so, but the appeal court were determined that they weren't going to give him chance! Were they!

Regardless the appeal court were supplied with enough evidence of a rigged trial to grant half a dozen appeals. Better still, what Johnny claimed he could disprove, he really could disprove, which was the vast majority, if not all of the claims made by Travis.

It would be inaccurate to say that the months were zooming past, but Johnny was kept extremely busy with the appeal, as well as with all the other things that he'd been doing in the education department. By now it was the beginning of April 2003 and was getting ever closer to his eventual release date. Johnny kept up his relentless bombardment of Mrs. Soskin with weekly letters. If he could get out of jail just one day early, then all the effort that both he and Frances had put into the appeal would have been worthwhile and the getting rid of the convictions could be sorted out later. The important thing was to get back to his family as quickly as possible.

In addition to everything else that he had sent the appeal court, Johnny also sent extra letters in an attempt to rectify the Chinese whispers and believe it or not he also had to send them a copy of the Travis transcript that he had purchased, as apparently the appeal court, with it's enormous amount of funds available to it, did not have a copy themselves. As with all of these letters, Johnny asked to be present at the hearing especially now that he had "real physical proof" that he wished to present to the appeal court, which would unambiguously show that absolutely everything that

Travis had said, relating to M316 XLV 's security, was completely and utterly untrue.

He also sent a copy of the letter that the auto electrician had written, which explained the exact procedure and costs involved in the duplication of immobilisers, complete with diagrams. The letter gave full details of his qualifications and explained that although technical knowledge was required, no specialised equipment was required for said procedure and that a fob could be duplicated anywhere, including at home. The electrician's letter ended with him saying that he was more than willing to attend any appeal hearing.

In addition to all of the other evidence that a mistrial, *or whatever* had taken place in July 2002, Johnny gave an extremely good example of a precedent for his own case for appeal, to the appeal court.

In February 2003, at the court of appeal in London, Mrs. Sally Clarke was granted an appeal against both her convictions for the killing of her two babies. She won her appeal on the grounds that the jury were not presented with the full facts of the case **because evidence was withheld by the prosecution, which in turn led to the jury being misled,** which consequently led to her convictions.

In Mrs. Clarke's case, it was the deliberately withheld evidence which caused the jury to find her guilty; basing part of their premise of guilt on the *coincidence factor*, which was extremely similar to the *coincidence factor* that had been created by the insertion of the United Carriers count by the prosecution.

Johnny pointed out that in his case, the primary cause for both convictions was that the identity of Travis and his so called evidence were **deliberately withheld.** Thereby leaving Johnny completely **unable to reply** to any of Travis' completely false evidence. Simply because he **did not get disclosure** on said false evidence. He continued by adding that as he was not able to put evidence before the jury to show just how uncomplicated it is to obtain ERF keys, or how uncomplicated it is to disable or bypass the old type immobilisers as fitted to M316XLV and asked the appeal court to bear in mind that **Travis never had to show any kind of proof whatsoever** of what he was allowed to say to the jury. Therefore, the jury were not presented with the full facts of the case, through no fault of his own.

Johnny made it clear to the appeal court that as Judge Farmer had told the jury to look at the whole case and each individual count, he was effectively telling them to consider how each of the counts interact with or resemble each other. Therefore the jury were comparing similarities and dissimilarities between each of the three counts.

FORMIDABLE, COMPELLING AND OVERWHELMING EVIDENCE

In count one, Bradford, Johnny did have (and always freely stated having) *possession* of goods that were later stolen whilst said goods were still in his *possession.* However, when it came to count two, United Carriers, Johnny never had (and always denied having) *possession* of goods that he was accused of stealing. For count three, Nottingham,—*ditto* count one.

So when the jury came to consider its verdict on count three it had relied on the false Travis testimony. The Bradford count closely resembled Nottingham in that Johnny did have (and always freely stated having) *possession* of goods that were later stolen whilst said goods were still in his *possession,* as he did with the Nottingham load, but there was no such similarity with the United Carriers bikes. So when the jury found him guilty for Nottingham, due to the false Travis testimony, he suffered another blow by being found guilty for Bradford the following day as a result on the premise that there was a similarity with the Nottingham count.

He also supplied the appeal court with a quote from *The Sun*, complete with a photocopy of the relevant page concerned, dated Wednesday, January 29, 2003. The age 27 quote from **Lord Justice Kay** read: **"Unless we can say that the evidence would have undoubtedly have been rejected by the jury we are bound to allow the appeal".**

He continued, by pointing out to the appeal court that if he was allowed to presume that both Mrs. Clarke (big time yuppie solicitor) and himself (penniless gob-shite lorry driver) were subject to the same set of rules governing evidence put (or not put) before a jury, then he too must have a valid case for appeal!

***

Finally a date for his second attempt for appeal was set for the end of April and in one of the very few replies, dated 16/4/03, that Johnny got to his unrelenting letters, he was informed that "the Lord Justice has refused you leave to be present at your application", the letter continued that, "should the applicant require time to obtain transcripts, etc. ***<u>at his own expense</u>*** then the court would not be unsympathetic towards an application to adjourn from 30th April 2003".

By now Johnny was totally conversant with the appeal courts tactics and he interpreted this letter as meaning that they would like very much indeed for him to be released from prison before he had a chance to go through with the appeal. In the hope that as he was now out and had done his time (their fucking time, more like) he'd let it drop. Johnny let it drop? You've got absolutely no fucking chance, Jimmy!

That evening Johnny phoned Frances as usual, informing her of the latest letter's contents. Both concurred that the Lord Justice had already made up his mind, but regardless they had to go through with the masquerade, if they were ever to "exhaust all domestic remedies". They needed to do this in order to get through to the European Court of Human Rights and have some chance of a real appeal. So plan B, number two was hatched and put into action.

The following morning a reply was in the post and on it's way back down to London, stating that due to their refusal to let it be shown, using the "real physical proof" that he had to show, that the undisclosed witness, Travis, lied in court. He intended furnishing them with a set of photographs and copies of receipts showing all of the locks, with their respective duplicated keys. As well as photographs of the immobiliser fob and it's receptacle, with it's FIVE COLOUR CODED wires sticking out of the back of it and the part of the dashboard from which it had been removed.

Meanwhile, *back at the ranch* in Menai Road, Bootle, Super Fran was busying herself with the above task!

***

A long time prior to this, Johnny had stopped telling anyone especially other prisoners about his appeal efforts, due to the level of animosity it caused with the moronic shite bags that didn't have the courage to stand up for themselves and just did whatever their solicitors had advised them to do. Which was almost always, make life as easy as possible for everyone, especially the solicitors and just plead guilty, even if you aren't. Johnny assumed that the main reason for the animosity was because each of these shite bags lacked the balls, determination, belief in their own innocence, not to mention self confidence. Refuse to take the easy way out, get up off your lazy idle arses, bite the bullet and make a stand!

Each and every single one of these shite bags repeated exactly the same twaddle about if you appeal you'll definitely get more time added on. That's what the lawyers had told them; they had affected yuppie accents, they were better educated than 'us' underclass. What these yuppies said went and that was that, but Johnny knew different, didn't he? He became every bit as adverse to them as they were to him, eventually coming to the conclusion that none of these moronic gob-shites could even spell non-disclosure, never mind having the brains to know what it meant. A lawyer was a yuppie and you were underclass, just like the shite on the bottom of their shoe. They could do whatever they wanted with you. That's just the way it was and these arseholes were content to just sit back and accept it!

Not Johnny though! That was what Gordon Spofforth, *et al.* had *misjudged*[12].

Johnny was under no illusions whatsoever that the threat to increase his sentence was indeed real. Probably all the more so in his case, because he actually did have a story to tell. He was actually innocent. He had actually been stitched up. Warrington Crown Court really did have something to hide; they had after all broken their own rules. Johnny was completely realistic about what might happen to him if he went ahead with the appeal. It was well possible that in an attempt to silence him, the appeal court could just bury him under a series of ever increasing prison sentences.

Johnny was compulsively driven; there were several major factors compelling him to continue, regardless of the possible consequences for himself. The first and foremost was his desire to get out of jail and return to his family, but what about his reasons for being in jail in the first place? He'd almost forgotten about the people that had originally stolen the two loads. His attitude was then (and still is) after spending so much time with so many thieves, most of whom were perfectly ok guys, was, well good luck to them. Surely they'd never have envisaged that the lorry driver's own solicitor could have been involved in stitching him up and him being sent to prison for what they had stolen.

Then there was the non-disclosure of a witness that had lied through his teeth, which had in turn directly led to the convictions. During the total of nine months that Johnny spent in prison, all but nine days of it were spent in Kirkham jail in Lancashire. The first nine days were spent in Altcourse jail in Fazakerley, Liverpool, which like most, if not all UK prisons, was overcrowded so the authorities in Altcourse were probably only too happy to categorise Johnny as being a low risk prisoner and move him on to Kirkham open jail.

As Kirkham was an open jail anyone who was sent there was either a low risk, like Johnny, with a relatively short time to serve or they were at the very end of a longer sentence, which meant that Kirkham had an extremely high turnover of prisoners. This in turn gave Johnny the opportunity to speak to several dozen other prisoners that had gone all the way through a trial. Trials that had quite obviously failed and these guys had been found guilty; otherwise they wouldn't have been here sitting chatting away to Johnny. However, there was one vast, enormous, major difference between Johnny's trial and all of their trials. When he told some of them about the difference in his trial to theirs some of them would squint and screw up their faces in disbelief. From the *non-believers* and believers alike, Johnny gleaned that he was the one and only person that anyone has ever heard of that **DID NOT get disclosure on a witness.**

---

[12] PUN INTENDED!

It came to the point where he'd seen just one too many *non-believers* with the screwed up face and now he was getting a sick feeling in his stomach. Right from the very beginning he'd expected the non-disclosure of Travis to have been at least, extremely unusual and that he would be part of an *elite*[13]group of convicts who'd had the same problem with heir own legal advisors. However, to Johnny's complete dismay, disgust and horror, he discovered that he was not part of an *elite* group at all. The truth was much worse than that; as far as he could tell the sneaking of Travis as the star witness into the trial via the back door and his subsequent lying through his teeth at his trial made Johnny (or at least his trial) completely and utterly *unique*.

Unique! Yeah sure, it sounds fine, but only if it had been for something good. However, in his case it was for something very bad and it was the last thing he wanted to be, especially if the cost of being *unique* was the price he was now paying. He thought *uniqueness* must be comparable to greatness—*some men were born great, some men achieved greatness and some men had greatness thrust upon them*. Johnny had *uniqueness* thrust right up his jacksy and it was extremely painful and very definitely bringing a tear to his eye. His *uniqueness* was the bitterest of pills, which no matter how hard he tried, he just couldn't bear to swallow.

On top of all that, he didn't do it! So why should not only he but also his entire family be made to suffer? His solicitor and barrister had both been under a duty of care to provide him with the best possible service they could and they were paid fantastically huge sums of money for representing him. These were supposedly highly trained professional people, that you could put your complete trust in. Johnny was the first to agree that he could have been more professional in his approach to both the wagon's and their security, but now he'd paid dearly for any incompetence he'd shown. Besides, he was way past the point of no return; whatever they intended doing to him, they'd do regardless of whether he continued or stopped. The letter which said that "the Lord Justice has refused you leave to be present at your application", convinced him that they had gone into full cover up mode and that their minds were already made up. There was no danger whatsoever, regardless of how much evidence Johnny provided, that they would take his side against Judge Farmer's. Even if they hated Judge Farmer's guts they were still going to stick together, because that's just the way it is. That's just the way it's always been and that's just the way it's always gonna be!

Following even more delaying tactics from the court of appeal, his case

[13] *elite,* is an extremely poor choice of word to describe Johnny's *status* (another poor choice), but it was the only word applicable to match up with *unique.*

for appeal was supposedly *reconsidered* by three Judges—Lord Justice Mantell, Mr. Justice Royce and His Honour Judge Mettyear—on 30/4/03. On the same day Johnny telephoned the Court of Appeal at twelve o'clock, three o'clock and again at five o'clock only to be told that his application had yet again been refused. No surprises there then! So now it was official; **Johnny did not have the same rights as Mrs. Clarke** (big time yuppie solicitor) and he was not subject to the same set of rules governing evidence put (or not put) before a jury. His poverty meant that he'd never have a valid case for appeal, no matter how much evidence he gave to the court of appeal!

On receiving the written judgement, it was clear that it was nothing more than a series of distortions of previous statements and a pastiche of the Court of Appeal's outside lawyers and the first judge's statement, with a notable repeat of the first judge's assertion that "... you were convicted on compelling if not overwhelming evidence... " as if they believed that by repeating this statement, it would somehow validate it. Whereas in reality, the convictions were based upon evidence that had no more credibility than Tony Blair's blag excuses for colonising another country in order to steal it's oil.

One of the major distortions in relation to Johnny's complaints was that they claimed that his **main complaint** was that he was now in a position to establish that duplicate keys, or fobs, are much more easily obtainable than the jury were led to believe. They then went on to claim that, for some miraculous reason this does not undermine the safety of the convictions.

How could the British Court of Appeal claim that **false evidence** given at the trial by an **undisclosed witness** did not affect the safety of the convictions?

The **main complaint** now as always has been the **non-disclosure** of the **secret witness,** who went on to give **COMPLETELY FALSE** evidence on ***everything of consequence*** that the ***undisclosed witness,*** Geoffrey Robert Travis, said at the trial on a vast array of points. Which was of course completely and utterly ignored in this latest judgement. Just as it had been throughout his appeal efforts so far.

Non-disclosure means exactly what it says: **Geoffrey Robert Travis** and his false evidence were **not disclosed** to Johnny. The **non-disclosure** issue becomes all the more conspicuous by the fact that each and every person that has been opposed to the appeal has consistently refused to acknowledge the issue.

The court of appeal also ignored all of the other **false** evidence their secret **un-disclosed** witness gave.

The *selective memory loss* was obviously extremely contagious, just like the Great Plague, the Black Death, or bubonic plague, or whatever it was called; it was now spreading to epidemic proportions.

Johnny was still as resolute as ever and so set out to make the *consistently ignored* issue of the **non-disclosure** to become the bane of not only his life, but also of every other single person who'd been involved in making sure that the convictions stuck, from the trial onwards.

For the most simplest of possible reasons :

If Geoffrey Robert Travis had been a genuinely impartial witness "with no axe to grind" and who "was not connected to the complainants", if the Crown knew that he would give *bona fide* evidence, that was truthful, accurate and reliable, then there would have been no reason whatsoever to have held him back as an ADDITIONAL witness who remained undisclosed to Johnny.

Chapter XIII
Appeal # 3

Immediately upon receipt of the three judge judgement ,Johnny began a Criminal Cases Review Commission (CRCC) based appeal. The CCRC was set up by the government after the Birmingham Six were freed on appeal after serving something like sixteen years in jail and it was allegedly intended to be a failsafe net to catch any unjust convictions that had failed at the Appeal Court in London. However, by now Johnny had been through it all before, at least with the British appeal system and by now he was the most sceptical of the sceptical. He resigned himself to the fact that the CCRC people in Birmingham were just the same as those in London and that it was merely just another way of the judicial system providing even more jobs for the boys and that these people would never shit on their own people and in turn would find any reason to disallow his appeal, regardless of how strong his case for appeal was.

However, he also knew that in order to get through to the European Court of Human Rights, where he would need to hope upon hope that he could get some kind of a semblance of justice, he would firstly need to completely exhaust all possible domestic remedies. Thus he reluctantly had to continue on with the charade with the British judicial system.

One of the letters that he received from the CCRC asked for evidence of his 'real physical proof' that the appeal court in London had been so reluctant to permit him to show them. After all they had to prevent him from showing it, didn't they, because it would completely disprove all of Travis' lies, wouldn't it?

Regardless, he had to continue on with the charade and telephoned the CCRC, saying that he wanted to deliver the 'real physical proof' consisting of the locks and fobs, etc. in person. As Johnny was only to well aware that if he didn't deliver them himself, they would just miraculously get lost in the post. So he dug even deeper into his bare pockets and bought a completely new set of all the locks and keys etc. Then made an appointment to deliver them personally and in due course Johnny and Frances travelled together in their rusty old fourteen year old banger to

Birmingham.

On arrival at the CCRC's address in Alpha Tower, Suffolk Street, Queensway, Birmingham, they found it to be a large high-rise office block. The concierge in the foyer telephoned the relevant department, but instead of being directed to an office on such and such a floor as he'd expected, Johnny was told to wait in the foyer instead and that a Mr. James Friend from the CCRC would come down to meet him. So far, so good.

Twenty five minutes later a young man, probably in his early twenties ambled his way into the foyer and introduced himself to Johnny as Mr. James Friend, saying that Johnny could now give him the bag of items he had brought with him from Liverpool.

Absolutely certain that the foyer of an office block wasn't quite the right place for such a transaction to take place, especially considering that the items in question were of such crucial importance to the entire rest of Johnny's life, Johnny took the precaution of asking."Well what about a receipt"?

With an over-affectedly astonished huff aimed at evincing scornful surprise at such a request from a distasteful character, such as this piece of worthless white trash before him, Mr. Friend condescendingly replied."A receipt"?

"Yeah. You know what a receipt is, don't you? It's usually given as some form of written proof, which verifies that someone has given you something into your care that is of very great value to them", retorted Johnny.

"So you want a receipt for these"? replied Mr. Friend, now widening his eyes and throwing his head backwards, in order to put on his best show of haughty indignation.

"Yeah, that's right, you seem to be getting the right idea at last"!

Mr. Friend went over to the concierge at the reception desk and came back a few seconds later with a scrap piece of paper that had obviously came from tearing up a bigger piece of paper into smaller pieces. He then began examining the contents of the bag that Johnny had handed him and started scribbling on the bit of paper.

"Is that what you intend giving me in way of a receipt"? Johnny barked at Mr. Friend, as by now he was getting extremely irritated at this person's attitude towards him. Johnny knew only too well that if he didn't get a proper receipt, then the evidence he had been so diligent in protecting and making sure came to the right place, was sure to go astray.

A stupid blank stare and silence was all Mr. Friend could manage by way of a reply. When suddenly Frances interceded, primarily to protect Mr. Friend. He might not have realised it, but she knew only too well the young Mr. Friend was rapidly heading towards a trip to the dentist and or the maxo-facial clinic. But she was also every bit as determined as Johnny that this little shit wasn't going to get away with discarding this absolutely vital evidence and then later claim that he knew nothing whatsoever about it.

"Get back up to your office and get us a proper receipt and by that I mean a full inventory. You know what a full inventory is"? growled Frances.

Indignantly, he stormed back off in the same direction from which he came and half an hour or so later he reappeared with a proper dated inventory, listing all of the items that had been given into his care.

On the return journey, Johnny and Frances discussed his prospects of getting any joy from the CCRC. Both concurred that if Mr. Friend's attitude was anything go by then today's journey was sure to be a total waste of time, money and energy. The proof would be in the pudding and only time would tell and neither Johnny or Frances were prepared to hold their breath.

On 19/8/03 Johnny received final conformation from the CRCC that they had no interest in his case. The CCRC enclosed a statemente of their reasons for not investigating his case. Which were nothing more than an almost word perfect repeat of what the three judges—Lord Justice Mantell, Mr. Justice Royce and His Honour Judge Mettyear—had said previously. Including of course yet another repeat of the first judge's assertion that "... you were convicted on compelling if not overwhelming evidence... " as if they believed that by repeating this statement, it would somehow validate it. So in total it had been firstly said by the first judge, the single judge, the Honourable Mr. Justice Langley, **(1)** the appeal court's outside lawyer **(2)** and all three appeal court Judges **(3)** and now the Criminal Cases Review Commission **(4)**.

"Baby, we're going to have to get ourselves inoculated, aren't we"? Johnny said to Frances.

"What the fuck are you going on about now"? She replied, with a concerned expression appearing on her face.

"We need some of that anti-*selective memory loss* serum, coz it's spreading like wildfire".

"Eh"?

"Oh Jesus Christ Frances it doesn't matter, just forget about it".

"What doesn't matter? Oh yeah, right, ok, why can't you just speak fucking English"? She snarled at him, as she didn't consider this to be a joking matter.

Johnny and Frances had both came to the same conclusion, no-one in the entire appeal system was ever going to bother looking at his case properly and all were quite content to simply repeat some kind of bog standard statement, that presumably was repeated to every single appellant in the entire country, relying on the fact that most appellants are too frightened to continue an appeal due to the threat of an increased sentence. Johnny and Frances also knew that everyone in the so-called appeal system were quite happy to suffer the same *selective memory loss* syndrome, whenever it suited them.

Neither Johnny or Frances collapsed in sheer and utter amazement at the decision to disallow his appeal and *coincidentally* on the same morning Johnny received another letter. This letter was from the Law Society to whom Johnny had written some months previously in order to complain about the *service* that he had received at the hands of Mr. Spofforth and Mr. Watson. The Law Society's letter *went all around the world* in order to state that it would do nothing in relation to the complaints that Johnny had made against one of it's own members.

Chapter XIV
Appeal # 4, Why Bother?

Frances looked much more sullen than she'd done for months and with more than a mere hint of pessimism in her voice she asked her husband,"So where do we go from here my lovely"?

Johnny was beginning to feel just that little bit apathetic himself, but only for a single fleeting moment. He was under no illusions that he was banging his head against a brick wall, but it was that same brick wall that Judge Farmer was relying on when he insisted that Travis be furtively sneaked into the trial. The more Johnny considered the brick wall, the more frustrated he became. The frustration soon turned to inner anger, but still in the back of his mind was the certainty that Judge Farmer was relying on that same brick wall and a brick wall's only a brick wall, now isn't it and like all brick walls, it could be either climbed over, tunnelled under, got round to the left, got round to the right, or even broken straight through!

Probably less than ten seconds after he had first detected that tiny little miniscule hint of pessimism and downheartedness in his beautiful loving wife's voice, he forced himself to reply with a blend of cheerfulness and recalcitrance."Onwards and upwards baby! Where else? Never Surrender! Never give up! These wankers have at least cleared the way for me to get through to the European Court of Human Rights. Just like any poor person, I'm obviously never going to get any kind of fair hearing in this shithouse country. Am I? There's every probability that I won't get one from them either, coz they're all going to stick together anyway, but I'll never know if I don't try. Will I"?

They both knew that he'd gone past the point of no return with the appeal and all the rest, a hell of a long time ago. Now no matter what, it had to be onwards and upwards, he could never surrender, nor could he ever give up! So he had to soldier on regardless.

Undaunted and now finding himself at the end of all domestic remedies, Johnny swiftly moved on to the European Court of Human Rights, in his relentless attempts at having the unjust and illegally gained convictions quashed.

By this time of course Johnny has been released from prison for over a month and so had plenty of time available to write down in fine detail most of his complaints as to his trial and consequent appeal efforts and in due course these were forwarded to the relevant address in Strasbourg, France. As of 17/9/03 he still hadn't received any reply from them.

In addition, whilst he had still been in prison, Johnny had sent off details of his appeal efforts to a solicitor in Rochdale, that apparently specialised in CCRC cases and appeals in general, but he'd heard nothing from them for several months and so went ahead with the European Court based appeal anyway. Thinking to himself that if it were possible, then he might as well have two appeals running together simultaneously. So if one failed then he'd always have the other to fall back on. On 8/9/03 he unexpectedly received a letter from them which stated:

"We write simply to inform you that we have not yet received your case file from your previous solicitors. We requested this on 11th July 2003. We have written to them again, once we are in receipt of your case file, we can advise you further towards your appeal".

Johnny interpreted this as meaning that if nothing else, then he'd at least succeeded in putting Gordon Spofforth's back against the wall. Now just like himself, Gordon Spofforth was also past the point of no return.

In collusion with others it could only have been Gordon Spofforth himself that had been *initially* responsible for the sequence of events that had led to Travis' clandestine entry into Johnny's trial at Warrington Crown Court. After all they could never have achieved it without Gordon Spofforth's help and his buddies at Warrington Crown Court would gladly hold him responsible for any consequent fuck-ups and instantly drop him like a hot potato at the very first hint of trouble.

Gordon Spofforth must surely have been aware of his own position, i.e. at the bottom of the pile, and as we all know, shit rolls downhill and if anybody was going to be the fall guy, it would surely be Gordon Spofforth. Now it was he that had no choice but to try his best to cover his arse and the most obvious means of escape open to him must surely be to rely on what he knew best and now he was back up to *his old tricks*—still withholding evidence.

By this time Johnny had already sent all the relevant documents off to the European Court, so he sat back and waited to see which he'd hear from first. As with the European Court, by 17/9/03 he still hadn't received any reply from them either.

However, on Monday 13/10/03 Johnny received an unexpected letter from the European Court, which asked for copies of several documents relating to his appeal efforts so far to be forwarded to them including:

FORMIDABLE, COMPELLING AND OVERWHELMING EVIDENCE

Fully completed application form, dated 14 October 2003
Copy of *CCRC* decision, dated 18 August 2003
Copy of *three judge* decision, dated 30 April 2003
Copy of *single judge* decision, dated 25 November 2002

On *page three* of the application form there was a section for Johnny to fill in his reasons for the complaint in his own words; Johnny wrote:

In July 2002, I stood trial at Warrington Crown Court, Cheshire, England for three counts of theft.

Prior to the trial I was assured by my solicitor and barrister that I had been given full disclosure on ALL the evidence that was to given against me at said trial.

During the course of the trial it was (became) very obviously clear that the prosecution's case was crumbling, until the point when an UN-DISCLOSED witness was sneaked into the trial. This same UN-DISCLOSED witness then went on to give ***(what I am now in a position to prove—but have been denied the opportunity to do so)*** *completely FALSE EVIDENCE.*

Two points

1/ Even in Britain, disclosure of evidence is ***supposedly*** *one of the very rights that we have left to us. YET this very basic right was denied to me!*

2/ I have made three separate appeal attempts in this country. Each time offering to ***prove*** *that the* ***undisclosed*** *witness* ***lied throughout his evidence****. Each time I have been denied the opportunity to do so. Also I have NEVER been allowed to get past the application stage of the* ***supposed*** *appeal process. Effectively denying me any kind of appeal. The British appeal court has done this with the* ***deliberate intention*** *of preventing my justified case for appeal being brought into* ***the public domain!*** *And into the open!*

Johnny checked over *page three* and the rest of the application, for spelling mistakes, etc. and concluded to himself that if this didn't make it clear what the basis of his complaint was, then nothing ever would! All of the documents were duly completed, photocopied and less than twenty four hours after this latest letter had popped through his letter box, the reply was back in the post on 14/10/03. Sceptical as ever, neither Johnny nor Frances held their breath whilst waiting for a reply from his latest submission to the European Court.

***

Johnny realised that most people would wonder why bother to continue trying to clear what is not an unblemished name. Well why not? He was just sick to fucking death of being a victim and besides, since coming out of prison he found himself to be completely unemployable, a situation that he didn't expect to change for the entire rest of his working life, another 24 years at least. In addition, he now found that it had become a hell of a lot more expensive to get basic building (bricks and mortar) insurance, never mind household contents insurance. In short the *activities* of Warrington Crown Court in Cheshire, England had by completely illegal means brought about the ruin of both his own and his entire family's lives and had left him with plenty of spare time to fill. Which, as you can see, he used to further his appeal efforts and the writing of this book. But apart from all that, why in the name of Christ should Johnny be made to accept being the one and only person[14] that he's ever heard of that's been transformed from being Mr. Mundane to being completely *unique*, all thanks to Gordon Spofforth, *et al.*? But there's got to be a hell of a lot more to it than that. Johnny bothered for his own sake and the sake of his family, but it doesn't end there and it doesn't stop there just because Johnny's said he's been innocent right from the very start. Right from day one throughout the police investigation, throughout the trial, throughout the multitude of appeals and then on throughout the book.

Johnny's innocence isn't the important matter here. The question of his innocence or guilt pales in significance, when you consider what's really important. Because what's really important here is the fact that several people that are involved in the judicial process in one way or another have taken it upon themselves to act together surreptitiously and with purely nefarious intent. These people at the very least deliberately ignored certain rules and laws laid down by the British government which are supposedly put in place **as a right** to protect each and every single person in this shithouse country.

So where do all Johnny's *problems* originate from? You can forget about the original thefts, because the level of *problems* that Johnny experienced would require a much higher level of organisation than a few minor criminals out to steal a few thousand pounds worth of goods. The

[14]During his entire time both in and since coming out of prison despite having discussed this with literally hundreds of other people to date he is still yet **the one and only** person that he has ever heard of that did not get disclosure on a witness. Let alone one who went on to lie through his teeth and give completely false evidence.

actual thefts themselves were just one of those everyday commonplace occurrences that we have to accept happens from time to time.

But what isn't supposed to be commonplace and what hopefully isn't an everyday occurrence, that you shouldn't need to accept as being one of those things that happens now and again, is the machinations that had evolved well before Johnny had an undisclosed witness[15]sprung upon him, out of the blue, at his trial. These aforementioned machinations must have evolved many months before Johnny ever set foot in Warrington Crown Court. They must have begun even before Gordon Spofforth decided that there was one witness in particular that he intended keeping secret from his client. The rationale for this being that he would never have done so ***unless*** this perfidious task had been requested of him. Which in turn has to beg the question—who made the request?

However, we don't need to get too bogged down with these questions, just yet. You can work it out for yourself. Just begin with Johnny's first contact in his *defence team.* Gordon Spofforth, who for whatever reason, decided to keep Travis and his false testimony a secret from Johnny[16], so we can consider Gordon Spofforth to be the first link in the chain that will eventually lead to Travis being furtively sneaked into the trial. Don't forget that it's the solicitor's job to select a barrister for his client.

Enter Tom Watson, who for reasons already discussed, we can deduce that Gordon Spofforth must have told about Travis, well before Johnny ever became aware of him.

From there we have to take a bit of a side step, in order to have a look at the (incomplete) Travis transcript. For the simple reason that it is incomplete and that there's a bit of it missing from the very beginning, right there on page one. Even now after all this time has elapsed, Johnny couldn't bring himself to believe that his own barrister, Tom Watson, willingly initiated Travis' entry into the trial. Simply because the first seven pages of the transcript showed that Tom Watson did indeed make several attempts to prevent Travis from being used as an *expert* witness. But Judge Farmer had vehemently insisted that *his star witness* was going to make his entrance, no matter what! Not only that, but Tom Watson also very nearly got the better of Travis on several occasions during his cross-examination of him, but on each of these occasions he was cut short by the judge, who came to the rescue of *his star witness*.

Without the missing part of the transcript, it would be impossible to

---

[15] Who incidentally lied through his teeth.

[16] Gordon Spofforth must have earmarked Johnny as being a moronic gob-shite, because he would never have tried this kind of blatant deceit with anyone that he considered to have even one single functioning brain cell in his head.

comment on whether it was Mr. Lewis-Jones or the Judge[17] himself that had *invited* Travis to join in the fun.

So even without including Travis and Rimmer, at the absolute minimum, you've got three separate officials of the judiciary working together in concert to *disobey* the government's own rules pertaining to the disclosure of witnesses.

But all that's by and by because Travis gains entry into the proceedings anyway and gives his utterly false evidence, without even being asked to or having to show the slightest minuscule shred of proof that what he was encouraged to say was somehow true and accurate. But why should he need to show any proof anyway? After all the jury must have been working on the assumption that any evidence given by Travis must have been thoroughly checked and verified. **If you'd been on that jury—wouldn't you?**

So anyway, the trial comes to an end and Johnny is found guilty on the basis of Travis' false evidence and a day later, because the integrity of the trial has been compromised by Travis' false evidence, Johnny also gets found guilty for the Bradford load, due to the premise of similarities between it and the Nottingham load, but not guilty on the United Carriers because the jury don't perceive any such similarity between that load and Nottingham. Besides it's quite impossible to steal something that's never been in your possession, now isn't it?

Then during the intervening period[18] between the verdicts and sentence, Johnny starts the ball rolling for an appeal, namely, buying the 1st ignition system which he tries unsuccessfully on several occasions to show to either Gordon Spofforth or Tom Watson and eventually has to settle for leaving it until the date of sentencing. Whereupon both Gordon Spofforth and/or Tom Watson immediately decide that such evidence is no good anyway and go onto do their utmost to dissuade Johnny from pursuing an appeal.

So all that's by and by, Johnny doesn't pass Go and doesn't get £200 and goes straight to jail anyway, and while he's there decides to have a go at a DIY appeal regardless.

Don't go to sleep on me now! I will get to the point soon enough!

So Johnny's been surreptitiously stitched up by completely illegal means. So fucking what? So have countless millions of other poor cunts, haven't they? These lawyers and judges always stick together and look after their own, simply because they know that they can sleep well at night

---

[17] Who had specifically asked for Johnny's case to be reserved for him.

[18] An unprecedented 7 week period, conveniently almost double the 28 day time limit within which you must lodge your appeal by.

in the knowledge that nobody, or at least very few people, have got the balls or the inclination to challenge their authority to do whatever they please, whenever they please. That's why they have so much power, because they're relying on people's fear of them; but you can only fear them if they've actually left you with something to lose. What if their illegal actions lead to total and complete penury, the stress of which in turn is tearing apart the one single thing in the entire world that you hold dearest to your heart, your own family!

After all, he's practically got absolutely nothing left to lose, does he? If he does nothing and accepts that what's happened to him is just another 'one of those things', then he's going to lose his family because neither he nor they can cope with the poverty that's resulted from Gordon Spofforth's illegal actions. But it's not just Gordon Spofforth's actions, is it? Because he was just a foot soldier (lackey) carrying out the orders of a *higher authority*.

So Johnny had no real option but to carry on with the appeals. And when they failed, as even number four was sure to, then he's got to write the book. How else can he hope to bring the *activities* of Warrington Crown Court out into the open? Which would be the one thing that Gordon Spofforth *et al.* must never have envisaged when they sat down together and decided to perform their nefarious deed. Which begs the question, does Johnny think he's something special? The answer to which is: he's not in any way, shape or form special, in fact he's a very ordinary guy, the epitome of banality; Mr. Average on a stick. Well not quite Mr. Average, because he's actually a lot poorer than the real Mr. Average and Gordon Spofforth knows that Johnny's a lot poorer than Mr. Average and he knows that because he paid Johnny a *home visit,* way back before the trial, when he'd carried out his reconnoitre patrol to see how much money Johnny had. After all, he could tell a hell of a lot about Johnny's income by the house he lived in. The house had probably been worth less than a 5th of the national average house price. Johnny's obvious lack of funds added to the fact that it was such an insignificant trial with only a relatively small amount of money involved and these two things would ensure that nobody in the media would ever have give it a second glance and it would never make the headlines and instead would go forever completely unnoticed.

Returning to the issue of the home visit paid by Gordon Spofforth. If you've ever been through a trial yourself, or if you haven't, just ask anyone that's had plenty of contact with solicitors: how often do solicitors make ***home visits*** to discuss official business that would *normally* be discussed within the confines of their office? I'm pretty sure, if not absolutely certain, that you'll find the answer is either pretty fucking rarely, or, as with the non-disclosure of a witness, absolutely un-fucking-heard-of! All of which would help to explain why a certain Mr. Chesney should now feel that he is so different! Completely and utterly fucking unique.

Johnny pondered his situation; I never used to consider myself to be unique, but nevertheless my own solicitor chose to transform me from the prosaic to the extraordinary. If someone's gone to a lot of trouble just to make you unique then it'd be downright rude not to give any credit, where it's due. So you might as well get up onto a soap box and start shouting about it. Shouldn't you?

So now that he'd become the reluctant recipient of this uniqueness, that was neither wished nor asked for, Johnny decided that he had to use it to his advantage, initially during the appeals and at a later point, in the publishing stakes, after all the poor bastard's still got to eat! Hasn't he?

Chapter XV
Release

Johnny pondered the word release, as opposed to the word freedom. Two different words with two very different meanings. Especially when the release involves being on an electronic tag. With Johnny's release he felt like a dog that was taken out for a walk but kept on the lead. Not only was Johnny kept on a lead, but the appeal court had also seen to it that he also had a muzzle, or a gag fitted as they would have surely preferred.

At last Johnny was out and promoted from a being on the outside of society, to the periphery, where he was still only permitted to look in on society and not actually be part of it. On his first day out, Johnny had to report to his local probation office where he was informed that someone would call round to his house a week later and from then on he would need to attend weekly appointments for the next month or so, until it was deemed that he could be reduced down to fortnightly visits to the probation office.

From there, Johnny and Frances went straight home to their little house on the Menai Road. Once there, Frances asked Johnny if he'd like something to eat. Despite the fact that he'd hardly eaten anything for months, food was the last thing on his mind at the moment. He grabbed her and held her close and told her that all he wanted to eat was her. He'd had none for nine months. She'd had none for nine months and so for the first time in years, she managed to ascend the stairs without the slightest of difficulty.

Johnny was a hell of a lot more agile than Frances, he was up into the bedroom and completely undressed in a jiffy. As Frances watched him undress, he noticed her eyes widen and her mouth opening into a wide gape. *Oh yabba fucking dabba do!* Johnny thought to himself as he eagerly awaited her next move in excited anticipation. Her mouth was growing ever wider as she approached him. "Yeah baby yeah! Come on baby! Help yourself! Fill your boots"! He thought out loud, growing ever more excited by the second.

She remained completely dressed, but he didn't care. She could still sort him out regardless. She crossed to him from the other side of the room and threw her arms around him, but instead of doing what he'd hoped for, she let out a muffled whine, followed by tears.

No, no this wasn't what Johnny wanted at all. *This isn't what I've been waiting the all this time for. Now was it!* He thought to himself, as she began to wail and cry even louder.

"What the fuck's up"? He asked, becoming increasingly alarmed and agitated.

Incoherent sobs were the best she could give in reply to his question.

He took her face in his hands and made her look straight into his eyes, but before he got the chance to ask her another question, she began wailing even louder than before. They stumbled onto the bed and he just held her in his arms as she sobbed.

After about five minutes of sobbing and crying, she began to control herself just enough to make some sense.

"Look at you. You're just skin and bones", she spluttered out as she continued to sob.

"Eh"?

"You're so skinny. Didn't you eat anything in there? What the fuck were they feeding you? I told you to eat, how could you let yourself get into that state"?

"For fuck's sake we've been through all this already, six weeks ago".

"You weren't anything near that bad six weeks ago when you came out for the weekend and besides I told you to eat whatever they put in front of you, didn't I"?

For the past six or seven months, Johnny had gotten completely used to his new concentration camp physique. He'd actually forgotten that he'd once been quite overweight. Frances hadn't seen him properly in his natural for nine months, so she could tell the difference in his figure. He thought to himself that it was probably just her emotions running wild that was getting her all worked up over his weight loss, what he considered to be a trivial concern.

Nine months previously he been a bit fat, but with it he had been a big strapping man, with plenty of muscle tissue to go with it. Now he was just skinny, not thin, not slender just skinny, too skinny, unhealthily thin, just like death warmed up. His muscular arms had turned to a string of piss. His formerly ample, firm bottom now sagged and looked like what you'd expect for a ninety year old man. His chest and shoulders were just bones everywhere. She could see his ribs sticking out, yes his ribs—that's what she noticed most. During the thirteen years or so that they'd been together, she'd never once laid eyes on his ribs, until now.

So much for the good afternoon session that he'd hoped and waited all these months for! By the time she'd pulled herself together, it was time to collect the kids from school. Johnny knew that he couldn't possibly demand sex, especially with her current emotional state, and so off to school they went.

As they waited in the school yard, Frances noticed a couple of other mothers who were talking to each other and would nudge each other as they looked over in our direction. Which Frances interpreted them as thinking that she had got herself a new boyfriend. They both laughed it off and he suggested that she introduce him to them as her new toy boy.

The school doors opened and Patrick the baby, came running out and straight into Johnny's arms, shouting at the top of his voice. Daddy! Daddy! Thereby obviating the need for the toy boy introduction.

Frank was next out and as always was much more reticent and merely walked over towards his dad and gave him a big but quiet hug.

Jack was Jack and that was that and Jack will always be Jack! And that's that! Regardless of his current title!

Overall, the children were made up to have their dad home and Johnny tried to split his time between Frances and each of the children. He had to re-accustom himself to the attention seeking from the kids and the noise emanating from them was terrific. Maybe this was just a wee bit of real life that they'd all forgot about.

Frances had cooked a nice big special dinner for the homecoming, but she'd neglected to take into consideration that Johnny's appetite had diminished down to child size proportions. He felt ever so guilty at not being able to finish off the great mound of food that she'd placed in front of him. He could see that each of the children, even Patrick, had eaten more than him, so he had to keep trying to cram more food into his mouth, despite that fact that he could feel his belly bursting at the seams. *What the hell? I might as well make the most of this while I can.* He thought to himself, as he crammed yet more delicious, nourishing food into his mouth, the likes of which he hadn't seen for the past nine months. Eventually he had to give in and confess to Frances that although he was ever so grateful for all the effort she'd put into his homecoming meal, he just couldn't manage another morsel due to the reduced size of his stomach.

She just laughed and said,"It's alright darling. I understand".

With the pain in Johnny's stomach, he wished to Christ that he'd had the courage to have spoken up a bit earlier and that he should have realised how considerate and understanding she'd have been.

Later that evening the 'Tag People' came round and as soon as they'd gone, the ale came out and the music went on.

Friends and family had wanted to come around but Johnny and Frances just wanted to be on their own, with their own immediate little family unit. The sad thing was that they were all completely emotionally and physically drained. By 10.30 pm they were all ready for bed. Especially Johnny!

Today's attempts at making love were totally ruined, but that was then and now was now. Johnny just hoped to God that she didn't start blubbering again, he was most definitely gagging for it, but it been nine months for Frances and so she was every bit as enthusiastic as Johnny. *Did she hear the sound of harps playing and waves crashing on the rocks or was it just in her imagination*? The lovemaking was slow and unhurried, so unlike Johnny had wanted it to be, but even better than he had ever expected.

Seven minutes later, when it was all over, they lay entwined together, as neither wanted to let go of the other. No talking, just quiet and silence. There was no need for words between these two such compatible people.

Suddenly the ice was broken, normality resumed, Johnny did it, yes, the passing of the wind!

"Oh my God"! exclaimed Frances.

Johnny just laughed and stared singing, "Where ever you may be, just let your wind run free, in church or chapel, let your arsehole rattle".

Frances was, as always, undisturbed by his singing. She had quite literally forgot all about this side of having a man in the house again, but she couldn't care less. The family was complete again at last and things looked as if they could return to normal. She pinched her nose with her index finger and thumb and laughed as she said, "I know you look like you've just escaped from Belson, but there's no need to bring the gas chambers home with you".

He laughed.

They both laughed together!

Within a few days of his release, Johnny was happily settling back into the real world. He got the children up and dressed them, fed and watered them, then walked them to school. By the time he returned to the house, Frances was busy cooking the breakfast. *Oh Christ, not more food*, he thought to himself, without making the lethal mistake of thinking out loud. It was a delicious, big, nutritious breakfast, but she was still making the same mistake that she'd made on his first day out. She was giving him adult portions that he just couldn't handle. Of course she was doing this deliberately and with the very best of intentions—trying to put a bit of meat back onto his protruding bones. Frances knew that although his belly was paining him, he'd be extremely reluctant to complain so as not to upset her.

***

Having served nine months of a two year sentence, for theft from an employer, he now had to undergo a further three months on home detention curfew (HDC) on an electronic tag. As the reason for his being in prison was theft from an employer, another painful reality he was going to have to get used to, was that in addition to being unemployed, he was also unemployable, leaving both the family and himself to rely upon state benefits.

Prior to the sentencing Johnny and Frances had sold their nice big house. They had made a reasonable, enough profit on the house and so used the cash from the sale to buy their current, much smaller and less expensive (but a hell of a lot more dilapidated) property outright. So as to ensure that Frances and the three kids were not also going to be encumbered with a mortgage in addition to all of the other strains brought to bear upon her with Johnny's being in prison.

While they were still in the old house in Fazakerley, Frances also had her own much newer car, but problems arose with it[19]and it was decided that they could manage with just the one car. As Frances was disabled, it was deemed absolutely necessary for her to keep hold of the much older and completely worthless 14 year old (F registration) Ford Escort, she couldn't care less about the age of the car, after all a car is a car, and as long as she didn't need to try and walk or get the bus, she couldn't give two hoots about what state the car was in.

Following the release from prison that he'd longed for so much over the months, Johnny suddenly now found himself both unemployed and on a very low income, and within the first week of being released he learned that Mrs. Chesney had been keeping secrets from him, during the time he'd been inside. No! You dirty minded fucker, not that kind of secret!

Johnny's wife Frances had throughout their almost ten years of marriage, always shown him the greatest respect, love and affection and never on any occasion put him under any kind of undue pressure. With a complete disregard for anything even remotely resembling self-pity for herself, in order to save him from any additional worries about her and their family's welfare, she had kept the extent of her own problems a closely guarded secret from him whilst he was languishing in prison. Each time she'd come to visit him, without fail she would always reassure him that she was doing fine and coping well with both the kids and money. However, it now transpired that the house that they had bought in haste, was now going to give them plenty of opportunity to repent at their leisure.

---

[19] An entirely new story altogether.

Due to their current financial state, which was far from indeed anything but healthy, this meant that he was now going to have the opportunity to test his DIY skills to their utmost limit and carry out the bulk of the necessary repairs by himself, on an extremely tight budget.

So no rest for the *wicked*, eh? Less than a week back out in the real world and poor old Johnny had to begin a series of absolutely essential DIY repair jobs on his home, which after his nine months in prison was beginning to look like the house that Jack built. All of these jobs should really should have been done before he went into prison, but at that time they both had a multitude of other more pressing problems to contend with.

Only the absolutely essential jobs were carried out, which included repairs to the windows and front door, plumbing work and roofing repairs at the end of which he was a great deal more than just slightly proud of having done a more than adequate job entirely by himself. However, despite not having to pay someone for these jobs to be done, the total cost for the materials and necessary tools required to carry out the work completely obliterated not only all of Frances' meagre savings, but also required her to pawn most of her beloved jewellery, which had been mostly family heirlooms. The house was also in desperate need of *a good lick of paint,* but that was just one of those things that was just like when the bulb goes in the fridge—destined to be put on the back boiler until only Christ knew when.

In addition to that, the 14-year-old car that they had retained was now in a quite desperate state of disrepair. It needed the clutch replacing immediately, in addition to lots of other less expensive, smaller jobs that needed doing—like the accelerator cable replacing and replacing burst door and ignition locks that had been damaged in an attempted theft of the vehicle, which they had to consider to be another essential job to be done.

During the middle of the school summer holidays in July 2003, all three kids were getting really bored, partly because the Chesney family couldn't afford to go on holiday during the school holidays, as usual. Which was primarily due to the lack of money in their household and besides, Johnny was still going to be on the tag until the first week in September, anyway. One evening while they were watching TV they seen an advert for a free month's trial on AOL, which stated that free internet access was available, for a one month trial period. Knowing that the children were due to finish their summer holidays and start back at school in early September, we decided to give it a try, for the free month, in the hope that it would enhance their academic interest, as well as keeping them occupied during the holiday. Frances phoned the AOL company and asked for the free month trial, specifically asking to make sure that it was indeed a free trial period; she was duly assured that this was the case and we were duly connected to the internet.

After less than a week, both Frances and Johnny began to notice lots of those little icons that come on the screen when you switch on the computer—such as *Hot Wet Lips* and *tranny porn.* Naturally each of the adults denied all knowledge as to who had been looking at porn sites on the internet, as did the children when asked about it—*it must have been that ghost, again, mustn't it?*

The obvious prime suspect had to be either *Jack the Lad, Jack the Nice Little Boy!* or more likely, *Jack the Twat.* Either way, Mother and Father knew exactly who the *usual suspect* was, after all, he was an extremely streetwise eleven-year-old and both Mr. and Mrs. Chesney assumed that the younger two wouldn't have known how to access these, or indeed any other internet sites.

Intrigued, whilst being far too terrified to imagine what the *tranny porn* site might hold in store for them, they decided clicked onto the *Hot Wet Lips* site, assuming or perhaps hoping that should be the *safer* option. In order to see just exactly what either Jack or perhaps all three of their sons had been watching. At this point they still believed that whatever came up on the screen, would still have come under the *free* access.

However, once they had got onto the correct site, they noticed that on the top right hand corner of the screen there was a message saying that this site would cost £1.50 per minute. Unperturbed, and desperate to find out more, they clicked on the continue flag and to the absolute horror of them both the £1.50 changed to £1.75 within a couple of seconds. A few seconds later it changed to £2.00, then £2.25 and still no sign of any *rudy nudy* pictures. Johnny's immediate reaction was to try to exit the website; he tried clicking on various flags, but still could not exit the site. By now the cost had risen to £4.50 and he still couldn't exit it. By this point they were both completely exasperated at being unable to exit the web site and worse still, Johnny hadn't seen even the slightest glimmer of a *bare naked lady!*

Both Johnny's and Frances' thoughts were now in perfect unison, with the other's. Both thought out loud, together, well how much did they spend to see any pictures? Plus how in the name of Christ were we going to get this web page closed down? The only answer they could think of for the second question was to turn the computer off at the electricity supply. At this point the cost had risen to £5.75. About half a minute later, Johnny switched the computer back on and to the relief of them both the web page had at last been turned off.

From the phone bills for the previous ten months, or so they estimated that their average phone should be about £45.00. With only about £9.00 of that figure being for actual phone calls. The rest of the bill being made up of line rental and the cost of the cable television and VAT.

The next more pressing concern was just how much damage had the kids done, as to the anticipated size of the next phone bill? Quite frankly they were both just too shit scared to ask the phone company how much of a bill they had run up. Besides, as always, the eternal optimist within Johnny came to the forefront giving him the remote glimmer of hope that these calls just might have been free after all and then there was an even more desperately remote chance that somehow it might go unnoticed by the phone company. In addition to all that, they weren't even too sure if it would be the cable company or AOL that would send the bill anyway, in which case it was supposed to be free months trial, so again they hoped upon hope that it would be free after all. So they decided that asking the phone company questions might just open up a can of worms and that their best option was to sit it out and wait for the next phone bill to arrive.

However, there was still the AOL problem that needed to be gotten rid of, so AOL was called using their free phone help line number. Which rang out for at least 15 minutes before getting through to a recorded message. From there Johnny had to press another number in order to get to speak to a *real person*, whom he told that he wanted to cancel their service. Rather than just agreeing to his request, the operator insisted on trying various enticements, even offering up extra free weeks to entice them into keeping the service connected.

Expediency forced him to persist to the point where he had to resort to forcefully, if not aggressively, insist in no uncertain terms, that he no longer required and definitely wanted to get rid of their service. Eventually he managed to get the message through to the operator and was finally disconnected.

Some two or three weeks, later the dreaded phone bill arrived on the doorstep. Johnny prepared Frances for the ordeal ahead by making them both a cup of tea and they sat down together at the dining table and she took in a big deep breath as she began to read the letter. Johnny watched her facial expressions intently, in order to try to decipher whether or not they would be laughing or crying.

Sitting opposite her, he could easily perceive her eyelids lowering, her shoulders sinking, her mouth opening up like a goldfish and a concerned frown appearing on her usually bright and cheerful face.

He tried his utmost to be as patient as possible as he watched her eyes repeatedly move from left to right and back to the left again, as she read down the letter, but he was also every bit as eager as her to know the details of said letter and by now his patience had completely run out. Realistically she probably only had the letter in her hand for a few seconds, but to him it seemed like ages and so without showing her the consideration she was due, he snatched the letter from her hand and a torrent of expletives flowed from both their mouths. Johnny cursed about the size of the bill. Whereas Frances was more upset at Johnny's uncharacteristic lack of tact and impatience and the worst of it was that she was absolutely right to berate him so.

"There's no need to grab the fucking letter like an animal", she growled.

Johnny sat in ashamed silence. Although she didn't expound her feelings she made him realise that he was indeed a very lucky man to have this devoted and considerate woman as his wife. Who else would have so unflinchingly stood by him throughout his hour of need? She could have abandoned him in jail, left him to rot and got herself another fella. She could have had umpteen affairs while he was inside and he'd have known nothing about it, but she didn't. He was absolutely sure of that. Their marriage had it's ups and downs throughout the years, just like everybody else's, but she'd never betrayed his trust. A claim that Johnny himself could never even attempt to make for himself.

She'd looked after the kids, the house, visited him every single week without fail and with complete and utter disregard to the financial costs that were digging into her meagre finances, come wind, rain or snow, which had the knock on effect of eating into the household finances. She got pennies from the assisted visits, but that money only covered the cost of one visit per month. Frances visited Johnny every week, to ensure that the children would see their father as much as was humanly possible.

She'd done her utmost to keep their household's finances in order, although it would soon transpire that she'd failed quite miserably in her attempts to keep their heads above water, but Johnny would always be the first to concede that if the finances had been left in his hands, they'd be in even deeper shit than they were at present. Above all she was the kind of wife that usually only appeared in romance stories. She was his rock, his lover, sister, mother of both himself and their children, she was the electrical impulse that kept his heart beating, the blood in his veins that kept his body nourished, *she was the lunatic in his asylum, eh?* his best friend and soul mate, nay more than a mere soul mate. All rolled into one, the kind of wife that the vast majority of men can only dream about having. For all the hardships that he had to endure, he thanked the God of his fathers, the God of Abraham, Jacob and Isaac for blessing him with Frances as his wife.

***

There was another letter in the mail that morning; concerning more of

Mrs. Chesney's little secrets.

"I just couldn't let you know how bad things were with money and all that, while you were in there. I was just too scared to tell you, coz you'd just have got yourself all worked up and with you being in an open prison, you'd have gone and done something stupid like jumping over the fence and only made things worse for yourself".

"Oh! Jesus, darling! Couldn't your dad have helped you"?

"Johnny! He's seventy fucking two years old and he's only got his pension, for Christ's sake"!

"Well we're going to have to do something, quick style, aren't we"?

"Well I'm very definitely open to suggestions, if you've got any bright ideas".

It was one of theses £30.00 letters you get when a direct debit or cheque has bounced. This particular one was from a store card and apparently it was the second one from the same company. So they sat down and Johnny tried his best to considerately and patiently extract the story from Frances, amid a torrent of tears. It now transpired that she'd managed ever so well with money up until Christmas and Christmas is Christmas, now isn't it? And she'd gone wild and totally overboard with it. She was trying to comfort herself with more than just a little retail therapy, and at the same time trying to make up for the children's father being absent at that time of year.

"It's all right darling, we'll get through this. There's no point in worrying about it, now is there? You know something will turn up, it always does", said Johnny.

This was his best attempt at trying to comfort her, though these words were sticking in his throat and even as he spoke them, he knew within himself that a miracle was going to be needed to sort out their financial problems. Not only that, but the worst was yet to come because she went on to tell him that today's letter was only one of several that head been landing on the family's doorstep. Ah well, in for a penny, in for a pound, eh?

Finally Johnny managed to get the full run down as to the extent of the debt and the upshot of it was that they were now quite literally up to their eyeballs in it. There had been £30.00 letters galore, especially in the last month leading up to his release.

At last Johnny was back in the real world and he'd came back to earth with an enormous, earth shattering thud. He thought, *Somebody lend me a razor or a rope, no wonder some of these people in jail are in and out all of the time; it's so much easier just to give in and hide away in there every time you get these kind of problems landing on your doorstep.*

The gods still weren't satisfied that enough tragedy had been inflicted onto the Chesney family, and as if that wasn't enough for them to contend with, by now the school holidays were almost over and it seemed like only yesterday that they finished the previous year, and so they also had to consider new school uniforms. The social security grant for all three kids came to the grand total of £56.00. The cost of Jack's uniform alone, who was due to be starting the high school, came to £108.00, almost double the entire allowance for all three children. Alas it didn't end there either; in addition to all of this, the younger two children also needed to have completely new school uniforms as well. The total cost of their uniforms came to £96.00.

So the social security grant had only managed to cover less than a third of the actual cost of the uniforms and that was with restricting themselves buying only the very cheapest of clothes for the kids.

***

Whilst in prison Johnny had been presumably reliably informed that the government only allocated the prison service a meagre £1.46 per day for each prisoner for food.

Now that they found themselves in such severe financial straits, they knew only too well that they'd need to make some drastic economies. They had absolutely no idea how much they were spending each week on food, but as they often threw food out in the bin it seemed an obvious to start making these necessary economies. So they sat down together and did some simple calculations, they worked out that £1.46 times five, times seven came to £51.10. So out of sheer desperation they decided to go ahead and make an attempt to survive on £1.46 per day per person for food.

The experiment began ever so seriously, with them intending to religiously stick to the £51.10 weekly allowance and only buy the absolute essentials on one main weekly shopping trip, but first they had to use up the supplies in the fridge, freezer and the stash in the cupboards. After a few days on surviving on these supplies, the cupboards were completely bare and every last bit of chocolate and biscuit had disappeared. Another good thing to come from their dilemma was that as they'd been cutting down on sweets and crisps and the like. The fruit bowl took a severe hammering, so at least the kids were eating healthy.

Looking at the bare cupboards, Johnny could clearly recall the days when once upon a time he couldn't move, or get anything else into the cupboards. Now he didn't have the slightest worry about being hit on the head by something falling out of the cupboard when he went to open it, and today he actually managed to see the back of the fridge for the first time since he didn't care to remember when.

As part of their attempts to cut down, they decided to go to cheaper shops and gave the Asda in Aintree a miss, in favour of the Netto in Orrel Lane, as it was both cheaper and within walking distance of their house in Menai Road, Bootle. But they still had to drive there regardless as Frances just couldn't allow Johnny out to the shops on his own. Even if she gave him a list, he'd still come home with all the wrong things. So they both went shopping together and all the daily essentials that they set out to get were purchased as planned and carried home in the carrier bags that they'd taken with them so as to avoid having to pay for new ones.

But, yes well there's always a but, isn't there? But old habits die hard. So in addition to the essentials, the trolley soon began to fill up with biscuits, crisps, fizzy drinks and the like. Although, they did at least buy smaller quantities of these luxury items than would normally have been the case. This excess was only permitted as a one off, on the pretext that theoretically they should have had plenty of spare cash left over from their budget, as they'd been using up the excess stock in the cupboards and fridge which wasn't intended to be used in the equation anyway.

The fifth day, their experiment began fine except that it fell on a Friday. It wasn't even the 13th of the month, but the fact that it was Friday was ominous in itself. The cupboards were looking a bit sparse and due to the empty spaces, over a year's build up of dust and grime could be seen easily. So it was decided (by Frances) that Johnny's task for the day was to give them a good scrub. When he'd removed all the contents in order to carry out his chore, he found several items were now out of date and had to be thrown away. Which was fine; good riddance to old shite and all that, but there was something else lurking discretely at the back of one of the cupboards which threatened to jeopardize the entire project.

Once the task of cleaning had been completed and what was left of the usable contents put back in, they sat down at the dining table in order to work out the budget for the forthcoming weekend's expenditure. They played about with the figures for a while, coming to the conclusion that they could indeed manage through to Monday with what still remained in the kitty and perhaps there might even be a little left over.

In a completely over-the-top obsequious tone, Johnny initiated the conversation.

"Well my beautiful darling love, my sweetness, oh light of my life, oh my precious gift from heaven above! Now, that we've done the calculations… "

"Mmmm"? She cautiously replied with a hint of more than a mere inkling of suspicion. The unctuous approach that he'd chosen was by far too out of character for him, which had set off alarm bells ringing in her head.

"Well, it's Friday today isn't it darling"?

"So, you've learned the days of the week. Well done".

"We're going to have plenty of money left over by Monday and if our experiment is to be realistic, then we shouldn't allow any money to rollover into following weeks. Especially as this week we've been using the old stuff already in the cupboards. Now should we darling… "?

"…I'm waiting! Ever so patiently! MY LOVE"!

"Oh my sweetness. Oh my Princess. My Queen. You know the half a case of Carlsberg and the bottle of red wine that we'd forgotten all about, that I found, while clearing out the cupboards as you commanded? Oh great one! It'd be an awful shame to let them go to waste, wouldn't it… "?

"…Oh would it now"?

"Yes my love, it certainly would indeed".

"Let's hear it then".

"Well I thought that it's not really enough to have a drink with. You know what you're like darling. Once you got started on it, it just wouldn't be enough for you, now would it? So I was just thinking… "

"Oh so it wouldn't be enough for me? Is that right"?

"Exactly my love. So what I thought was we could use the left over money from this week and get some more ale in and we could have a toast to how successful we've been so far. Now doesn't that sound like a very good idea"?

"And we are still serious about trying to live off £1.46 a day, are we"?

"Oh absolutely! My love"!

"Well, my love. You know that my love for you is stronger than Samson, Hercules, or even Arnold Swhazrenegger himself. You know that it's greater than the highest mountain and longer than the greatest river and deeper than the greatest sea… "

"Yes, my love".

"Which believe it or not, is even deeper than the great river Mersey, upon the banks of which our great city has been built and the bottom of that great river is where you'll find yourself if you think for one second that I'm going to waste our fucking money on fucking ale"!

"Yes, my love".

"Do I make myself clear"?

"Crystal, my love".

So Johnny's plans were put on hold. It was only day five and Johnny at least was beginning to wane in his determination. Frances however, was still resolute, but quite not that resolute.

Almost an entire year previously, Frances had meticulously planned a surprise victory (not guilty) party for Johnny. Her plans were that he was supposed to get found not guilty on all three charges, she would then suggest that they stay in Warrington and go for a celebratory, romantic candlelit dinner for two. She'd then phone her mother under the pretence that it was purely to arrange for her to pick up the kids from school, but she'd actually be secretly arranging the go ahead and exact time for the surprise party, that was already pre-arranged weeks ago.

Terrific idea! One small problem! Mr. Travis. The undisclosed witness had been furtively sneaked into the trial via the back door, been encouraged to lie through his teeth and Johnny had been found guilty. So no party had ever taken place, not even a consolation party.

So Frances planned another party instead. This would be a yellow ribbon party, no oak tree, not even a bonsai tree, but the apparently big, huge stash of ale that she had hidden at her mother's house, well out of sight from Johnny's eyes, was supposed to come in handy for that.

Johnny hadn't even been in prison a month when one of Frances' nephews asked her if he could dip into the big stash to use at a 21st Birthday party, promising to replenish whatever he used when he was a bit more flush for cash. Well it would have been a terrible crying shame to let it go to waste now. Wouldn't it?

So practically the entire Fitzpatrick family sang, danced, laughed and partied their way into the wee small hours, thoroughly enjoying the nice big stash of commandeered ale. They quite happily swallowed the whole lot down and duly pissed the whole entire lot against a wall. Meanwhile, back in Kirkham jail, poor old Johnny was *rotting his back out* all alone in his cold lonely cell, completely and utterly oblivious to what was going on in the big world outside, which was just as well, because if he'd known, he just might have given into temptation and put his pole vaulting skills into practice.

Now almost a year later than planned, it was time for Johnny to do a bit of singing and dancing himself and so the debt was called in. One phone call and less than 24 hours later, Johnny was folding the back seats of the Escort down and loading a very substantial amount of booze into the boot of the car.

"Thank Christ I got found guilty, or I wouldn't have a liver left", he joked with Frances.

"Well you ain't gonna have one tomorrow, are you"? she replied.

That evening several of their friends came found to the house, the kids got threw to bed, the CDs went on and Johnny did his usual highland fling. Frances did her best at an Irish jig and everybody else done something else and a concerted effort was made by all to reduce the size of the heap of cases of drink that was taking up too much space anyway!

Half past eleven on the Sunday morning and Johnny and Frances were still in bed, each with their own big, giant, enormous head. Johnny ventured down to the kitchen; the two younger kids were playing in the back yard. When he looked out to see if they were ok, the yard looked more like a battle zone, with piles of empty bottles and cans strewn everywhere, some of which were half in and half out of bin bags. All of this was amid a mass of other clutter, including an upturned Bar-B-Q that the two little ones, Frank and Patrick, were playing with. He watched them for a minute and realised that they were playing quite safely. By now Frank and Patrick had abandoned the Bar-B-Q and began making rows of bottles, each in their respective order, one row of Bud, another row of Carlsberg, etc.

The mere thought of the task of cleaning up was just too much for him to contemplate at the moment. Watching the kids playing made him smile and he thought to himself, *Oh fuck it! That lot can wait until tomorrow*.

He filled two glasses with water and added a spoonful of Andrews Liver Salts to each and told the kids "now you two be careful, if you break any glass, come and tell me straight away". They nodded in assent and he retreated to the warmth and comfort of the bed with Frances where she gulped down the Andrews, then turned to Johnny and set about him for the next hour and a half, only releasing him on the condition that he go and clear up the back yard.

By the time Monday morning arrived, the weekend's doings had ensured that the cupboards were now well and truly completely empty, which meant that they would need to spend every single penny of this week's allowance today, just to ensure that the kids didn't starve altogether. So they bought only the absolute essentials for one week and the bill came to just slightly over the entire weeks allowance.

By the time the following Thursday had arrived they'd gone through the entire £51.10 weekly allowance worth of food and they hadn't bought any sweets or luxuries which had the knock on effect of enticing the kids to eat all the fruit and then work their way into and completely deplete all the supplies that were supposed to be for the whole week. This meant that they were now short of the food which was supposed to see them through to the following Monday and the start of another week's allowance. Neither Johnny nor Frances were prepared to allow their children to starve for the sake of a silly little experiment based upon the government's supposed limits. You could bet your bottom dollar that the Blair family were spending more than the entire £51.10 weekly allowance just for one breakfast alone. Never mind trying to survive on that for a whole week.

Thus the grand experiment that they had so meticulously planned, with the very best intentions, ended in a sad pathetic debacle with Johnny selfishly insisting on spending unnecessary cash on soft drinks in order to use in the whisky and vodka that had survived from the previous Saturday, with the intention of polishing the whole lot off this coming weekend. Alas it would later transpire that this sad pathetic debacle was an omen of what lay ahead for the Chesney family, if they were to continue trying to make ends meet on benefits.

***

Johnny was determined that release wasn't going to be all bad news for the Chesney family. Before being released, he was well aware that finding new employment was going to be comparable to the forty year trek around the wilderness that the Israelites who had followed Moses into the wilderness had to endure. Both he Frances and the children had come though the police investigation, trial and prison together. He felt an overwhelming sense of duty towards them; he just couldn't find it within himself to sit back and allow himself to *decay* in front of the children, or Frances, for the next forty years, until he was dead and buried. The twelve tribes of Israel had wandered through the desert for forty years, at the end of which, ten of them decided to sit on their arses, too frightened to forge on ahead and into Canaan. If Johnny had been there all that time ago, Joshua and Caleb would have had another partner with whom they could return to the promised land.

Not content with just merely tackling an uphill struggle, Johnny set his sights on achieving a bit of advancement in his life. Just like Joshua and Caleb, Johnny felt the need to set his sights on greater things and within two weeks of being released from prison, he applied to the Liverpool Polytechnic, now known as Liverpool Johnny Moores University, in order to do a masters degree and finally make some use of the degree that he'd obtained several years previously. The course was due to start on 22/9/03, which gave him about three months worth of time that needed to be filled in.

***

Bearing in mind that release is not the same thing as freedom, and the freedom to go and look for a job is not the same thing as actually being able to find one, and having the freedom to earn a living was a different thing to actually being able to do so.

Whilst in prison, Johnny had taken a course for driving a fork lift truck because at the time, he thought he might as well. After all, he be dammed if he'd ever be stupid enough to go back to driving lorries. Considering what he knew about filling in the declaration on job applications, he carefully pondered his options. What about lying and getting a job as a lorry driver or getting a job that requires a fork lift licence? If he were to do so, he'd only need one single box of whatever to go missing and the police would become involved. They'd take his details and check him out on the computer and it would be adios to Johnny, for at least another year, or perhaps even more. Even that was beyond the limits of Johnny's stupidity. He'd be risking his neck, just so he could pay tax to a government that would be only too happy to build even more prisons. He started imagining all sorts of silly scenarios, like one with a cell marked reserved for Chesney, J. GT8329. Paid for by Chesney, J. GT8329.

He could always turn to crime. Well, why not? If you're going to get put in jail, it might as well be for something that you actually did! He decided that was a ridiculous option. It would fuck up any appeal. It would play right into their hands, give them what they wanted on a plate. It would give them the perfect justification for their illegal actions. They'd come out with a pile of shite—like saying we knew he was a thief, we just couldn't prove it by legal means and so we had to frame him in order to protect society.

So what now then? Completely out of great ideas, it now seemed that Johnny was destined to help swell the ranks of the masses of unskilled workers who had to survive with a job *on the side.* What a fantastic prospect—looking into the abyss at forty years of age, with less prospects than someone with Down Syndrome; at least they could get a job with their green card.

Well Johnny could just sit there moping, moaning and bitching about it all day long. Get the violin out and sing a sad, sad song. He could be a country and western star in no time at all. Or much more likely, just another sad wanker with no guts, no balls, no get up and go, and worst of all, no fucking hope. Or he could always try and be positive about it. What could be positive about being just out of jail with no job and no money? Mmmm? Yeah positive! Why not? What about the Jewish refugees at he end of WWII, way back in 1945, a long time before he was even a twinkle in his mother's eye. Wasn't he after all one of their descendants? They must have had to start all over again from absolutely nothing. He didn't need to start from nothing. He had a home, a wife and a family to return to. There was no denying that he was in a rut, a big rut even, but a rut's only a rut; a bottomless chasm's a bottomless chasm, but this was only a rut! A little tiny insignificant indentation on life's highway! Hardly significant at all! Something that Johnny knew he could and must climb out of. Not only for his own sake, but what about Mrs. Chesney, his gift from heaven? Then there were the kids to consider. What kind of example was he for the children if he was gong to act like some old loser that decided to just lay down and die?

So at the very least he needed something to keep himself occupied with between now and September if he was going to start the masters course. So perhaps his best option would be for a career change, even if it was only going to be for a short time, but as what exactly? It would very definitely need to come in the form of some type of self-employed type of work. Problem was, he was absolutely skint, so how could he set himself up in any kind of business without any money? Just yet another 'catch 22' situation for him to try to ascend from.

He trawled through the job ads in the local freebie paper and amongst the multitude of shite jobs that would only pay pennies, were lorry driving jobs and there was absolutely no danger whatsoever of either Johnny or Frances even considering them no matter how skint they were.

The only thing in there that would be suitable, i.e. a self-employed job, with little or no starting capital involved, was the plethora of sales jobs. He'd tried them in his youth and knew only too well that the reason for there being so many of these jobs available was that in reality it was extremely difficult, if not absolutely impossible to actually make even a modest living with these jobs. However, borne of a combination of lack of choice and sheer desperation, he sat himself down at the computer and began to type out a letter in reply to one of the sales job advertisements. The letter was drafted and completed in less than thirty minutes and on proof-reading the letter, Frances remarked on the speed and skill that Johnny had demonstrated in the writing of said letter and added that,"with all the shit that's happened to us you could write a book on it".

"Yeah, too right babe. I bet you a shilling you don't realise just how right you are. All that time while I was in jail, whenever I was bored shitless, I'd lock myself in my cell and read. I read literally hundreds of books, many more than I've ever read before in my entire life, but the overwhelming majority of them were complete and utter absolute, fucking shite. Frank or Patrick could have written a better book than some of them. I could hardly believe the kind of shite that actually makes it into print. In the jail's library there's millions of them True Crime books; I read dozens of them as well. I was actually so bored that I was reduced to reading that Jeffery Scratcher book about when he was in jail. It was all right, nothing special though, just readable, that's all, and I'm pretty sure that even I could have done better than that myself".

"Yeah"?

"Yeah! I really could have and you know what"?

"What"?

"When Gordon fucking Spofforth, *et al.* decided to stitch me up, you can bet your very last penny that they'd never have put me ignoring them and going ahead with an appeal anyway into the equation. Now would they? But much better than that, they'd never in a million years have thought that someone they'd stitched up would have the nouse to go and write a book about their doings and bring their activities out into public view. Now would they"?

"Well what the fuck's stopping you then"?

"Well, what the fuck is stopping me"?

"Have you got something better to do"?

"Guess not, darling".

"You ain't writing Johnny".

"Oh yes I am dear"!

Chapter XVI
Two Fridays

Two Fridays…

Printed in the United Kingdom
by Lightning Source UK Ltd.
101273UKS00003B/172-195